ARTHUR E. BRANDT
JUNE

D0387302

Sport and Society

Series Editors

Benjamin G. Rader
Randy Roberts

A list of books in the series appears at the end of this volume.

Cowgirls of the Rodeo

☆ **Mary Lou LeCompte**

Cowgirls of the Rodeo

Pioneer Professional Athletes

University of Illinois Press

Urbana and Chicago

©1993 by the Board of Trustees of the University of Illinois
Manufactured in the United States of America
C   5   4   3   2   1

This book is printed on acid-free paper.

Library of Congress Cataloging-in-Publication Data
LeCompte, Mary Lou, 1935–
     Cowgirls of the rodeo : pioneer professional athletes / Mary Lou
LeCompte.
        p. cm. — (Sport and society)
     Includes bibliographical references (p.) and index.
     ISBN 0-252-02029-4 (alk. paper)
     1. Cowgirls—West (U.S.)—History. 2. Rodeos—West (U.S.)
3. Cowgirls—West (U.S.)—Social conditions. I. Title.
II. Series.
GV1834.55.W47L43 1993
791.8'4—dc20   92-42635
                                                              CIP

Contents

List of Illustrations

Acknowledgments

The seven years I have spent researching and writing this book have been most rewarding, and I am indebted to the many individuals and institutions who have assisted me. Foremost among them, my husband Melville LeCompte, without whom I would never have started, much less finished, the project. This work would not have been possible without the financial support of the University Research Institute, University of Texas at Austin, for which I am most grateful. Also invaluable were research assistants Annie Laura Moerbe and Laura Mae Sodolak, and the students in KIN 330: History of Sport and Physical Activity, at the University of Texas, who spent countless hours surveying periodicals. Special thanks go to Joan S. Hult of the University of Maryland and David McComb of Colorado State University, and my many other friends and colleagues in the North American Society for Sport History for their support and encouragement, and to Katherine Stansbury of Mulhall, Oklahoma, for sharing her insights, ideas, and photo collection.

I am grateful for the opportunity to meet and interview a number of outstanding cowgirls. My visits with them were the highlight of the research, and made for many delightful as well as informative hours. The women, all honorees in one or several halls of fame, include Mary Ellen "Dude" Barton, Nancy Binford, Margie Greenough Henson, Dixie Reger Mosley, Alice Greenough Orr, Isora DeRacy Young, and the late great Tad Lucas.

This book could not have been completed with out the help of Margaret Formby, National Cowgirl Hall of Fame and Western Heritage Center, Hereford, Texas, and Jackie Hammett, also formerly of the Cowgirl

Hall of Fame. They opened their doors and their archives for my research, arranged my interviews with Nancy Binford, Mary Ellen Barton, and Dixie Mosley, and welcomed me back for induction ceremonies and festivities. I am also grateful to the late Willard Porter, Bobby Weaver, and Don Reeves of the National Rodeo Hall of Fame at the National Cowboy Hall of Fame, Oklahoma City, Oklahoma; Patricia A. Florence, ProRodeo Hall of Fame and Museum of the American Cowboy, Colorado Springs, Colorado; and Susan Kooyman, Glenbow Museum and Archives, Calgary, Alberta, Canada. All were extremely cooperative and hospitable.

The records of the Women's Professional Rodeo Association were unavailable for study. This is regrettable, as many of the dedicated women who worked on behalf of that organization will remain unrecognized. Fortunately, many of the WPRA founders donated their personal memorabilia to the Cowgirl Hall of Fame. Recently WPRA president Jimmie Gibbs Munroe has been most helpful.

Portions of this book have been derived from previously published material, and are included with permission:

"Home on the Range: Women in Professional Rodeo, 1929–1947," *Journal of Sport History* 17 (Winter 1990).
"Cowgirls at the Crossroads: Women in Professional Rodeo, 1889–1922," *Canadian Journal of History of Sport* 20 (Dec. 1989).
"Champion Cowgirls of Rodeo's Golden Age," *Journal of the West* 28 (Apr. 1989).
"Col. William Thomas Johnson, Premier Rodeo Producer of the 1930s," *Canadian Journal of History of Sport* 23 (Summer 1992).

Introduction

On March 1, 1992, Charmayne James Rodman, nine times national bar-rel racing champion, won $18,546 at the Houston Rodeo. This total set "a new world record for earning the most money at a regular-season rodeo by any contestant, male or female, in any single rodeo event, PRCA or WPRA."[1] Rodman, the Women's Professional Rodeo Association's first million dollar cowgirl, is surely the beneficiary of the many changes in women's sports during the past twenty years. She also shares the legacy of the almost-forgotten pioneer rodeo cowgirls who were among the first American women to succeed as professional athletes.

During the late nineteenth century, women began competing in rode-os and cowboy tournaments that ranch communities staged for local amusement. From the turn of the century through World War I, cowgirls were popular stars of some of North America's biggest and richest con-tests. They also competed successfully in big-time rodeo during the twen-ties, sometimes labeled America's Golden Age of Sport. Women head-lined the Madison Square Garden and Boston Garden rodeos, and even in the Great Depression some earned as much as ten times the average per capita income. During World War II, many changes took place in the world of rodeo, diminishing women's role to almost zero by 1948. That year, cowgirls from a new generation formed the Girls Rodeo Association (GRA), which is now the Women's Professional Rodeo Association (WPRA). The organization aimed to provide females with new competi-tive opportunities and orchestrate their return to the mainstream of the sport. As Rodman's achievement clearly demonstrates, their efforts final-ly succeeded, but only after a struggle of nearly thirty years.

This is the story of more than six hundred women who competed in professional rodeo between 1896 and 1992. Some had long and successful careers, but almost two-thirds remained in the business for only one or two years. That is not surprising. Although almost all women born and raised on ranches could rope and ride, only a few possessed the exceptional skills required for a professional rodeo career. Just as only a handful of the millions of Little League baseball players ever make it to the major leagues, so only a few men and women from ranching backgrounds ever made it in professional rodeo. Most who enjoyed successful rodeo careers had achieved recognition since early childhood. Highly skilled and intensely competitive, they joined the rodeo to follow a dream. Aspiring to compete against the best in the business for the coveted title of world champion, many also perceived a professional career as their only hope for escape from endless drudgery and sometimes grinding poverty. These top cowgirls had the psychological makeup necessary for a life-style where home was mostly on the road, travel long and arduous, income unreliable, and the possibility of crippling injury ever-present.[2] Yet to the women involved, the glamor and excitement more than compensated for the difficulties. Hall of Fame cowgirl Ollie Osborn, who rodeoed from 1913 to 1932, summed it up this way: "We can't say it isn't dangerous, we know better, it is dangerous. But . . . when you're young, and everybody's feeling good, and the band's playing, it just gives you a go-ahead."[3] Despite the hardships, most not only survived, they thrived; some remained in the business for thirty years or more. Of the 607 women in this study, 218 had professional careers of three years or more. Women with longer careers were far more versatile than their less-successful counterparts, and therefore better able to earn a living through their sport.[4]

Cowgirls came from a special segment of the population. Most were and are from ranches west of the ninety-eighth meridian. Until World War II, virtually all were working-class, first- or second-generation Americans with no more than an eighth-grade education. As a matter of economic necessity, they grew up roping, riding, and working on their family ranches. Shelly Armitage calls their home area the "cattle frontier," and correctly suggests that its unique environment contributed to the development of heroic women. She notes that while most frontiers depended on settlement for progress, the cattle frontier thrived on uncivilized expanses. The ranch women were part of a self-sufficient unit, "and often had to take a nontraditional view of the home, division of labor, the land, and even the law."[5] Whether independent women or ranchers' wives, widows, or daughters, they all experienced the violence and the values of the range, and thereby shaped their lives.[6]

Rodeo cowgirls were products of this culture where athleticism, skill, competitiveness, and grit were acceptable traits for women. They were largely unencumbered by Victorian middle-class notions of womanhood. Therefore their self-image and sense of womanliness were never at odds with their athletic skills and ambitions. Most champion cowgirls have been true heroines in their western communities, and highly sought after as wives by both professional cowboys and ranchers. Cowgirls never had to make the choice between career and marriage that many professional women faced until quite recently. From the nineteenth century through World War II, more than 90 percent of all rodeo cowgirls married rodeo cowboys.[7]

Some cowgirls did come from eastern states, and a few were European immigrants. However, I found no record of participation by either African-American women or Chicanas during the years covered by this book.[8] This situation was also true for males. There were few black cowboys on the rodeo circuit because most rodeos barred them. Hispanic women as well as men participated in Wild West shows, but although their numbers remained small, males were more successful than females in competitive rodeo. The absence of black and Hispanic women may have been due to differing cultural attitudes toward female sport participation as well as racial discrimination. They may also have lacked the opportunity to learn the needed skills.

Before World War II, many rodeos in the Far West had special events for native Americans, including races for "Squaws." As a requirement for competing, the Indians had to camp on the rodeo grounds and provide "native entertainment." Only a few of the men and women who took part in the Indian activities went on to compete in mainstream rodeo. The best-known males were Jackson Sundown and Tom Three Persons. Several females, including Emma Blackfox, Good Elk, and Princess Redbird, also moved beyond the special events to succeed in standard competition. Rodeos no longer hold special contests for Indians, and Indians have their own rodeo circuit. Today, some of the top athletes from that circuit progress to the big time. The most recent example is Shelly Bird-Matthews, 1990 barrel racing champion at the Indian National Rodeo Finals. In 1991 she was a rookie qualifier for the barrel racing finals at the National Finals Rodeo (NFR), the world's richest rodeo.[9]

Like Good Elk and Princess Redbird, cowgirls selected their professional names. Some like Tillie Baldwin adopted stage names, whereas Mrs. Ed Wright and a few others insisted upon being known by their husbands' names.[10] Most, like Bertha Kapernick and Reine Hafley, who were single when they began competing, changed their professional names when they married, becoming, for example, Bertha Blancett and Reine Shelton. Women like Tad Lucas and Fox Hastings who used nicknames instead of first names also changed their last names when they married. Many more, including Lucille Mulhall and Marjorie and Alice Greenough, used their maiden names throughout their careers. In this book, I use the professional name by which each woman was best known.

Regardless of their names or backgrounds, most female rodeo contestants readily adopted the customs and life-styles of rodeo veterans, and ultimately considered themselves "real cowgirls." They succeeded as professional athletes long before the athletic revolution of the seventies. Rodeo cowgirls proved that women could compete in a rough, physically demanding, and theoretically macho sport, endure falls, breaks, and bruises, and still earn the respect and admiration of millions. They showed that athleticism and femininity were not mutually exclusive. Most were married and many had children, disproving the widespread beliefs that athletic women were incapable of child bearing and unsuitable for marriage. Finally, they demonstrated that outstanding female athletes could earn favorable headlines and several hundred thousand dollars through sport without having to be exceptionally beautiful or deemed "sex symbols" by the press. Therefore, though few if any cowgirls were feminists, and several insisted they certainly were not, they still helped to change the public image of women and advance the feminist cause.

I hope that *Cowgirls of the Rodeo,* a story of a group outside the mainstream of American life, will contribute to the history of both western women and western sporting women. Most of the literature on western women has focused on the "westering" women who made the cross-country trek by covered wagon and assisted in the early settlement of the West.[11] This book, on the other hand, focuses upon a special group, the cowgirls, and their organization, the WPRA. It attempts to place them within the framework of western history, that is, within the context of western ranch culture and a special world of commercial entertainment arising from the West. Furthermore, this book aspires to locate the cowgirls within the framework of women's sport history. Rarely have sport organizations formed by women, for women, with women's needs and interests uppermost, survived for long. The WPRA, the oldest organization of female professional athletes in America, is a striking exception. Although it has always been governed solely by women, it is totally absent from the literature of women's sport history.[12]

This work is unique among books about cowgirls because of its exclusive focus on cowgirls who competed for prizes in professional rodeos. It is also unique in its exhaustive use of archives, newspapers, and rodeo trade publications. These materials enabled me to piece together the history of rodeo cowgirls despite the lack of official organizations or records. They also allowed me to provide a clearer picture than has previously been available about the careers and achievements of individual women and the group as a whole.[13] Tables containing numbers and percentages of cowgirl participants, career length, and events for the entire group, as well as for the subjects in each chapter, are included in the Appendix.

This book is limited to professional athletes. Although other "professional cowgirls" performed in Wild West shows, circuses, and films, I did not include them. I also made no attempt to trace women's participation in Little Britches, Junior, high school, intercollegiate, Indian, Bill Pickett, or international rodeo. All of these subjects merit study in their own right. It is also limited in the number of actual interviews conducted. However, since two earlier works on cowgirls utilized oral history almost exclusively, I chose to emphasize archival data heretofore ignored. Still, the greatest limitation was lack of information; much of the history was never recorded, and many records are lost.

One final note: feminists and others sometimes oppose the term *cowgirl*. To date, no one has found an appropriate substitute, and it is doubtful Americans would embrace the Australian Jill-a-roo (and Jack-a-roo). Therefore, as long as the term *cowboy* remains standard, *cowgirl* will probably do likewise. As *Texas Monthly* magazine said in 1987, the word *cowgirl* is not necessarily bad: "Like it or not, the word [cowgirl] calls up a range of resonant images: the coquettish trick rider in a wild West show; the self-reliant ranch woman who brands and doctors her own calves; the suburban mother who spends every night and weekend running barrels, the bull rider who drives hundreds of miles to an All-Girl rodeo, hoping to win maybe a couple hundred dollars."[14]

Chapter One

Overview

American Rodeo

American rodeo owes its very existence to the public's continuing fascination with the cowboy hero, and what the Pulitzer Prize–winning historian William H. Goetzmann and art historian William N. Goetzmann call "the West of the Imagination."[1] Although rodeo originated in Mexico, it moved north with the cattle business, and during the early nineteenth century passed from Hispanic to Anglo along with the skills and traditions of ranching.[2] Cowboys, *vaqueros,* and others who worked with cattle devised a variety of equestrian games and contests that eventually led to ranch-versus-ranch rodeos in North America. Many rodeo contests first began as part of community fairs and holiday festivals like the Fourth of July during the 1860s. Professional rodeo really began in 1882, when Buffalo Bill Cody packaged the contests as part of his highly successful July Fourth Celebration at North Platte, Nebraska.[3]

Intending to show spectators what life had been like in the "real west," Cody hired cowboys, Indians, and Mexican ropers and riders to reenact stagecoach robberies, war dances, a buffalo hunt, and the famous Pony Express rides. In addition, he persuaded merchants to donate valuable prizes for the winners of contests in roping and riding wild broncs, steers, and buffalo. The event enjoyed enormous success, drawing the largest crowd in the history of the Nebraska territory. Because of Cody's fame as a buffalo hunter, dime novel hero, and vaudeville star, it also drew considerable media coverage.[4]

The following year, Cody went on the road with his Wild West show. He sold the production to the eastern United States and ultimately the world as an authentic representation of the vanishing frontier life-style. Consequently, Cody gets credit for making the cowboy a hero, and popularizing rodeo as the cowboy sport.[5] Cody's show and its hundreds of imitators remained significant entertainments through 1917, and did much to establish the image of the cowboy as a romantic idol and acrobatic horseman rather than a manual laborer, as well as to develop many great cowboy and later cowgirl stars. It also served as the prototype for the rodeos that followed.

Cody's West was considerably more accurate than many of the Hollywood versions that followed. Hispanics and Indians were significant performers. They earned headlines and star billing, and were treated with dignity and worth. Mexican *charros*, whom Cody called *Vaqueros*, or simply "Mexicans from Old Mexico," were responsible for the development of trick and fancy roping as a rodeo event. Despite their pride in being "true charros" they had only minimal success in introducing that term in the United States.[6] Following the lead of sharpshooter Annie Oakley, the first female Wild West superstar, other women also attained headliner status. The same could not be said for blacks. Sarah J. Blackstone reports on their status in the Wild West this way: "Another exciting riding event seen during the season of 1883 and 1884 was an 'Indian from Africa' who saddled and rode an elk as it kicked and bucked its way all around the arena. This was the only event featuring a black rider in Cody's show until he added a black cavalry unit in 1894."[7] Clearly, neither the "Indian from Africa" nor the cavalry unit depicted the black cowboys who helped tame the American West. The first, and probably the only, black star of the Wild West was Bill Pickett, creator of the modern rodeo event of steer wrestling or bulldogging. Promoter Guy Weadick discovered Pickett at a small Texas rodeo. Weadick became Pickett's agent and booked his successful appearance as a contract act at the Cheyenne Frontier Days. This led to a starring role with the 101 Ranch Wild West where Pickett spent the remainder of his career. Unfortunately, his success did not lead to greater opportunities for blacks in the Wild West, but it did reveal the persistent racism in contest rodeo. According to his biographer, Col. Bailey Haynes, the true extent of Pickett's talents remains a mystery: "Pickett would have been a contestant at many more rodeos between 1910 and 1930 had it not been for the color line at many of them, both large and small. This restricted his activities and prevented him from compiling a better record as a bulldogger, bronc rider, and steer and calf roper."[8]

As Wild West entertainment expanded, cowboy contests gradually got more publicity and bigger prizes all over the West. Cattle towns organized community celebrations, often called "Frontier Days," to preserve and perpetuate their heritage.[9] Competition was the central focus of these events, but they also featured a variety of entertainments modeled on the Wild West show. Throughout the late nineteenth and early twentieth centuries, informal community festivals and ranch-versus-ranch rodeos continued to exist even as larger contests became professionalized. During the same years when tens of thousands of dollars in prizes were being awarded at rodeos in Calgary, Alberta, and New York City, local cowboys and cowgirls continued to compete for little more than bragging rights at small community contests in which local citizens sometimes formed arenas with their parked vehicles.[10]

Women rarely participated in ranch-versus-ranch rodeos, because they were not hired hands like the cowboys. Usually their parents owned small ranches where the children learned to ride almost before they could walk and were expected to help with the chores as soon as they were able. Since many rodeo events (such as bronc riding and calf, steer, and team roping) derive from ranch work, and demand a high degree of roping and/or riding skills, these youngsters were learning the fundamentals of rodeo when they went about their chores. Most also rode to school, and played equestrian games with siblings and neighbors. Large groups of people from ranching areas frequently gathered in the small towns on Saturdays, with ranchers bringing along outlaw horses and ornery bulls. Children competed with one another in attempting to ride these creatures, sometimes winning coins tossed by the onlookers, other times taking prizes offered by local merchants. On festive occasions, youngsters sometimes participated in contests during the community fairs and festivals. Women also took part in these local activities, and many cowgirls got the "rodeo bug" in that manner.[11] Some cowgirls were discovered at local contests, while others began their professional careers as jockeys, or made their way to the contest circuit on their own. Regardless of how they began, professional athletic careers provided talented ranch girls an exciting alternative to unending drudgery, while apparently posing no threat to their perception of their own femininity.[12]

The Cheyenne Frontier Days, introduced in 1897, achieved dominance as the most prestigious of the early western contests. Women quickly joined that competition, and in 1904 the *Denver Post* donated a trophy for the "Champion Lady Rider" at the Frontier Days. Mrs. Bill Irwin (Etta McGulkin), winner of the cowgirl cow pony race, was the first recipient of the award. Officials at other locations soon began adding women's contests to their programs as well.[13]

From the 1890s through the 1920s, these western heritage celebrations, held in the out-of-doors, were America's premier rodeos, with Cheyenne Frontier Days the undisputed leader and model. Many of the same stars who competed in frontier days also performed in Wild West shows, and both forms of western entertainment often traveled with circuses, carnivals, and the like. Until after World War I, Wild West shows were far more significant than rodeos. During those years, numerous Wild West show performers earned good livings, while even the best athletes found it impossible to make ends meet with rodeo winnings alone.[14]

Nonetheless, this era offered great opportunities for cowgirls, who could and did compete directly against men in steer roping, trick roping, trick riding, and Roman racing. Rodeo was the first, and perhaps the only, sport in which men and women truly competed as equals. Even with the growth of special cowgirl contests in bronc riding, trick riding, trick roping, and relay and cow pony races, women continued to compete successfully against men in a variety of events, and still enjoyed the respect and friendship of the cowboys.[15] Lucille Mulhall, who often competed against men, told reporters that the cowboys treated cowgirls like one of themselves, and liked to see them succeed in public. She also noted that cowboys "admire a girl who can handle a horse well."[16]

As contestants began traveling greater distances to compete, and as rodeos grew to several days in length, it became the norm to pay the winners after each day's performance. The daily prizes became known as day money, and the various performances rounds or go-rounds. Usually the champions were those with the best times or scores, not those who had collected the most day money in their respective events. Champions collected their purses after all events were over, sometimes at special ceremonies held for that purpose.

Throughout these years, every rodeo in America was an independent production, with its own rules and often its own unique events. Almost every contest claimed to be a "World Championship" in some event so that title meant very little unless won at a major rodeo like Cheyenne Frontier Days or Calgary Stampede. Most Americans knew little of western sports until 1916, when promoters decided to bring the competition to cities where Wild West shows had drawn huge crowds for years. The early eastern contests took place at racetracks and ball parks in New York and Chicago before the first Madison Square Garden rodeo in 1922. The first important indoor rodeo, that Garden event changed the sport forever. Soon, Madison Square Garden, not Cheyenne Frontier Days, was the most prestigious rodeo, and subsequently Boston Garden and other indoor venues joined the circuit. Of course limited space left no room for the long races, Indian ceremonials, and other traditional fare. To shorten the length of performances many popular contests like trick riding and trick and fancy roping became paid performances called contract acts, leaving bronc riding as the only competitive event for women in the prestigious eastern contests, while races remained the most popular in the West.[17]

The spread of rodeo would have been impossible without the introduction of new methods of organization. Local citizen committees usually ran the western frontier days. They handled every aspect of production including constructing the arena and acquiring livestock from local ranchers, with profits returning to the community. On the other hand, all elements of eastern rodeos had to be imported, usually by independent producers or traveling rodeo companies. Although these organizations were essential to the growth of rodeo, they also created a situation in which dishonesty flourished. Because it was difficult to distinguish fraudulent operations from legitimate ones, contestants lost countless dollars and the integrity of rodeo was compromised.[18]

At the same time, honest independent producers like Tex Austin and Guy Weadick did much to improve rodeo, and many others copied their techniques. Entrepreneurs hoping to make a profit underwrote the Stampedes Weadick staged at Calgary, Winnipeg, and New York in 1912, 1913, and 1916. They paid Weadick a salary to organize and produce the rodeos. His duties included soliciting entries, hiring and paying contract entertainers, and obtaining livestock. For the 1912 Calgary Stampede, he not only advertised for participants, he sent personal invitations to top athletes in the United States, Canada, and Mexico, while at New York he hired a huge contingent of reservation Indians to provide entertainment.[19]

Unfortunately, the 1916 New York Stampede drew small crowds, and closed with a deficit. Although Weadick made a concerted effort to obtain needed funds from his backers, it appeared that neither winners, contract performers, nor Indians would receive the money owed them. Fortunately for those participants, four New York newspapers kept up an unrelenting barrage of negative publicity until the backers capitulated. They eventually awarded contestants approximately 25 percent of the amounts they had won, and provided all other performers and participants transportation to their next destination.[20]

Weadick was really an honest producer whose rodeo simply failed to make expenses. However, to cowboys and cowgirls who competed in the New York Stampede, he appeared to be just another "bloomer." That was the term used to identify dishonest producers who traveled to smaller communities to schedule rodeos. They advertised heavily for contestants, and although they often charged higher-than-usual entry fees, everything about their rodeos appeared legitimate at the outset. Then, during the last round of competition the bloomers took all the entry fees and gate receipts and skipped town, leaving the winners empty-handed and with no hope for collecting their prizes. The most notorious bloomer was Milt Hinkle, whom award-winning rodeo writer Bill King called the "King of the run out boys," but there were many more.[21] They caused extreme hardship and often left contestants stranded and penniless.[22]

Bronc rider Marie Gibson described such a situation in a poignant 1927 letter: "I play [sic] a show at Lexington Ky. I won 340 dollars and it did not pay up. It sure hit me hard. . . . I may have to go to work here for a few weeks . . . there are a lot of shows in California but its too far and I ain't got the fair [sic] up."[23] At the time, Gibson was attempting to support her husband and children through her winnings, because their crops had failed the previous year, and they were unable to obtain a loan for spring planting.[24]

While bloomers defrauded countless cowboys and cowgirls, a second problem, "fake rodeos," undermined the entire profession. The fakes began at about the same time as the bloomer rodeos, and closely resembled the legitimate traveling rodeo companies that ultimately dominated the sport. Like the honest operations, fake rodeos were performed by touring groups that included producers, announcers, livestock, and a cadre of cowboys and cowgirls. These employees staged both the entertainment and the contests themselves, rotating the "victories" among the cast members, and distributing the "results" for publication. In some cases, they allowed outsiders to participate in the contests. Of course those who unwittingly paid entry fees to these operations were wasting their dollars, because the winners had already been determined. Local papers often printed the results, assuming that actual competition took place, but trade publications rarely did so. Rodeo columnists for *The Billboard* condemned the dishonest practices for years, and frequently reiterated their refusal to publish results of rodeos they knew had been staged rather than legitimately contested.[25] Despite their vigilance, however, some very questionable results appeared in print. In more than one instance I found an obscure rodeo company whose results listed the same group of individuals, albeit in a different order of finish, week after week.[26] In the mid-thirties, columnists for *Hoofs and Horns* joined the effort to "clean up" the rodeo business.[27]

It is reasonable to ask who participated in fake rodeos? There is no single answer, partly because rodeo was such a financially risky business for all participants. Honest producers risked going broke, as Weadick learned in 1916. Rodeo companies honest and dishonest often disbanded because they could not meet expenses, leaving their employees penniless and far from home. For these and other reasons, there were always cowboys and cowgirls temporarily down on their luck who would take almost any means of employment, whether as fake rodeo performer, stable hand, or dishwasher. Marie Gibson would certainly have been tempted to sign on with almost any company that offered a paycheck and transportation out of town when she was stranded in Kentucky. Dishonest producers also appealed to starry-eyed youngsters who answered ads to join a rodeo company. Several fake rodeos were former Wild West shows, while others were once-legitimate rodeo companies that changed their formats in an effort to reduce expenses and become more profitable. There were also a variety of different formats and combinations, including Wild West Rodeo Thrill Circuses, so that in some cases new employees didn't even know what kind of outfit they had joined.

Outsiders could rarely discern the difference between the fakes and legitimate companies that communities or organizations could hire to stage their rodeos. Like the fakes, real rodeo companies owned livestock and employed laborers, announcers, and a contingent of cowboys and cowgirls to serve as contract performers, pickups, and the like. Although honest companies advertised widely in hopes of attracting large numbers of contestants who would pay entry fees and increase income, they too allowed employees who paid entry fees to compete in the rodeo contests. This practice made all rodeo companies vulnerable to charges of fraud. Groups who investigated the operations often expressed doubts about the legitimacy of any contest in which employees of the producer competed for prize money.

The problem began with the prototype rodeo company, which cowgirl star Lucille Mulhall and her partner Homer Wilson formed in 1916. Mulhall thus became one of the few female producers in rodeo history, as the organization provided her with the unique opportunity to compete and entertain, without the usual financial risks. Financial responsibility lay entirely with the backers, who paid her company a fee for organizing and promoting the rodeos. Once the company was established, Wilson spent most of his time traveling and advertising the business, while Mulhall headlined the entertainment and also competed for prizes in the rodeo events.[28] After producing contests at places like Fort Worth, San Antonio, and Kansas City for two years, Mulhall's business diminished. While World War I was partly to blame for the downturn, that was not the only reason. Sponsors of the Fort Worth rodeo also questioned the integrity of an operation in which a majority of the contestants were already on the payroll. Their doubts cost Mulhall her 1918 contract with the Fort Worth rodeo, and the following year she left the business for good.[29]

Even with the apparent conflict of interest and the competition from fake rodeos, many new rodeo companies appeared following World War I. They dominated the business through the fifties. They succeeded in spite of the problems because they were a financial boon to competitors, as salaries usually covered expenses, leaving winnings as profit. The steady employment also protected athletes from financial disasters caused by a downturn of luck, and made encounters with bloomers less likely. Finally, the companies facilitated the spread of rodeo across the country and throughout the year, so that it could become a full-time profession for the contestants. The entire situation benefited women especially, since they always had fewer opportunities to compete and needed the steady employment.[30]

Top rodeo stars like Tommy and Bea Kirnan, Tad and Buck Lucas, and Alice Greenough and Joe Orr, as well as former Wild West show owners like California Frank Hafley, all owned rodeo companies at one time or another. While the most enduring was Col. Jim Eskew's J. E. Ranch rodeo, the most famous were unquestionably Gene Autry's Flying A Ranch Rodeo Company and Gene Autry's World's Championship Rodeo Company.

Fortunately, honesty ultimately triumphed, although bad coexisted with the good for many years. In her book *The Cowgirls*, the folklorist Joyce Gibson Roach suggests that many of the cowgirl contests throughout rodeo history were fraudulent.[31] A related issue pertains to "chippies," women who supposedly joined the rodeo to chase the cowboys and won their titles by bestowing sexual favors on the judges. Chippies too have become part of the folklore of rodeo, and some must surely have existed, but supporting data is scarce. To date, no women have stepped forward to admit having been chippies and won titles in that way, so the charge is impossible to substantiate.[32]

The only evidence I could find to support either claim came from Alice Greenough. She maintained that the victory in one bronc riding contest in which she participated was actually promised in advance to another contestant. Two other women who participated in the same rodeo did not agree with her on this point. It is my belief that the major contests such as Cheyenne Frontier Days, Pendleton Roundup, and the Madison Square Garden and Boston Garden rodeos, as well as the other contests staged by major producers such as Tex Austin, Guy Weadick, W. T. Johnson, Fred Beebe, and Jim Eskew, were legitimate. The dishonesty occurred at the lower echelons of the rodeo world, in the nether land of fake companies, Wild West rodeo thrill circuses, and the like. Today, the history of all of them has become so intertwined that it is almost impossible to separate the good from the bad.

The first significant attempts to regulate rodeo began with the 1929 formation of the Rodeo Association of America (RAA).[33] Although the RAA had little enforcement power, it did use the pages of *Hoofs and Horns,* its original "official publication," to blacklist crooked operators like Milt Hinkle and the equally notorious Larry Sunbrock.[34] The RAA also provided contestants with the assurance that all RAA-sanctioned rodeos would be conducted in accordance with their published guidelines, which were designed to eliminate undesirable practices and establish rodeo as a sport. Rodeos had to include bronc riding, steer bulldogging, steer roping, and calf roping, conducted according to RAA rules, in order to be sanctioned. Through an intricate point system based on dollars won at their sanctioned rodeos, the RAA also proposed to name the true "world champions" in the four required events, as well as the all-around cowboy each year.[35] The RAA system never included any events for women.

The problems did not end with the formation of the RAA, which was most powerful in the West, because eastern rodeos remained in the control of powerful independent men who did not join, while bloomers and other questionable operators continued to flourish. Contestants themselves remained virtually powerless until 1936, when a series of factors led to a successful cowboy strike at the Boston Garden. The most immediate result of that action was the formation of the Cowboys Turtle Association (CTA), now the Professional Rodeo Cowboys Association (PRCA). Working with the RAA, the CTA ultimately succeeded in getting more equitable prizes, standardized rules and events, and the right to sanction rodeos.[36] The RAA subsequently merged with another organization, and for a time competed with the PRCA. By 1955 the PRCA had driven out all competition, leaving the professional cowboys themselves in control of big-time rodeo.[37] It was only after the PCRA gained credibility and could both blacklist dishonest promoters and cancel the permits of cowboys who participated in nonsanctioned events that the unscrupulous operations finally disappeared.

The major beneficiaries of the CTA/PRCA success were white males. Females, African-Americans, and Hispanics, already few in number, disappeared from rodeo's mainstream. In the CTA/PRCA's defense it must be said, however, that their records give no evidence of institutional racism. In fact, they were more than fair in that regard, while sexism was pervasive.[38] Therefore, women were the biggest losers of all. This was particularly true since another result of the 1936 strike was that new promoters took over the Madison Square Garden and Boston Rodeos. By 1943, they discontinued the cowgirl bronc riding contest that had been featured at New York since 1922.[39]

Rodeos throughout the country followed the New York lead, leaving cowgirls with few options. Of course, rodeo control had been almost totally patriarchal since Buffalo Bill. Local committees and independent promoters and producers had almost all been male as well. Even though a few females did become producers or coproducers, women had no opportunity to participate in the governance of the RAA or the CTA. Still, the old-time cowgirls tried to work within this system, even as their disadvantages continue to mount.

The same was not true of women born in the thirties and beyond, who also aspired to be legitimate athletes. Unlike their predecessors, the post–World War II generation of cowgirls took matters into their own hands. In 1948, a group of them founded the Girls Rodeo Association (GRA), now the Women's Professional Rodeo Association (WPRA), and began working with both local rodeo producers and the PRCA itself. The WPRA soon made cowgirl barrel racing a standard rodeo contest at a majority of PRCA-sanctioned rodeos, and recently also succeeded in getting women prize money equal to that of the men. The WPRA also sponsors a series of All Women rodeos, but these draw limited crowds and prize money is insufficient even to meet expenses.[40]

For the PRCA, the problem of determining true world champions remained until 1959, when the first National Finals Rodeo took place at Dallas. Since that time, the NFR has become America's premier rodeo. The top fifteen money winners in six cowboy events: bareback and saddle bronc riding, bull riding, calf and team roping, steer wrestling, and, since 1967, WPRA barrel racing, compete in the week-long rodeo. Prize money won at the NFR is added to the year's winnings, and the contestant with the highest total winnings is the national champion of his/her event. The contestant earning the most money in two or more events combined is the all-around cowboy, the highest honor.

In 1985, lured by a hefty increase in the purse, the NFR moved from Oklahoma City to Las Vegas, Nevada, where it has gained enormous popularity and publicity. There, in 1986, world champion barrel racer Charmayne James (Rodman) brought her annual earnings to over $200,000, more than any cowboy or cowgirl had ever won in a single event. Charmayne's achievements during the past nine years show that women can once again attain stardom and top earnings in professional rodeo, although they have yet to regain the status they once enjoyed.

American Women and Sport

The women's sport revolution of the past two decades has seen opportunities and attitudes toward female athletes change dramatically. Funding and prize money have skyrocketed, so that some women athletes, amateur and professional, have begun to realize the kinds of financial benefits heretofore available only to men. Equally significant have been the changes in the social attitudes toward female sport participation. Today, a vast majority of American parents believe that sport is equally important for women and men; few believe that sports are unladylike. More significant, less than 3 percent of female adolescents now feel that males denigrate female athletes.[41]

These changes are very recent. From the mid-nineteenth century until the 1960s, mainstream attitudes toward female athleticism often reflected the views of Pierre de Coubertin, founder of the modern Olympic Games, who stated that women's sports were against the laws of nature, while the proper role for females was to reward male athletic victors with applause.[42] Medical beliefs dictated that women refrain from vigorous physical activity or risk destroying their reproductive capabilities. As a result, social norms and lack of opportunity kept all except the most daring women out of the sports arena. A majority of Americans continued to believe that sports were not for females.[43] Sport sociologists such as Stanley Eitzen and George H. Sage noted that the combined role of successful athlete and woman was virtually impossible in North America until recently. Women found that they could not compete actively in sports and remain feminine; instead they faced social isolation. "By choosing the physically active life, the female was repudiating traditional female gender-role expectations. Female athletes did not suit the ideal of femininity, and those who persisted in sport suffered for it."[44]

Still, these attitudes applied primarily to urban, eastern, educated, middle- and upper-class white women. Very different attitudes, standards, and practices applied to women from other geographic, racial, and socioeconomic groups. The Victorian ideal of the pale, frail woman incapable of exertion was never relevant for women who toiled in fields and factories, and certainly not for those who actually made the arduous trek west with the wagon trains and established homesteads under the most difficult and physically demanding frontier conditions.[45] As the historian Elizabeth Jameson observes, the roles prescribed by the "Cult of True Womanhood" could only be achieved by urban, leisure-class women.[46]

Yet for most American women, these attitudes died hard. The number of socially approved sports for elite women increased during the late Victorian period, a time when a more athletic "new woman" appeared as an alternative to the ideal of feminine frailty. While this new woman initially appeared to increase the acceptability of female athleticism, exactly the opposite occurred. There were several reasons for this. One was the contention that athletics, like suffrage, would teach women male traits, thereby destroying their femininity. Psychologists like Richard Krafft-Ebing went even farther, linking female athletic participation to lesbianism, and suggesting that girls who preferred boy's games were exhibiting the initial symptoms of perversion.[47] Also, because the new woman was dedicated to a career, marriage was not possible. These factors combined to change the upbeat image of athletic, enthusiastic young women to the negative stereotype of masculinized lesbians, a specter that has haunted athletic women ever since.[48] The Canadian feminist Helen Lenskyj noted that "Throughout the century of women's mass sporting participation, femininity and heterosexuality have been seen as incompatible with sporting excellence: either sport made women masculine, or sportswomen were masculine at the outset. In the last half-century, the term 'masculine' has often implied lesbian."[49] Detractors have been able weaken support for both women's sports and feminist activities by implying that the participants were lesbians. Even with recent progress toward eliminating discrimination based on sexual orientation, homophobia remains pervasive, and some women avoid participating in activities that have lesbian connotations.

Several female athletic heroines did earn the enthusiastic support of the masses during sport's golden age in the twenties and thirties. All who did so were young, exceptionally attractive participants in track and field and traditionally feminine, noncontact sports of the upper classes. Female amateur athletes such as tennis star Helen Wills were quite popular, but professional athletic competition remained outside the realm of generally accepted female behavior.[50]

One female athlete whose popularity actually increased when she turned professional was figure skater Sonja Henie, but she did not compete professionally. Instead she performed with skating shows and starred in films that emphasized her feminine grace and charm and always depicted her beautifully coifed and costumed, and in the films at least, always getting her man. Conversely, the greatest American woman athlete of the thirties, and perhaps of all time, Mildred "Babe" Didrikson Zaharias, never reaped the glory or financial rewards of her Olympic triumphs. Donald Mrozek has suggested that "great as her athletic achievements were, her final social acceptance came only when she had passed beyond athletic success and emerged as a *mater dolorosa* and moral paragon during her fight with cancer."[51]

Throughout these years, women physical educators, in cooperation with the medical profession, continued to stress the dangers inherent in intensive, competitive sport. Through a network of national organizations, these educators labored tirelessly to keep American women out of the Olympic Games, and to remove varsity competition from American high schools and colleges. Nervous breakdowns and infertility were high on the list of problems they associated with physical activity for women, although the idea that sport masculinized women was always lurking beneath the surface. Consequently the actions of the physical education groups reinforced existing negative stereotypes and helped keep athletic women outside the bounds of social acceptability.[52] While the physical educators did not totally eliminate women's athletics, they did deprive several generations of middle- and upper-class urban women of a legitimate opportunity to compete and excel in sports other than ones traditionally learned at country clubs. Varsity sports for women did continue in rural high schools and a few small colleges, while urban women sometimes competed in Amateur Athletic Union (AAU) and Industrial Leagues.

Since this situation had prevailed during the "Golden Age of Sport," it is no surprise that it intensified during the period following World War II, an almost neo-Victorian era when women's clothing became much more modest, and home and family values dominated. Attitudes toward sport during the late forties and fifties echoed Coubertin's nineteenth-century beliefs, and women were expected to avoid actual athletic competition, becoming instead cheerleaders and pompon girls that encouraged the men's teams.[53] Not until the late fifties did the Division for Girls and Women in Sport (DGWS), one of the physical education organizations involved in diminishing women's competition, finally capitulate and begin endorsing varsity competition and supporting the Olympic movement. By that time, the DGWS was really acknowledging what was already happening. A majority of their younger members had already made known their support of varsity competition, and approximately one-third of colleges were conducting such programs for women.[54] Subsequently, the DGWS organized the first intercollegiate championships in women's team sports.[55] This reversal, the passage of Title IX of the Educational Amendments of 1972, which barred gender discrimination in education, and the women's movement itself, finally turned the tide. The combined effects of all of these produced the attitudes found in the 1988 Wilson Report.[56]

Rodeo Cowgirls and Western Women

To date there has been little research on the sporting experiences of women outside the mainstream.[57] Janice Beran, one of the few sport historians to study the subject, has shown conclusively that the frontier heritage left a lasting impact on Iowa women, who refused to accept the idea that they were somehow less capable than men. As a result, Iowa educational institutions ignored the dictates of physical educators and provided physical education and sport for women from earliest times. Iowa women have played basketball since 1898, with the Iowa girls high school basketball tournament beginning in 1926. Iowa's female basketball stars are superstars in the truest sense, and remain genuine heroines long after their competitive careers have ended.[58] While there are undoubtedly numerous other examples of the relationship between frontier and/or homesteading experiences and the development and promotion of women's sports, research on these topics remains unpublished.

Recent research on pioneer women from the trans-Mississippi West does provide some insights into the life-styles and attitudes that enabled female athletes to flourish there. Scholars have found that westerners held widely divergent ideas about sex roles, and that those ideas changed over time, place, and generation. Some writers found that once women became settled in the West and their conditions improved, they attempted to return to a more genteel style of living, while other scholars found that for many families hardship and primitive conditions remained for decades, if not generations. Some also believe that women born on the frontier were usually more liberated in their ideas about gender roles and stereotypes than their parents.[59] This is consistent with my findings on rodeo cowgirls.

Scholars have also found that the homesteading experience was a positive one for many women, whether or not they personally staked a claim. It appears that even wives who could not themselves enter claims "probably acquired some psychological benefit from the unprecedented opportunities for land ownership available to their daughters and to others of their sex."[60] The ranching environment, where women could perform all manner of tasks and enjoy the freedom of owning and caring for their own horses and of working for pay, also opened up new vistas.

Experiences of homesteaders in northeastern Colorado between 1873 and 1920 were in many ways similar to those reported by pioneer cowgirls in this book. In both cases, all family members worked, with tasks assigned on the basis of ability, not gender.[61] This was certainly a reality for future rodeo cowgirls Alice and Margie Greenough. Born in 1904 and 1911 respectively, they grew up on a ranch near Red Lodge, Montana. Like their brothers, they began riding horses while very young, and could rope and ride quite well even as children. While they enjoyed these activities, they also had to use them to contribute to the family income by working both on the ranch and at outside jobs.[62] Gender clearly mattered little when there was work to be done either in their own or neighboring families. Alice recalled one occasion when a local rancher came by seeking to hire one of the Greenough boys for a seasonal job. Noting that all his sons already had work, her father said: "take Alice, she'll work just like a man." Alice spent the next several months driving six to eight horses on a gang plow with an otherwise all-male crew, and that was not her only experience with "man's work." When Alice was fourteen, Ben Greenough took a rural mail route and turned it over to his daughter to drive. She carried the mail thirty-seven miles a day, even when the weather was forty degrees below zero. These experiences did nothing to harm her sense of womanliness, nor did it ever occur to her that such arduous labors might preclude her eventually marrying and having children, which she did.[63]

Like Alice, most female ranch children learned the traditional homemaking skills of cooking and sewing along with their liberating and empowering experiences. Mothers frequently encouraged them to aim for a more genteel and feminine life-style. Several cowgirls remembered their mothers as tiny, quiet, gentle, or shy, and quite different from themselves. They also recalled mothers urging them to ride sidesaddle, and reminding them that ladies never went out without their corsets.[64] Since experience had taught them different attitudes and values, they often took or created opportunities to quit ranch life for the rodeo business. Even there, women received mixed signals. It was not unusual for cowgirl winners at early western contests to be awarded lemonade sets or sidesaddles.[65]

Whether they won sidesaddles, western saddles, or cash, cowgirls' thrilling performances inspired countless younger women to follow their lead. Everywhere that cowgirls appeared, they provided new examples of women's potential. They proved that women could enjoy independent, apparently glamorous careers, and also be physically strong and competent. While there is ample evidence that cowboys who participated in rodeos, Wild West shows, and films had a dramatic impact on young males in America, little has been written about the influence of cowgirl performers on young women. Research for this book has uncovered many cases in which girls were inspired in early childhood by professional cowgirls, and had new dreams and ambitions as a result. This was true not only of girls on the cattle frontier but of eastern women as well. Several who rode well ran away from home to follow their rodeo dreams. Even girls with no interest in joining the rodeo might have gained a new understanding of women's potential for independence, strength, and physical achievement from watching the professional cowgirls in action.

As late as World War II, women raised on the cattle frontier enjoyed many of the same experiences as their foremothers. Almost all ranch women could ride, and most had selected and trained their own mounts since they were children. Many also mastered a variety of ranch skills from dehorning and castrating cattle to shoeing horses, as fathers continued to encourage both daughters and sons to perform these chores. Both male and female children competed in a variety of rodeolike activities with siblings and neighbors.[66] Like their predecessors, many of these youngsters aspired to professional rodeo careers, often as not motivated by men and women they had seen in person when the rodeo came to town.

The situation remains essentially the same today, as more than 85 percent of professional cowgirls still come from the old cattle frontier.[67] Richard Slatta maintains that ties between rodeo and ranch life are now largely "cultural and nostalgic."[68] It is true that the skills of ranching and rodeo have become dissimilar, but it is equally true that excellent horsemanship is the basis for all rodeo skills except bull riding. In the 1990s as in the 1880s, ranch youngsters begin riding in infancy, and frequently become proficient with the lasso as well. Elizabeth Atwood Lawrence shows conclusively that ranch youngsters are socialized into rodeo at a very young age.[69] She reported that Little Britches contestants' enthusiasm is supported by parents, several of whom told her about their children, stating they "rode before they could walk." The mothers also reported that the youngsters "are constantly roping; they rope anything that moves." Several parents summed it up this way: "my kids eat, breathe, and sleep rodeo."[70]

These youngsters frequently progress from Little Britches to Junior Rodeo, High School Rodeo, and Intercollegiate Rodeo without ever leaving home. Children who grow up in an eastern or urban environment have no similar opportunities. Top cowboys and cowgirls still come from the cattle country, perhaps more now than in the pre–World War I era, when eastern youngsters were still likely to run away and join the rodeo. Among 114 participants at the 1991 NFR, 94 percent were from states and provinces west of the ninety-eighth meridian. Texas and Oklahoma accounted for more than 40 percent of the total, sending thirty-one and thirteen athletes respectively. Montana, home of rodeo hall of fame honorees Fannie Sperry Steele and the famous Riding Greenoughs (Margie, Alice, Bill, and Turk), produces rodeo stars far out of proportion to its population. Montana and California had eight contestants apiece at the NFR, even though California has almost thirty million more inhabitants than Montana.[71] Among the Montana contingent was cowboy Deb Greenough, carrying on a proud family tradition, and three cowgirls, two of them from Cut Bank.[72]

The pioneer rodeo cowgirls were also products of a very different culture from their eastern, urban counterparts. They had disparate attitudes toward sport, work, and femininity. Cowgirls' sporting experiences differed in many significant ways even from those of other female athletes who managed to succeed despite the odds against them. According to the sport historian Joan Hult, a major factor contributing to the success of most great female athletes has been the support, encouragement, and coaching they received from their fathers.[73] This was true of very few cowgirls other than Lucille Mulhall, and women like Reine Shelton and Dixie Reger Mosley, who were literally born on the rodeo circuit. Although cowgirls did learn their roping and riding skills working on the family ranches, and some like the Greenoughs were encouraged by their fathers to compete in other sports, their career choices were made quite independently, and sometimes without family approval. The situation did not begin to change until the thirties and forties when champion cowgirls like

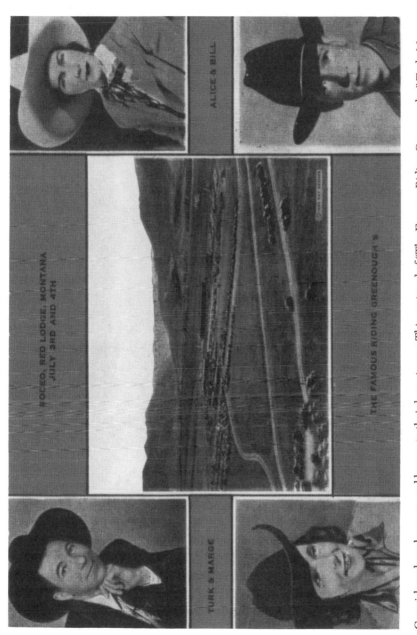

Cowgirls and cowboys are real heroes in their hometowns. This postcard of "The Famous Riding Greenoughs," Turk, Marge, Alice, and Bill, is still for sale in Red Lodge, Montana. Courtesy of Alice Greenough Orr, Tucson, Arizona.

Dixie Reger (Mosley) making her rodeo debut at age five. Photo courtesy of Dixie Reger Mosley, Amarillo, Texas.

Isora DeRacy Young and Jackie Worthington received tireless coaching and support from their fathers. Since that time, many rodeo cowgirls have come from rodeo families.[74]

Hult also discovered that exceptional beauty was virtually essential in order for American women to become "glorified athletic heroines."[75] Few cowgirls were beauties in the classic sense. Those who enjoyed the glory, the headlines, and commercial endorsements were outstanding athletes like Fannie Sperry Steele, Lucille Mulhall, Tad Lucas, Mabel Strickland, and Alice Greenough, rather than great beauties. These women were certainly attractive, but they earned their fame through skill, dedication, and victories in cowgirl contests at important rodeos like Cheyenne Frontier Days, Pendleton Roundup, Calgary Stampede, and Madison Square Garden. The few cowgirls who were considered exceptionally beautiful were often selected to pose for publicity stunts, but were not the most famous or the most financially successful contestants.[76]

Skilled cowgirls did reap the rewards of athletic victory because they usually enjoyed much better press than most other female athletes. Of course, media coverage of women has been so minimal as to be called "symbolic annihilation."[77] It is not surprising, given public attitudes toward athletic females, that their exploits have largely been ignored. What is perhaps worse is that the limited coverage women's sports have received has been overwhelmingly biased and sexist. Scholars in the United States, Great Britain, and Canada have reached essentially the same conclusions. They note that while male athletes are subjects of action shots and in-depth interviews about their training, records, and goals, with their achievements endlessly analyzed, females seldom get such treatment. Photographs of women athletes are more likely to be cheesecake than action shots, if they appear at all. A 1977 study found that women were the subjects of 30 percent of all newspaper photographs, with only 8 percent of the pictures found in sports pages.[78] Articles about female athletes have generally focused on beauty, domesticity, marital status, and culinary skills, with few interviews and only minimal attempts to analyze athletic skills and strategies.[79]

The thousands of articles consulted for this book, from trade papers and countless American and Canadian newspapers published between 1896 and 1992, gave cowgirls far more extensive and unbiased press treatment than female athletes usually received. From the earliest major rodeos, cowgirls were interviewed and photographed. They shared headlines with cowboys, and their events were often reported in great detail, with explanations of their triumphs and their secrets to success. Reporters did show a great deal of interest in the fact that most cowgirls were married, but this was clearly news, given the widespread belief that female athletes were unfeminine and not desirable to men.[80]

This does not suggest that the media treatment of cowgirls was universally equal and free of gender bias. Some papers did omit the results of cowgirl contests, or give them scant notice. It is also possible to find such statements as "Alice Van, the blonde cutie from Burbank" took second in the relay,[81] or "Amazons of the Arena ready for today's semi-finals."[82] Far more common were headlines like: "The most daring performance of the day was also given by the cowgirls . . . ,"[83] "One of the greatest exhibitions ever seen in a rodeo" (referring to Florence Randolph),[84] "All American Girl, Expert at All Sports" (Alice Greenough),[85] or "one of the most remarkable exhibitions of rough riding ever seen here" (about Bertha Blancett).[86]

Words like these must have been an inspiration to the women who read them. When Gertrude Ederle in 1926 became the first woman to swim the English Channel, doing so in a time faster than the males who had preceded her, Carrie Chapman Catt called it a feminist victory. Boston *Daily Globe* writer Uncle Dudley suggested that "Ederle's success gave women 'new physical dignity.'"[87] Enthusiastic accounts of cowgirls' victories over men and horses and their achievements in and out of the arena may well have had a similar effect.

Another way in which cowgirls received different treatment from other women athletes was in media reaction to serious injuries. When female athletes in other sports experienced injuries or exertion-related problems, there was often an outcry against both the participants and the events, while cowgirls under the same conditions received praise for their courage and determination. At the 1913 Winnipeg Stampede, Tillie Baldwin collapsed following the Roman race, and was taken to the hospital. Despite doctor's orders to rest four to five days, she returned to the arena the following day, and reporters singled out her performance as one of the day's best.[88] In 1928 headlines exclaimed: "Rodeo Girl Star at Performance," "Knocked unconscious, Florence Randolph does stunt after recovery."[89] Randolph's accident occurred during the trick riding competition at the San Antonio rodeo. To the amazement of all present, Randolph awoke, waved off the stretcher, and resumed her ride, completing the trick that had caused her fall. She finished to thunderous applause, and in an interview afterward said simply, "It's all in the game."[90] On the other

Tillie Baldwin defeated an otherwise all-male field to win the Roman race at the 1913 Winnipeg Stampede. Photo courtesy of the Glenbow Museum and Archives, Calgary, Alberta, Canada. Photo #NA-1029-18.

hand, the collapse of some female runners following the 800-meter race at the 1928 Olympic Games produced an outcry against women participating in such an arduous event. One American reporter called the participants "wretched women." As a result of such negative press, Olympic officials dropped the 800-meter race, leaving women with no races longer than 200 meters until 1960.[91]

Overall, cowgirls got the kind of coverage many female athletes could only dream of until quite recently. Even during the forties and fifties, when their opportunities were almost as limited as those of other female athletes, cowgirls continued to enjoy unprecedented family and community support, and generally favorable and unbiased press. The many articles written about them, along with other data, make it possible to draw some generalizations about their lives and the significance of sport to these women. This information may help enhance understanding of the chapters that follow.

The attitudes and traditions of the cattle frontier were adapted to life on the rodeo road, where for many years a homogeneous and amiable group of competitors traveled the circuit and often camped together, referring to one another as the "rodeo family."[92] Even though they competed with one another on an almost daily basis, they also worked together for the betterment of their sport. When a member was seriously injured, fellow contestants raised money to pay doctor and hospital bills, as no insurance was available to rodeo professionals. When donations were not sufficient, they staged benefit performances.

Bank loans were similarly unavailable, but cowboys and cowgirls with a few dollars to spare usually made loans to their friends in need. They also shared costs of accommodations, cooked meals for one another, and helped out with child care. These men and women also worked hard transporting and caring for their stock and practicing for their contests and exhibitions. Women probably had the additional responsibilities of cooking, sewing, and homemaking tasks. While the women I interviewed remembered the long hours of practice and training, they never mentioned any domestic matters except the sewing, in which they took great pride. Most of them sewed costumes for themselves and their husbands. Single women often made extra money by designing and sewing fancy shirts for bachelor cowboys at a cost far lower than would have been available elsewhere.[93] Comfortable for most, life on the road was difficult for outsiders, and the group not always friendly to young, single women. This may have contributed to the fact that most cowgirls married rodeo cowboys within a year or two of joining the circuit.

Among the dramatic illustrations of the significance of rodeo in the athletes' lives are elaborate weddings in which bride, groom, and all attendants were on horseback. The ceremonies took place at Boston Garden and Madison Square Garden rodeos, as well during Wild West shows, with cast, crew, and spectators in attendance.[94] Almost all of the couples married in equestrian ceremonies stayed together, as did many of the other cowboys and cowgirls who met and married on the circuit. Some of the better-known rodeo couples who remained married as long as both were alive included Fannie and Bill Steele, Tad and Buck Lucas, Bea and Tommy Kirnan, Mayme and Leonard Stroud, and Ed and Tillie Bowman.

Others were not so fortunate. The fact that large groups of rodeo professionals lived and worked in close proximity inevitably created temptations. It was not unusual for a cowgirl to divorce one rodeo cowboy only to marry another. Many cowgirls married at least twice, and some had several husbands. From the evidence available it appears that more than 98 percent of the cowgirls in this book were married at one time or another. Of that group, 33 percent divorced at least once, and 16 percent divorced two or more times.

Without question, there were more divorces among this group than in the population as a whole. For reasons not entirely clear, the stigma that divorce carried in some areas was clearly absent from the rodeo fraternity. Although she specifies no time period, Sara Deutsch notes that the West had more liberal divorce laws and higher divorce rates than the East.[95] Cowgirls would therefore have grown up with more liberal attitudes than their eastern counterparts. This was probably compounded by their joining the entertainment world, where frequent marriages and divorces were typically accepted. With so many rodeo contestants active in films, vaudeville, and Wild West shows, they probably also picked up some of the mores of show business. Finally, cowboys always outnumbered cowgirls by a sizable margin, creating a situation that mirrored the Old West itself.

Far less data is available on cowgirls' children than on their marital status. It appears that at least during the period before World War II, professional cowgirls were less likely to have children than other women. A few cowgirls did raise their youngsters on the road and in the limelight, while others went to great lengths to prevent their offspring from pursuing rodeo careers. In some cases, the children themselves made the choice. Tad Lucas said this about her two daughters: "Dorothy hated the rodeo and wouldn't go, Mitzi loved it and wouldn't stay home."[96] Mitzi began riding with her mother while still a toddler, and made her professional debut at age four.[97]

Evidence is also scarce concerning many other issues and problems that inevitably developed within so large a group, but some of the difficulties experienced by the cowboys must have been true for the women. Slatta notes: "Like the early cowboy, rodeo riders gained unsavory reputations for wildness, fighting, and drunkenness."[98] The extent of women's participation in these activities is unknown, but they were surely involved. Ella Gangler, a native of Pendleton, Oregon, who participated in the first three Pendleton Roundups at ages ten through twelve, had vivid memories of the professional cowgirls who came to her home town. She recalled that they smoked, drank, played cards, and were always around men, "we didn't know that kind of life."[99]

While I found no other accounts like Gangler's, I did find evidence that two cowgirls were alcoholics, at least in their later years, and both were active during the years Gangler recalled. Another, from a later time, admitted that excessive drinking contributed to her disastrous personal problems. She was among three cowgirls indicted for murder. Two were tried and found not guilty, while the fate of the third is unknown. Several cowgirls died in automobile accidents, and one committed suicide.[100]

Of course, rodeo itself is dangerous, and career-ending injuries were possibilities that cowboys and cowgirls lived with throughout their careers. Six women did die as a direct result of rodeo accidents, while the number of injuries is beyond calculation.[101] Despite the risks, most professional cowgirls lived remarkably long lives. For those on whom data is available, the average life span was seventy-five years. The oldest lived to be ninety-seven, and of the ten who died before age sixty, only two died of "natural" causes.[102]

As mentioned earlier, many of these women had enjoyed long and successful careers. Sixty-seven women had careers lasting eleven to twenty years, and thirty-two continued in professional rodeo for twenty-one years or more. The average career for those who remained in the business three years or more was twelve years, with the longest being fifty-seven years. On the other hand, 389 women dropped out after only one or two years. The women with shorter careers clearly lacked the skills needed to make a go of professional rodeo. More than three-fourths of the women whose careers lasted three years or longer competed in two or more events, while only 14 percent of the women with shorter careers did so. Almost all of the successful cowgirls also gave performances, known as "contract acts," at the rodeos, thereby greatly increasing their incomes. Only 5 percent of the women with short careers were contract performers.[103]

The real driving force behind many long careers was a trait shared by almost all successful cowgirls through the years: their special love for horses and unique ability to train and handle them. Often, riding, working with, and being around horses was the central focus of their lives.[104] Along with this love came an amazing skill with animals that enabled them to select and train the horses that would be their partners in competition, thus enhancing the significance of their victories. It is equally true of the top cowgirl of the eighties and nineties, Charmayne James Rodman. She selected and trained Scamper, the "wonder horse" that she has ridden to nine consecutive world barrel racing titles.[105]

Many rodeo couples who enjoyed long lives and successful marriages were able to take advantage of their shared expenses and combined incomes. They amassed sufficient savings to purchase properties for their retirement years. While poor financial planning and impoverished retirements are common in both the entertainment and sports worlds, I could find only one example of similar distress in all of the data collected for this

Charmayne James Rodman with Scamper, the horse she has ridden to nine world championships in WPRA barrel racing. Photo by Kenneth Springer, Waxahachie, Texas.

book! On the other hand, success stories of pleasant retirements, comfortable homes, and long, healthy lives abound.

All of the women interviewed for this study agreed that their rodeo years had been the best of their lives, and that they would certainly select the same careers again.[106] Most of them, along with cowgirls who wrote about their feelings, seem to agree with the sentiments expressed by pioneer rodeo star Fannie Sperry Steele. In a 1967 interview, seventy-five-year-old Fannie told a reporter: "I've never seen one rodeo too many nor ridden one ride too long in my life."[107]

Vera McGinnis, another early-day cowgirl who has been honored by two halls of fame, wrote emotionally about the day she decided to quit her office job and join the rodeo: "If I'd pulled up right then, I likely would have missed the years of hardship, heartache, fun, adventure, a smidgen of fame, and finally, a broken body. But I'm glad I didn't, for I can honestly say the glamor never faded. It dimmed once in a while when I was hurt or overworked, but after a rest I always felt that I wouldn't trade being a rodeo cowgirl for any other profession."[108]

Chapter Two

Wild West Frontier Days, 1880s–World War I

Commercial rodeos and Wild West shows both began with Buffalo Bill's successful 1882 Fourth of July celebration at North Platte, Nebraska. Until that time, western contests were merely local folk festivals where neighbors gathered to watch one another participate in a variety of events. Consequently, most of the winners' names are lost in the mists of time. It was only after Cody's venture that western contests became more formalized, and athletes and entertainers began to make headlines. From the 1880s through World War I, the major beneficiaries of the publicity were Wild West show performers, rather than rodeo contestants.

Buffalo Bill had no women other than actresses in his original cast until he signed legendary sharpshooter Annie Oakley in 1885. He added "lady riders" the following year.[1] From 1886 until the turn of the century, at least twelve women performed with various Wild West shows.[2] Exactly how Cody recruited these women is uncertain; he probably found them in the same way he found his cowboys, by scouting local contests for outstanding athletes. It is therefore likely that the first Wild West show cowgirls had also been among the earliest female rodeo contestants. Two women who earned local reputations as bronc riders in the 1890s were Annie Shaffer and Lulu Belle Parr. By the turn of the century, both had quit competitive rodeo to become full-time Wild West show performers.[3] Many others followed their lead, while approximately one-third of the professional cowgirls active before 1912 combined performing and competing for most of their careers.[4]

During the 1880s, at least sixteen women participated in rodeos, Wild West shows, or both. Seventeen women competed in rodeos during the

Miss Lulu B. Parr, Lady Broncho rider, 101 Ranch Real Wild West Show.

Lulu Belle Parr was one of the first famous cowgirl bronc riders. She was notorious for extravagant costumes like the one shown here as she rode a bronc for the 101 Ranch Real Wild West in 1913. Photo courtesy of Gilbert Pittman, Wichita, Kansas.

years between 1886 and 1911, while twenty-one others performed in one of eleven Wild West shows that employed female riders. There were enough small town rodeos to comprise a kind of circuit that both cowboys and cowgirls could follow, during those years, but few records exist of men's or women's contests.[5] Both rodeo and Wild West shows grew tremendously between the late 1880s and 1917, when World War I brought them to a virtual standstill.

Those cowgirls who competed before the war had few peers in sport. In the 1870s and 1880s, women and men had competed in professional pedestrian races, but the contests died out before the cowgirls rode into the picture. The only other female professional athletes during the late nineteenth and early twentieth centuries were a few sharpshooters and professional weight lifters. Like the cowgirls they longed for genuine competition in which to prove their prowess, but found limited opportunities other than specially arranged challenge matches. Also like the cowgirls, they found it necessary to perform in circuses or vaudeville in order to earn a living from their sports. These women had other things in common. All defied traditional gender roles by becoming professional athletes in traditionally "male" sports. Yet virtually all of them were married, and they enjoyed reasonably fair treatment from the press. Many not only competed in sports but also invaded the male domain of business, forming partnerships with husbands or other male friends.[6] All of this made them a distinct minority among white married women, only 3 percent of whom were in the work force.[7] Although ranch women engaged in virtually all of the chores associated with the cattle business, western women as a group were less likely to hold jobs outside the home or family business than their eastern counterparts. Leaving home for professional rodeo careers made the cowgirls even more unusual when compared to other women from their region.[8]

There were some differences of course. One was that competitive situations for sharpshooters and weight lifters really never improved over the years, whereas cowgirls eventually had a regular rodeo circuit on which to compete.[9] The greatest contrast was in the clothing the women wore while competing. The differences were partly a result of different backgrounds. Most weight lifters were from families of entertainers, while a majority of cowgirls and sharpshooters emerged from conventional backgrounds where women's dress remained quite modest and conservative. The weight lifters' dress was very theatrical, and certainly risqué by traditional standards of the times, as they usually appeared on stage wearing revealing tights and sleeveless leotards with plunging necklines. Their outfits not only allowed them maximum freedom of movement, they were also showy and attractive.

Cowgirls needed costumes that enabled them to perform their skills successfully without violating the restrictive dress codes of the cattle frontier. Western women rarely wore trousers to work on ranches, even under the most adverse conditions, until the late twenties.[10] Glenn R. Vernam dates the invention of the divided skirt at 1902, and states that western women rode sidesaddle until the turn of the century.[11] He was wrong by at least a decade on both counts. When British expatriate Evelyn Cameron rode into Miles City, Montana, in 1895 wearing a divided skirt, authorities threatened to arrest her. The following excerpt from a letter to her family explains the event: "Although my costume was so full as to look like an ordinary walking dress when the wearer was on foot, it created a small sensation. So great at first was the prejudice against any divided garment in Montana that a warning was given me to abstain from riding on the streets of Miles City lest I might be arrested! After riding into town forty-eight miles from the ranch, I was much amused at the laughing and giggling girls who stood staring at my costume as I walked about."[12]

Resistance remained strong for several years, with Cameron insisting that divided skirts, or even her husband's old trousers, were much safer for ranch work than dresses. When one of her friends incurred serious injury in a riding accident, Cameron stated that more sensible clothing would have prevented it. Eventually her pioneering efforts paid off. Female ranchers like the neighboring Buckley sisters, Mabel, May, and Myrtle, found new freedom to pursue their tasks in divided skirts.[13] By the time the Miles City Roundup was organized soon after the turn of the century, divided skirts were a common sight around Miles City, and cowgirls who came to participate in the rodeo never encountered the problems Cameron had endured.

By then the standard rodeo cowgirl costume consisted of simple, floor-length divided skirts and shirtwaists devoid of any decorations. Even in 1912, many cowgirls still competed in very plain shirtwaists and sometimes old sweaters, while others paid great attention to their appearance. Some wore large hair ribbons beneath their ten-gallon hats. Their rodeo outfits are virtually identical to work attire worn by the Buckley sisters, who never competed in a rodeo or performed with a show.

Anglo women in southwest Texas wore similar attire through World War I for recreational riding.[14] However, women who actually did ranch work in those remote regions found divided skirts unsuitable for their tasks. When newlywed Hallie Crawford Stillwell first appeared in her divided skirt to assist her husband with the ranch chores on the Big Bend frontier, he immediately vetoed the outfit: "Hell, you can't ride in that thing. There's not a horse in this part of the country that will let a thing like that on it. . . . You'll have to have some pants."[15] Only after one of the ranch hands agreed to loan her a pair of his trousers was Hallie allowed to proceed with her work.

Even though rodeo and ranch outfits were similar, Wild West show costumes were much more ornate. Female performers often wore leather riding skirts decorated with fringes and conchos, leather fringed gauntlets, and embroidered vests. Women like Lucille Mulhall and Florence LaDue dressed much more conservatively while competing than when performing in shows, but always appeared in divided skirts. Even though competition attire became more decorative, it never paralleled the most elaborate Wild West costumes.[16]

The problem of finding acceptable and practical competitive attire was by no means limited to the rodeo arena, but was evident wherever female athletes appeared. During the first years of the twentieth century, female amateur athletes, mostly from the eastern social elite, gained prominence. Although not permitted at the 1896 Olympic Games, women did compete thereafter. In 1900, several American debutantes attired in voluminous skirts and petticoats participated in tennis and golf at the Paris games, with Margaret Abbot winning the golf title.[17] At the 1904 games in St. Louis, archery was the only contest for women; in 1908 they competed in both tennis and figure skating. The foremost female amateur athlete of the era, however, was not an Olympian. During a lifetime of active partic- ipation, socialite Eleonora Sears, great-great-granddaughter of Thomas Jefferson, won more than 240 athletic trophies in sports ranging from ten- nis to long distance walking.[18] She also earned praise from the press for her athletic grace and skill, and really made headlines with her dramatic efforts to break down some of the barriers to female sport participation. In 1910, Sears created a sensation on the polo field. She rode astride and competed against men, things rarely seen in the East. Cowgirls had been doing the same things to little notice for decades, but Eleonora's social position made her actions newsworthy.[19] Sears gained even greater noto- riety when she appeared in public wearing trousers more than a decade before the cowgirls made such a radical move. When cowgirls did perform in the East, they got favorable reviews from the press, often for doing the same things for which Sears was castigated. One possible explanation for the difference is that the public still viewed cowgirls as visitors from the mythical West, an almost exotic culture with distinctive customs and mo- res.

"America's First Cowgirl"

The most famous pioneer cowgirl, and the first to charm the New York press, was Lucille Mulhall. Lucille became "America's First Cowgirl" be- cause of widespread belief that the word *cowgirl* was coined for her. That is incorrect. The *Police Gazette* called Gertrude Petran "a genuine and fascinating cowgirl" in 1893,[20] four years before Mulhall's first public ap- pearance. Lucille was, however, the first famous cowgirl, and probably the best-known woman in western entertainment other than Annie Oakley. Like Oakley she received nationwide publicity. Fictionalized and roman- ticized biographies later described her as a typical, wholesome, outdoor- loving all-American girl.[21] Katherine B. Stansbury, of Mulhall, Oklahoma, finally revealed the true story. The woman she describes in her privately published 1985 book *Lucille Mulhall: Her Family—Her Life—Her Times* (revised and reissued in 1992 as *Lucille Mulhall: Wild West Cowgirl*) is a complex and somewhat troubled individual from a very unusual family.

Lucille was born in St. Louis, Missouri, on October 21, 1885. When she was four the family moved to a ranch near Guthrie, Oklahoma. While she attended boarding schools, she also spent a great deal of time on the ranch. She became an excellent roper and rider, and enjoyed both, for unlike most frontier cowgirls, Lucille never had to do ranch work as a matter of economic necessity. For her it was all play until her father, Col. Zack Mulhall, decided to capitalize on her talents. Thereafter, he dominated her life and her career, and probably contributed to the breakup of both her brief marriages.[22]

Her first public appearance was at the 1897 St. Louis Fair, and she was a seasoned performer by her 1900 New York debut. Later that year, the Mulhall troupe entertained at the Rough Riders' Reunion. Theodore Roosevelt thoroughly enjoyed Lucille's performance, and encouraged Zack to exhibit his talented daughter to the entire country.[23] During the next six years, the Mulhall family show, under a variety of names, performed throughout the United States at fairs, conventions, and rodeos. Lucille competed whenever possible, and during the winter months she and a small contingent from the show joined the vaudeville circuit.

In 1907, apparently unbeknownst to her father until after the fact, she married the vocalist from her vaudeville show, Martin Van Bergen. She gave birth in 1909 to a son, William Logan Van Bergen.[24] Soon after, Zack summoned her back. As in so many other instances, she did as her father asked. Leaving young Logan with his paternal grandparents, she hit the trail once more. She and Martin made their last public appearance together in 1910, and she saw her son only twice thereafter.[25] In March of 1914, at Olathe, Kansas, Van Bergen filed suit for divorce from Lucille.[26]

Except for a brief time during her marriage, Lucille was usually with her father, brother, and sisters. Among the siblings with whom Lucille performed was "sister" Georgie. In truth, Georgia Mulhall was Zack Mulhall's adopted daughter, his mistress, and the mother of two of Lucille's other "siblings," Mildred and Charley, whom Lucille's mother raised as her own.[27] In spite of the strange relationships, the group seemed to get along amicably. Lucille and Georgie traveled together frequently, and when Lucille left the show for competition, Georgie sometimes took her place. During Lucille's 1917 San Antonio Round-Up, journalists followed participants to the Cowboy's Ball at the Gunter Hotel. They reported: "Miss Lucille Mulhall and her sister, Miss Georgia Mulhall, were the belles of the evening, all the girls were very much in demand."[28]

Although she had two failed marriages, Lucille never lacked for suitors, one reportedly film star Tom Mix. Her closest male companion, other than her father, was her business partner Homer Wilson. Self-centered and temperamental, Mulhall nonetheless had an excellent rapport with the younger women who joined the rodeo circuit during the second decade of the twentieth century. They recalled her as invariably kind and helpful, even to those against whom she was competing. For some, like Ruth Roach, she was not only a role model but a personal mentor and friend.[29]

While Mulhall was the most famous cowgirl of the era, Cheyenne Frontier Days, begun in 1897, was the most notable early rodeo, and the first to publicize women's contests. During the years between the introduction of Buffalo Bill's Wild West show and the opening of the first Cheyenne Frontier Days, seven western states joined the Union. In 1885 Congress enacted new laws prohibiting the unauthorized fencing of public lands. "In 1886, . . . Geronimo gave up to U.S. troops, signaling the end of organized resistance on the part of free-roaming Indians on this entire continent."[30] Four years later, the last battle between Indians and United States troops took place at Wounded Knee.[31]

Far removed from western developments, one of the most famous American women of the late nineteenth century began her career. Jane Addams, who with Ellen Gates Starr founded the Chicago Hull House in 1889, helped launch the American Settlement House Movement. Addams soon became one of the most respected and idealized women in the United States.[32] Partly as a result of her endeavors, countless mostly middle-class women participated in a variety of voluntary organizations, working with settlement houses, and for suffrage and other benefits.[33]

An 1893 financial panic set off a devastating depression throughout the United States, flooding the settlement homes with impoverished victims. Even with the economic downturn, several 1893 events had lasting impact on the nation. The World's Columbian Exposition, popularly known as the Chicago World's Fair, was the most memorable. The largest, most influential and successful world's fair to that time, it marked a turning point in the cultural history of the United States.[34] One scholar described it as: "A shared and inspiring experience for Americans representing every segment of the population."[35] As with any such event, exhibitions ranged from the ridiculous to the highly intellectual. Belly dancer Little Egypt and professional strong man Eugen Sandow were among those displaying their unique skills.[36]

The three-day World Congress of Historians, held in conjunction with the annual meeting of the American Historical Association, was the most successful of the intellectual events. "Fair-sized" crowds came to hear more than thirty scholarly presentations, including one by Fredrick Jackson Turner, history professor at the University of Wisconsin. His seminal paper, "The Significance of the Frontier in American History," theorized that the process of conquering the frontier had forged the American character and transformed its people. Even though Turner's speech had little immediate impact, his frontier thesis ultimately became the foundation of western history, and has been "the subject of American historiography ever since."[37] Still today, the thesis sparks lively debate in academic journals and the popular press, and textbooks still follow Turner's basic outlines.[38]

Part of Turner's legacy was to keep the ideal of the mythical West in the public imagination. This bolstered the audience for rodeos, Wild West shows, and western films and novels. At the same time, Turner's theories extolled the achievements of heroic, rugged males, and created the perception of a West virtually devoid of females. This had far-ranging consequences, and was one reason that cowgirls had difficulty establishing their essential and rightful place in western entertainment. Sarah J. Blackstone discussed the problem as it related to Wild West shows and came to this conclusion: "The heroine of the mythic West was never as clearly established as the hero. Perhaps it was too difficult to reconcile the need for someone for the hero to protect with the emerging realization that the women of the West had shared equally with the men the dangers and hardships of frontier life and had emerged quite able to protect themselves."[39]

Thanks in part to Annie Oakley, women did have a place in Buffalo Bill's Wild West, and several cowgirls performed with his 1893 production. Although not officially a part of the Chicago fair, Cody set up his extravaganza on a lot between Sixty-second and Sixty-third streets by the Exposition entrance. This show was probably the pinnacle of Cody's success, and thousands seemed to agree that "You hadn't seen the fair unless you had seen the Wild West." For the time, it was the most successful venture in the history of outdoor amusements and netted between seven hundred thousand and one million dollars.[40]

One reason for the great interest in the show, besides its ideal location, was the tremendous success Cody enjoyed in Europe, where his show had played every season but one since 1888. The public was anxious to view a show that had entertained the crowned heads and given command performances for Queen Victoria. The elaborate presentation did not disappoint. A cast of 640 took part in nineteen different acts including a reenactment of the Battle of the Little Big Horn.[41] Also featured were Oakley, fancy roper Vincente Oropeza, and "Racing between Prairie, Indian, and Spanish Girls."[42] The success of the show and the huge crowds who saw it increased the already abundant interest in western entertainment. The many other Wild West shows touring the country at the time gave additional evidence of the genre's popularity. Pawnee Bill's Wild West, starring his wife, May Manning Lillie, "Champion Girl Shot of the West," ran Cody a close second until the two merged.[43] By the first Cheyenne Frontier Days, western amusements had achieved new heights of popularity throughout the United States.

Cheyenne Frontier Days: "The Daddy of 'em All"

Rodeo writers have devoted a great deal of attention to the Cheyenne Frontier Days, yet never agreed on when women first competed there. Several, myself included, have stated that the first cowgirl contestants talked their way into the Cheyenne bronc riding competition against the men. Most frequently cited are Bertha Kapernick (Blancett) in 1897, Prairie Rose Henderson in 1901, and Kapernick again in 1904.[44] These conflicting accounts, plus irrefutable evidence that women's races existed at Cheyenne as early as 1899, led me to reexamine all the evidence, particularly primary sources. Kapernick was certainly the first woman to ride broncs at Cheyenne, but she did so in 1904, not 1897. As Kapernick herself stated in a 1971 letter: "1904 was the first year, my first year at rodeo and the start of women competing at rodeos a long time ago."[45] Officials invited her to give a bronc riding exhibition after cowboys stopped the 1904 Frontier Days competition due to rain and a muddy field. She put on an outstanding show despite these problems, leaving the cowboys little choice but to go on with the scheduled activities.[46] Even then, Bertha did not compete against cowboys.

Local reporters gave a lengthy description of Kapernick's ride and her successful battle with the "long lanky roan, full of deviltry, with eyes blazing at the injustice." They concluded: "It was one of the most remarkable exhibitions of rough riding ever seen here, and would have been exciting had the rider been a man. As it was, the great multitude cheered . . . this extraordinary young lady who has conquered the west."[47] Bertha's reputation soon spread far and wide, but she was already a local legend closer to home. Daughter of German immigrants, Bertha was born in Cleveland, Ohio, in 1883, and moved to a Colorado ranch in 1886. Soon after her father first sat her on a horse, she became a typical cowgirl, and spent most of her time riding. She mastered almost every phase of rodeo, frequently beating men.

Those who suggest that Kapernick made her historic ride in 1897 seem to have misinterpreted Warren Richardson's 1947 article "History of the First Frontier Days Celebration." Despite its title, the article covers more than the 1897 contest. It discusses several Frontier Days, including the one in 1904.[48] Richardson states that Kapernick's ride took place during *one of the early* (emphasis mine) Frontier Days, several days into the contest, and after a terrible rainstorm. This eliminates the 1897 contest, which lasted only one day under ideal weather conditions, and without any participants named Kapernick. As noted above, the press did report on her 1904 ride along with the rain and muddy conditions. Since that was the year Kapernick herself said was her first in rodeo, it seems reasonable to conclude that Richardson too was discussing Bertha's appearance at the three-day 1904 Frontier Days.[49]

While this solves the Kapernick riddle, I found no evidence of Prairie Rose Henderson's participation in any of the early Frontier Days. Neither Richardson, the Cheyenne newspapers, nor the Frontier Days archives make any mention of her before 1910.[50] Since neither Kapernick nor Henderson rode broncs at Cheyenne before 1904, it is safe to say that the first contest for women at the Frontier Days was the cow pony race, introduced in 1899. By 1901 the race drew a popular following and a dozen entries. The local press called it the most interesting and exciting contest on the program.[51] In 1904, the year of Kapernick's first bronc riding exhibition, the winner of the cow pony race received the inaugural Denver Post Trophy for the outstanding lady rider. It was not until 1906 that cowgirl bronc riding and relay racing contests became part of the Cheyenne program.[52]

The success of the Cheyenne Frontier Days led other communities to hold their own contests. The next major western event, the Pendleton Roundup, began in 1910. It was there that Kapernick caught the eye of cowboy bulldogger Dell Blancett, whom she soon married. As Bertha Blancett, she added another dimension to her versatile career, riding as hazer for her husband's bulldogging contests.[53] She continued to be a major figure at Pendleton. There in 1914 she won the cowgirls bronc riding and relay races, as well as the Roman race—coming within a few points of the all-around cowboy title.[54]

Bertha also starred in Wild West shows and western films, the newest entertainment form to employ cowboys and cowgirls. The first western, *The Great Train Robbery*, filmed in 1903, was such a resounding success that several companies began producing westerns exclusively. They achieved enormous popularity and within nine years produced three memorable stars: Bronco Billy Anderson, William S. Hart, and Tom Mix. Mix, "King of the Cowboys," made more than two hundred western films between 1909 and 1917.[55] Blancett's employer was Bison Films, one of the pioneer companies.

At the time, the western films depicted remarkably authentic western women, who were self-reliant, athletic, and also appealing. Rodeo stars like Dorothy Morrell, Mildred Douglas, and Mabel Strickland also portrayed these roping, riding, robust cowgirls. They sometimes captured bandits at gunpoint, or galloped wildly across the plains with the cowboys.[56] Their films helped publicize rodeo and maintain the image of true cowgirls in the public imagination.

While in Hollywood, Bertha issued a $10,000 challenge for any cowgirl who could beat her in a bronc riding contest. She had also developed quite a local reputation by winning steer roping matches against cowboys.[57] Steer roping, now illegal in most states, is one of the oldest rodeo events. It was extremely popular with audiences before World War I, when contestants faced full-grown longhorns weighing more than one thousand pounds. The beasts often got head starts of as much as 150 feet before ropers could grasp their lassos and take chase. Then as now, the contestant who roped, threw down, and tied the animal in the shortest time took the prize. At some early competitions, ropers had to remount their horses before giving the finish signal to the judges, whereas others required them only to stand and raise both arms.[58]

While Blancett was among the premier woman steer ropers on the West Coast, Mulhall had gained fame from Texas to New York by roping steers better than men. During the early twentieth century she won a number of specially arranged steer roping contests at places like San Antonio, Texas, and McAlister, Oklahoma.[59] At El Paso, Texas, her father Zack won $10,000 betting on Lucille to beat the local cowboys. At the 1906 Fort Worth Cattlemen's Convention she won a gold medal worth $1,000 for defeating the "most expert cowboys and riders of the plains from Texas, Indian Territory, Oklahoma, Arizona, New Mexico and even more distant places."[60]

While she was a successful competitor, Mulhall still spent most of her time performing with the family show, since there were not enough contests and prize monies to support the clan. Mulhall and Blancett apparently never competed against one another in steer roping, but both did participate in the cowgirl trick and fancy roping contest at the 1912 Calgary Stampede.

Today, 1912 is best remembered for a tragedy, the sinking of the "unsinkable" luxury liner *Titanic.* It also marked the outbreak of the first Balkan War. In the United States, the entry of Arizona and New Mexico into the Union and the publication of Zane Grey's *Riders of the Purple Sage* once again put the mythical West in the forefront of the popular culture. The years before World War I were also a time of increased interest in women's rights, particularly the suffrage, a movement in which cowgirls had minimal involvement.

When Calgary reporters questioned Mulhall about her feelings on the suffrage, she declined to give any opinions, stating that she was "not much interested in it."[61] On the other hand, *The Billboard,* in addition to its traditional Wild West and rodeo column, "The Corral," also published a cowgirl column known as "Wimmin's Writes," penned by Whistling Annie. Although no proof has been forthcoming, several have suggested that Whistling Annie was cowgirl trick roper Florence LaDue. It is certain that her husband, rodeo producer Guy Weadick, was "Corral" columnist Rowdy Waddy for many years. Whoever wrote it, "Wimmin's Writes" lived up to its name. In addition to news and gossip, it also served as an advocacy forum for cowgirls, a place to air disputes and grievances and to propose rules changes.

Because of their nomadic life-styles, few cowgirls ever had the opportunity to become involved with any suffrage organizations, or even to know about them. One who did was Dorothy Morrell. In June of 1915, she addressed the Congressional Union for Women's Suffrage Conference at San Francisco, and received a huge hand for her "typical western speech." Nothing else appeared in the press regarding her activities in the organization or the movement.[62] The only reason Morrell was home and able to make the speech was that she was injured. She made her presentation just days after being released from the hospital, long before she could resume her rodeo career.[63]

Few cowgirls expressed an interest in suffrage, and the ideas espoused

Dorothy Morrell (Robbins), one of the top cowgirls of the pre–World War I era, riding a bronc. Morrell, a native of Canada, also starred in western films and in 1915 addressed a women's suffrage conference. Photo courtesy of ProRodeo Hall of Fame, Colorado Springs, Colorado.

by pre–World War I followers of the feminist movement would surely not have attracted them.[64] Women like Morrell, Mulhall, Henderson, and Blancett felt they had already achieved feminist goals such as Crystal Eastman expressed: "How to arrange the world so that women can be human beings, with a chance to exercise their infinitely varied ways, instead of being destined by the accident of their sex to one field of activity, housework and child-raising."[65] Even though most did not actively participate in the feminist or suffrage movements, cowgirls did serve as examples of women who enjoyed freedom of choice and the opportunity to follow their dreams and achieve their potential.

Beyond the realm of world and national politics, sports continued to flourish. Most remember the 1912 Olympics because of Jim Thorpe's achievements. After winning both the pentathlon and decathlon, Thorpe earned the accolade "world's greatest athlete," and achieved the widest fame of any Olympic winner to date. Olympic officials stripped away his medals and titles a few months later because he had violated the rules of Olympic eligibility. Women's competition in 1912 expanded to include swimming in addition to the fashionable and genteel sports of tennis, golf, and archery. American women, however, could not take part in the new contest. The AAU, which then controlled most of America's Olympic sports, and which subsequently revoked Thorpe's eligibility, also refused to sanction female participation in swimming.[66] Rodeo cowgirls were much more fortunate. They enjoyed greatly improved competitive opportunities in 1912. (See table A.2.) The three most important and widely publicized contests that year were the Pendleton Roundup, the Los Angeles Rodeo, and the Calgary Stampede. The latter two were new in 1912, and all three were typical of the major outdoor contests of their day, though primitive by today's standards.

Most rodeo arenas then included three-mile racetracks. These were ideal for their intended purpose, but caused problems for the other events. They kept much of the action in the steer roping, bulldogging, and bronc riding beyond spectators' view, since the beasts raced to the far side of the infield immediately after their release. The absence of chutes and gates also slowed the proceedings. Broncs had to be snubbed and blindfolded in the infield, and released only after riders had mounted and signaled their readiness. The contests then continued for several minutes until the rider bucked off or the horse stopped bucking.[67]

Both men's and women's bronc riding contests then and now were judged, with zero to fifty points awarded to each rider and to each horse. The winner was the contestant with the highest combined score. As with any contest in which subjective judging takes place, there were inevitable cries of bias, and occasionally the accusation of a fix. These problems were especially acute in the early years when there were no regulatory bodies, and no standards or established qualifications for judges. The situation was obviously ripe for abuse, and led to charges of favoritism, and accusations that women were chippies.

Despite the more primitive conditions, the early rodeos had far more contests than contemporary ones, sometimes as many as twenty in a single day. Promoters had a vast array to choose from, as more than two hundred different events have at one time or another been included in the sport now called rodeo. Among these colorful contests were a variety of races.

Roman races, relay races, and cow pony races were three in which women excelled. Trick and fancy roping and trick riding also enjoyed great popularity. Neither trick roping, trick riding, nor racing required contestants to capture or subdue animals; instead, contestant and horse worked as a team. Events of this type outnumbered the roping and busting contests that dominate contemporary rodeo, so that the entire focus of the rodeos was different. It was a festive atmosphere, and one in which talented women earned acceptance and success.

The 1912 Los Angeles Rodeo staged by the legendary E. J. "Lucky" Baldwin was a good example. Held at the Santa Anita Race track March 9–25, Baldwin's contest received excellent publicity, and several times drew crowds in excess of ten thousand. The *Los Angeles Times* covered the rodeo extensively, and gave excellent write-ups to the female contestants. Unfortunately for future historians, the papers failed to mention the final winners.[68]

Henderson and Blancett participated in the bronc riding, with Bertha also winning day money in the women's fancy roping, maverick race, and the coed Potato Race.[69] Another notable was the gifted Hazel Hoxie, who won day money in the cowgirls' half-mile race, relay race, fancy roping, and steer roping.[70] Various sources have credited both Hazel Walker and Tillie Baldwin with winning the cowgirl bronc riding competition.[71] The winner probably was Baldwin, since the *Times* did list her among the finalists, whereas Walker's name never appeared in any articles about the rodeo.[72]

Tillie Baldwin was a Wild West show star, a phenomenal athlete, and most unlikely cowgirl. Tillie was a native of Norway where she had excelled at skiing, skating, and canoeing. She came to the United States at age eighteen, speaking no English. She lived with an aunt in New York and learned to be a hairdresser. During an outing on Staten Island, she

Tillie Baldwin in the bloomer costume she pioneered for rodeo competition, circa 1913. Note that she wears a simple "gym suit," unlike her more flamboyant followers. Photo courtesy of the Glenbow Museum and Archives, Calgary, Alberta, Canada. Photo #NA-446-107.

saw some Hollywood cowgirls practicing trick and bronc riding, and immediately decided she wanted to learn. Friends who owned a stable taught her to ride. She taught herself enough cowgirl tricks to land a job in a small Wild West show owned by a man named Baldwin. Taking the stage name Tillie Baldwin, hairdresser Anna Matilda Winger became a professional cowgirl. She continued to improve her skills while earning a living with the show, and by 1912 was a star of the prestigious 101 Ranch Wild West. Her competitive nature led her to take leave of performing to participate in the Los Angeles rodeo, her first major contest.[73]

Even though Tillie was exceptionally skilled, her costume contributed to her success. Most cowgirls in 1912 still wore divided skirts. In keeping with street wear of the day, some did wear them shorter than in the nineties. Many had also begun adding decorations like fringes or conchos, but the attire still restricted their movements. Baldwin also wore elaborate divided skirt outfits in the Wild West shows, but for competition she dressed much more athletically.

Baldwin's competition wear is instantly recognizable as a gym suit, consisting of bloomers and a middy blouse.[74] This costume was much lighter and less cumbersome than what the other women were wearing, and it enabled Tillie to perform headstands and other riding tricks impossible in skirts. She earned higher scores as a result, since trick riding was judged much like gymnastics or figure skating, and the more difficult tricks produced higher scores. The reason for her choice of costume was likely her background. In her native Norway she competed in a variety of sports, and probably selected rodeo attire much like the athletic costumes she had worn all her life. It was a good choice, and eventually revolutionized cowgirls' costumes and the range of skills they were able to perform in the trick riding competition.

Since athletes were always looking for a competitive edge, and almost all of the cowgirls made their own costumes, it is amazing that they were slow to follow Baldwin's lead.[75] This is particularly true of costumes for relay races, where the skirts actually posed a serious hazard. Ella Gangler, for example, competed in relays at the first three Pendleton Roundups, always in the traditional divided skirt. She was injured in the 1912 race, and her mother never allowed the twelve-year-old to compete in rodeo again. Her injury occurred the same year Tillie Baldwin first appeared at Pendleton wearing bloomers, and Ella never forgot the outfit or Roundup that ended her own career. Even at age eighty-two, she maintained that had she been wearing bloomers the accident would never have happened.[76]

Tradition does die hard. Lucille Mulhall participated in almost every rodeo event including relay racing. When reporters asked her about the bloomers in 1912, she stated with some disgust that she would never wear them, and indeed she did not.[77] Several other women also wore divided skirts throughout their careers. Others began experimenting with more appropriate attire by 1913. First they put elastic in the hems of their divided skirts, and later made bloomers in a variety of styles.

Baldwin in her bloomers and Blancett in a long leather divided skirt won the women's contests at the 1912 Pendleton Roundup. Blancett took the bronc riding championship, and Baldwin the trick riding and the all-around cowgirl title.[78] Most of the publicity went to Hoot Gibson, who parlayed his all-around cowboy title into a successful career in western movies.[79] Gibson and Tom Mix were among the first stars to have their films distributed internationally, attracting some of the same fans who had once flocked to see Buffalo Bill's Wild West.[80]

Calgary and Winnipeg Stampedes

Although the Los Angeles and Pendleton rodeos were important, the most renowned contest of 1912 was the Calgary Stampede. Trick roper Guy Weadick conceived and organized the Stampede, which he presented with the same flair and publicity as the top Wild West shows. It created the first real cowgirl superstars, and helped establish women's place in professional rodeo. While Calgary is certainly in the West, the Stampede advertisements circulated much more widely. Announcements in the United States, Canada, and Mexico attracted participants and spectators from all three countries. Because it offered the richest prizes in rodeo history, $20,000 in gold, contestants found it worthwhile to travel great distances, and even forego other employment, in order to participate.

The big prizes, elaborate publicity, and Weadick's personal efforts to bring in the best athletes in the business attracted the most talented group of cowgirls and cowboys ever assembled in one place.[81] Along with rodeo veterans like Blancett, Walker, and Mulhall, female vaudeville and Wild West show stars with no competitive experience also took part. Annie Shaffer made a brief return to the contest arena for the occasion. The most important thing for the women was neither the money nor the publicity. It was the opportunity to test their skills against the best cowgirls on the continent for the coveted title of world champion.

Weadick had envisioned a world-class contest like the Stampede for

The STAMPEDE at Calgary Alberta
Programme
September 2nd, 1912

Galloping parade of all mounted people around track.
Presentation of Characters to audience
Fancy and trick riding by cowgirls
Stage Coach Race
Roping of steers by cowboys
Cowgirls relay race
Bareback bucking horse riding by cowboys
Roping of steers by cowboys
Fancy roping by cowgirls
Fancy roping by cowboys
Cowboy relay race
Bucking horse riding by cowgirls
Bucking horse riding by cowboys
Roping of steers by cowboys
Fancy and trick riding by cowboys
Steer riding by cowboys
Indian Relay Race
Wild Horse race

Any other special events will be announced from the judge's stand, and
displayed under the heading of extra on the bulletin board.

Contests are set in boldface type. Note that there are several "heats" of some contests, but also that aside from the parade there are no exhibitions. Program for September 2. From Glenbow Museum and Archives, Calgary, Canada.

several years before getting the financial backing of the four wealthy Calgary businessmen who were ultimately responsible for the Stampede. These men hired Weadick and paid him $425 to manage, promote, and produce the affair. For the occasion, Indian tents and teepees surrounded Calgary, and two thousand mounted Indians rode in the opening parade.[82] The Canadian Pacific Railroad offered half-price fares to tourists making the round trip to Calgary. More than forty thousand took advantage of the bargain. They helped account for the seventy-five thousand who saw the opening-day parade, and the one hundred and twenty thousand who paid to see the contest during its six-day run.[83]

I have been unable to determine the reasons Weadick decided to include a full complement of women's contests. Certainly one was his desire to produce a cowboy [sic] contest that had all of the color and excitement of the best Wild West shows. It is also significant that Weadick's wife and vaudeville partner was trick and fancy roper Florence LaDue, an international star who had never participated in a roping contest.[84] Since their 1906 marriage, Weadick and LaDue had toured the United States and Europe with their vaudeville act. They also performed in a Broadway extravaganza entitled "Wyoming Days," before settling in Calgary to produce the Stampede.[85] Weadick might have viewed the contest as an opportunity to increase LaDue's fame, as winning the contest would enable her to reap the rewards of being a world champion. Perhaps he included the contest for her benefit, or perhaps it was her idea.

While hardly a typical westerner, LaDue had certainly lived a colorful life. Born Florence Bensel at Montevideo, Minnesota, in 1883, she grew up on a Sioux reservation where her grandfather was a government agent. An accomplished horsewoman and roper, she began her professional career in 1905 with Cummins [sic] Wild West and Indian Congress. It was there that she met Guy Weadick.[86]

The trick and fancy roping at which both Weadicks excelled was introduced into the United States by *charros* such as the great Vincente Oropeza and popularized by Will Rogers. Oropeza won the first world championship in 1900, and trick and fancy roping remained a popular cowboy and cowgirl contest through the mid-thirties. As the name implies, it actually included two skills. The more common, trick roping, involved catching one or more running animals by throwing some kind of loop. Favorite tricks were roping as many as ten animals at one throw, and roping running horses by all four legs. Fancy roping was the name given to twirling the rope at various speeds to make different shapes and positions, such as

Florence LaDue, spinning her rope on horseback at the 1912 Calgary Stampede, where she won the first of three world championships in trick and fancy roping. Photo courtesy of the Glenbow Museum and Archives, Calgary, Alberta, Canada. Photo #NA-628-4.

Oropeza's spelling his name with the spinning lasso. Contest rules required trick and fancy ropers to exhibit their skills both on foot and from horseback. They usually had to be ready to perform any time the arena director asked.[87]

LaDue's major challenger in the trick and fancy roping at Calgary was Mulhall, whom the *Calgary Herald* called the "Defending World's Champion." Blancett and the other participants attracted little notice in the press. The contest between Mulhall and LaDue was very close and thrilled audiences and reporters alike. Mulhall "won repeated applause by her graceful and smooth handling of the twirling loop, and by her roping of a rider by flipping the rope with her foot."[88] Ultimately, LaDue took the championship. She showed great versatility and amazed spectators when she tied a double hitch in her slack rope with just two wrist movements.[89]

The reason we know so much about that long-ago cowgirl contest is that journalists at the 1912 Stampede took the female athletes seriously, and reported women's and men's contests in the same manner. They also photographed and interviewed female athletes, all of which was most unusual, since coverage of women's athletic contests has traditionally been both minimal and biased. Reporters rarely described the skills and techniques that led female winners to triumph, or explained the nuances of the sport. Coverage typically stressed women's beauty, charm, attire, personality, and domesticity, while ignoring or belittling their athletic achievements.[90]

Fortunately, favorable reporting like the account of the Mulhall-LaDue roping contest and other women's events at the 1912 Stampede continued as the big-time contests moved eastward to Winnipeg, Chicago, and New York City. There for several decades cowgirls received some of the fairest newspaper coverage accorded female athletes. Even when the rodeos were relative failures, women reaped headlines. While the New York Stampede attracted primarily negative press due to the financial problems, New York papers carried elaborately illustrated and very favorable articles about cowgirls Florence LaDue and Tillie Baldwin.[91]

One of the women whom Weadick invited to compete at Calgary was Fannie Sperry, a famous Montana bronc rider and relay racer.[92] Fannie was born in 1887, and raised on a Montana ranch located at the foot of Bear Tooth Mountain near Helena. Horses fascinated her from earliest childhood, and she had her own horse by age six. With her four siblings she often courted death by riding across the rough waters of the Missouri River. Throughout her childhood, she lassoed and broke her own horses, and was determined to spend her life working with them in some manner.[93]

By the time she was sixteen, Fannie had achieved statewide fame as an equestrienne. She gave riding exhibitions at community festivals and horse shows and rode in relay races at Montana fairs. Relay races were the most difficult of all the cowgirl contests. They required the rider to make three laps of the track, changing horses at the end of the first and second laps. In the early years, riders also had to unsaddle each horse and saddle the next one before continuing the race.[94] From 1905 through 1908, Fannie earned $100 a month plus expenses as a relay rider. During the off-season, she competed in rodeos and performed with a Wild West show, although neither of these endeavors could match the income she earned racing.

Fannie and her racing teammates, the "Montana Girls," wore racing silks and trousers, just like male jockeys. This is somewhat surprising given the very conservative Montana attitudes discussed earlier. Perhaps that conservatism explains why, after enjoying great freedom in her racing wear, Fannie did not transfer it to the rodeo arena, but she never did. There she appeared in long divided skirts throughout her career.[95]

After a lengthy correspondence with Weadick, Sperry agreed to enter the cowgirl bronc riding and relay race at Calgary. She also asked to enter the wild horse race,[96] but Weadick denied her request, with this explanation: "The wild horse race is open to cowboys only, and I would not advise any lady to participate in this particular event as it is rough enough for the men let alone the ladies."[97] Weadick's position is difficult to understand. Women and men had competed together in wild horse races since the earliest rodeos. They still do today.[98] Nonetheless, Sperry did not protest, apparently satisfied to enter only two events.

Fannie also had questions about the bronc riding, then the most popular and most controversial cowgirl contest. Although most early cowgirls rode slick just like the cowboys, some favored an easier, and far more dangerous, method known as hobble riding. Hobbling the stirrups meant tying them together beneath the horse. Rodeos rarely made rules specifying which technique women should use, but many of the major contests awarded bonus points to women who rode slick. Even without special rules, slick riders enjoyed an advantage.[99] Fannie naturally wondered what rules would be in effect at Calgary, and Weadick had this reply: "We allow lady contestants in the bucking horse event to hobble their stirrups if they so desire. It is needless for me to say that any lady riding the horse slick and clean will certainly be considered by the judges much better than those who hobble their stirrups."[100]

Sperry and other slick riders such as Bertha Blancett and Tillie Baldwin took advantage of the extra points and/or extra consideration they received from the judges to dominate the event. Since few spectators could tell the difference, fans sometimes selected flamboyant hobble riders as their favorites and expressed their disapproval when slick riders defeated them.

Goldie St. Clair, perhaps Fannie's biggest rival at Calgary, was one popular hobble rider. The twenty-two-year-old St. Clair (Irene Wooden) had won the world championship at the 1907 Jamestown Exposition and World's Fair and was also a seasoned performer on the Wild West show and Broadway circuit.[101] Calgary reporters named her the favorite during the first day of competition after she successfully rode Red Wing, a bronc that had killed a cowboy the previous week. Goldie herself did not escape injury. Before the ride was over, the horse's bucking and scraping her against the wall had severely lacerated her leg and torn her skirt. She finished the ride in triumph, then fainted in the pickup man's arms. She received accolades for her courage and showmanship, and continued to ride throughout the Stampede.[102]

Fannie realized she was in for a tough fight. She felt that if she rode well every day, and could stay aboard Red Wing, her extra points for riding slick would provide the margin of victory. She drew Red Wing on the final day, and made a spectacular ride. Soon after, the announcer named Fannie "Lady Bucking Horse Champion of the World." She won $1,000, a saddle, and a belt buckle. She also placed third in the relay, winning a total of $1,125, almost as much as she had made in four years on the racing circuit. Probably the most popular athlete at Calgary, Sperry received a tremendous ovation at the awards ceremonies.[103]

The multitalented Blancett won the relay race, took second in trick riding, and third in both bronc riding and trick roping. She was the only woman to enter all four cowgirl events at the Stampede, and earned $1,150, even more than Sperry.[104] Dolly Mullins, winner of the trick riding title, never achieved the fame enjoyed by the other Calgary winners, and apparently never won another cowgirl contest. She subsequently performed for several years with the 101 Ranch Wild West. Sperry, on the other hand, returned home to a hero's welcome, and like champion athletes of today, was much in demand for public appearances. At one such event she met rodeo cowboy Bill Steele, whom she married in 1913. As Fannie Sperry Steele, she became one of the top rodeo stars in the country.[105]

Sperry Steele, Mulhall, and other Calgary veterans met again in 1913, during another series of major western contests. The second Los Angeles Rodeo, produced by Col. J. Raley of Pendleton, attracted fifteen cowgirls. Winnie Brown won the pony race and took second in bronc riding, won by Rose Henderson. Tillie Baldwin took both the relay and the trick riding titles.[106] These three winners, along with Hazel Walker and Rose Wenger, were among the ten Los Angeles veterans who competed in Weadick's 1913 Stampede at Winnipeg, Ontario. Joining them were most of the Calgary contestants, except for Blancett and Mullins.[107]

One significant newcomer at Winnipeg was Vera McGinnis. Unlike most of her peers, she was not born on a ranch, and actually spent little time there. Until she was three years old, she lived in the small Missouri town where she was born. The family then moved to a New Mexico ranch where her father worked as a country doctor and her mother ran the cattle business. They had no baby sitter, so her parents tied young Vera onto the back of a donkey where she spent many lonely and unhappy hours. When she was old enough to ride without the ties, she quickly learned to ride bareback, to enjoy the out-of-doors, and to make friends with the cowboys.[108]

This idyllic life ended only two years later as her father's ill health forced the family to move to town. Her father died soon thereafter, and an uncle, later her stepfather, joined the family. He kept them moving from place to place at a distressing rate, all the while enchanting Vera with tales of faraway lands. These stories left her with a lasting desire to see the world. He also saw to it that she always had a horse to ride, which kept her content despite the constant moving. Her mother taught her to sew and to ride sidesaddle, a skill for which she saw little use.

There were no rodeos in any of the towns where Vera lived. When she was thirteen, the town of Norborne, Missouri, did hold a street carnival with a contest for the best lady rider. Despite her young age, Vera talked her parents into letting her enter, and her mother made her a new riding habit for the occasion. She won the event and took home a gold-handled umbrella. She was thrilled with her victory, though disappointed with the prize. Her parents deflated her ego somewhat when they told her: "Likely you won because the older girls were all riding cross saddles. Some people frown on ladies riding astride" (17). Still, the victory stirred a latent competitive urge that ultimately led to her rodeo career.

She continued riding both cross and sidesaddle, and finished high school and business school by age seventeen. Although she had anticipated a career as a housewife, no marriage was in the offing, and she sought gainful employment. Vera worked as a movie extra in Hollywood, and then accepted a "real job" in Salt Lake City. There for the first time in her life, she had no access to horses. When some of her California acquaintances arrived to organize and promote a rodeo, they called her, and began taking her out in the evenings to ride their stock. This was her first contact with rodeo, and the sights and sounds immediately fascinated her.

When a relay horse owner announced he was looking for a rider, Vera volunteered. Her friends thought it rather ridiculous for her to attempt something so difficult in so short a time. The owner did not realize she had never even seen a relay, so he was willing to take a chance. Despite this obvious disadvantage, her lifetime of riding paid off, and she learned very quickly (18–37). A week after her first relay lesson, McGinnis competed in the rodeo. She finished third in the first go-round, but recalled: "I was the most exhausted girl in the whole world when the struggle was over. My lungs ached, my knees buckled under me, and I wished wholeheartedly that my long corset was in Hades" (35). The following day, she junked her corset *for life* (her emphasis), and again finished third. The last day's finish was not better, and in the process she lost several teeth in a spectacular accident. This left her friends pleading with her to resume her office job. However, as Vera recalled later, that job was no longer interesting. Instead she asked her friends to help her improve her skills, so she could follow the rodeo career that now beckoned her. She signed a contract as a relay race rider and was off down what she called the "rodeo road." She summed up her feelings as follows: "This is the life I've been looking for, the continual challenge! I love it" (35–37).

Relay race riding was probably the best way for a novice to enter the rodeo profession. Horse owners normally paid riders an agreed-upon percentage of any winnings, along with room, board, expenses, and sometimes a monthly stipend. Unfortunately, Vera's only guarantee was a share of prize money. She quickly realized that to have any financial security she needed to compete in more than one event. After surveying the possibilities, Vera selected trick riding and convinced a member of the entourage to give her lessons. A phenomenal athlete and quick study, she made rapid progress. When the group arrived at Winnipeg she saw a beautiful saddle that was the prize for the fourth place finisher in the ladies trick riding. She made it her goal to win the saddle, and employed a former cowboy trick riding champion as her new coach. They worked out for long hours, and she made two new costumes especially for the contest (38–45).

Winnipeg was a burgeoning city eight hundred miles east of Calgary, not a cow town like most rodeo sites. Sometimes called the Chicago of Canada, it was in the midst of a real estate boom, the population having risen from sixty-seven thousand to more than two hundred thousand in ten years.[109] Organizers intended the Stampede to lure prospective land buyers, and promoted it widely. Weadick faced a new challenge in attempting to get the community involved in an unfamiliar activity like rodeo. Community involvement had been the hallmark of successful contests like the Cheyenne Frontier Days and Pendleton Roundup. Of course, it was easier in those places where rodeo was an integral part of the life-style, and local committees ran the rodeos for the benefit of all citizens. Even though Winnipeg lacked both rodeo tradition and community ownership, Weadick elicited excellent support from the business sector.

The familiar trappings of more western venues, such as the Indian village, were missing. Stores did close the morning of the opening parade, and merchants offered "Stampede Specials" on everything from men's suits to ladies' undergarments. Baseball games were moved to mornings

Lucille Mulhall, "Champion Lady Steer Roper of the World," roping a steer at the 1913
Winnipeg Stampede, where she competed against the cowboys. Photo courtesy of the
Glenbow Museum and Archives, Calgary, Alberta, Canada. Photo #NA-1029-27.

throughout the week to avoid conflicting with the rodeo.[110] Both the *Manitoba Free Press* and the *Winnipeg Tribune* had special rodeo sections, and
reporters covered the event thoroughly.

They provided information on contests, disputes with officials, and audience reactions, as well as the appearance, demeanor, and attire of both
male and female participants. Like the Calgary journalists, they were
more than fair in their treatment of cowgirls.[111] Oddly, these papers gave
only minimal coverage to the trick roping and trick riding. They omitted
details of the Mulhall-LaDue contest, which Florence again won. Lucille
did get a great deal of publicity for her steer roping once reporters discovered that "the 'cowboy' to take the premier position was a 'cowgirl.' Lucille Mulhall . . . roped and safely hogtied a big wild steer in 53.35 seconds."[112] Significantly, that contest did not get the circuslike treatment it
might have attracted, probably because the cowboys accepted Lucille's
participation without question, and the press and fans did likewise. Mulhall won the first two rounds, clearly establishing herself as a legitimate
contender. Even though a cowboy ultimately won the event, Lucille became "Champion Lady Steer Roper of the World," a title she cherished
for the rest of her life.[113]

Mulhall was not the only woman to challenge the cowboys at Winnipeg.

Tillie Baldwin was even more successful, defeating an otherwise all-male field to win the Roman standing race.[114] In that grueling event, contestants rode two horses. Standing with one foot on each mount, they raced one lap around the half-mile track daily. The winner was the one with the best average time for the entire contest. Describing the race of August 13, the *Winnipeg Tribune* noted: "Tillie Baldwin, the wonderful cowgirl trick rider . . . drove her twin mounts at a gait which would frighten many men . . . to death."[115]

Baldwin also competed in the relay and won the trick riding title, making her the only two-event winner at Winnipeg. However, McGinnis really challenged her in trick riding. Vera recalled that after the final round of competition the judges summoned her and Baldwin to their stand: "Mr. Tanner, the good-looking young judge from Oklahoma, said, 'You two girls are tied for first. You'll have to ride it off.' I almost fell off my horse. Tillie looked so lovely on a horse I couldn't imagine tying her in anything. 'We'll allow you one more trick,' he went on, 'so give us your best.'"[116] While she had made rapid progress since beginning trick riding, McGinnis was no match for Baldwin in the tie breaker. She had already used the few tricks she had mastered in her fledgling career. Nonetheless, her second place finish was far better than anything she had expected, and reinforced her determination to succeed as a rodeo professional.

Things were far from easy outside the arena. Some of the difficulty no doubt stemmed from the fact that Vera had a very different background from the other members of the entourage. Not only had she lived most of her life in an urban setting, she had far more education than most rodeo professionals. Her two diplomas surely created something of a gulf between her and a group whose education ended at eighth grade or below. To add injury to insult, Vera had enjoyed virtually overnight success, without really "paying her dues." She was extremely young, attractive, and single, all of which created animosity and jealousy. Some of the women even called her a chippie, causing her to fight back with words and fists. Although the physical battles soon ended, the problems persisted for some time.[117]

Fannie Sperry Steele never experienced difficulties of that sort, although she did have the dubious distinction of being both heroine and villain at the Winnipeg rodeo. Reporters were quick to note the superiority of the relay stock from C. B. Irwin's stable, and predicted that Irwin's riders would sweep both men's and women's events. They also discovered that Sperry Steele was by far the "fastest relay horsewoman in the world" and the most popular with fans.[118] Even with slower horses, Fannie's outstanding athletic ability enabled her to win the relay two of the racing days. In so doing, she defeated two of C. B. Irwin's daughters, Pauline and Joella, and the crowds cheered enthusiastically when they learned that she had edged Pauline out to finish second overall.[119]

The story was quite different in the bronc riding. Blanche McGaughey became the crowd favorite after a dazzling display reporters called "one of the most sensational exhibitions of horsewomanship ever seen in Western Canada."[120] Blanche retained her popularity throughout the Stampede. On the last night her fans thought they had a winner when Sperry Steele bucked off a horse all the other women had ridden. However, Fannie protested vociferously that the ride was unfair because her horse was released prematurely. The judges apparently agreed, and awarded her a re-ride. She succeeded on her second attempt, and due to her added advantage as a slick rider, won the contest.

Reporters and fans alike were furious at this news. They had no understanding of the differences between slick and hobble riding, and could see no justification for Fannie's triumph over McGaughey. Their displeasure increased when they heard that McGaughey was not even alone in second place, but tied with two others. This controversy brought more headlines and more press coverage to the women, as the *Manitoba Free Press* exclaimed: "Much Dissatisfaction over Women's Bronc Riding Title Won by Fannie Sperry Steele."[121]

At the final award ceremonics, Fannie received a warm greeting for her relay performance, but fans had little applause for her as the ladies bronc riding champion. This was quite a contrast to her enthusiastic ovation for taking second in the relay, and to the standing ovation she had enjoyed after winning the bronc riding at Calgary the previous year.[122]

The Stampede drew at least one hundred thirty thousand spectators, including a holiday crowd of sixty thousand; the largest ever gathered in western Canada. Even so, the public did not agree on its success. Some locals felt attendance was poor. Others expressed delight that no one lost money, and all contestants received the prizes they had earned.[123] Certainly winners like Fannie, who pocketed more than $1,000 at each of Weadick's Stampedes, hoped the successful ventures would continue.

Life on the Rodeo Road

Many of the contestants from Winnipeg traveled together across Canada, staging rodeos and exhibitions at various towns until they arrived in Oregon for the Pendleton Roundup. There Tillie Baldwin again thrilled crowds with her outstanding exhibition of steer bulldogging, a dangerous feat no other woman performed.[124] Bulldogging (or steer wrestling) contestants jump from the back of a speeding horse onto a bull. Grabbing the bull by the horns, they wrestle the beast to the ground. The winner is the one who accomplishes this in the fastest time. In Tillie's era, some cowboys still followed Bill Pickett's style of biting steers on the lips to subdue them. Several other cowgirls eventually followed Tillie's lead, and earned headlines as bulldoggers in the twenties, but I found no evidence of female bulldoggers biting their quarry.

The number of rodeos that included women's contests increased steadily after 1912, and exceeded twenty for the first time in 1916. By that time, more than 100 cowgirls had joined the competition, although the 140 women who were Wild West show performers exclusively still outnumbered them.[125] One reason women's opportunities improved was the growth of rodeo itself. Western towns attempted to promote themselves and build community spirit through the festive events, while promoters also began to see business opportunities in the sport, and they too aided its spread. The women added to their own popularity by displaying exciting skills and also wearing colorful costumes, which soon became a cowgirl trademark. Bloomers gradually surpassed divided skirts in popularity, and remained so through the early twenties.

Unique costumes enabled the women to express their individualism, while getting the kind of publicity that would enhance their popularity and incomes through additional contract appearances.[126] Most of the cowgirls designed and made distinctive and attractive outfits, while some went to extremes. Pioneer bronc riders Lulu Belle Parr and Prairie Rose Henderson designed clothing that even their fellow professionals considered somewhat outrageous. Photos depict Henderson wearing cowboy boots, silk stockings, and knee-length bloomers beneath a skirt trimmed in ostrich feathers.[127] Parr posed for photographers beside a live buffalo, clad in a divided skirt and cape of spotted fur.[128] Yet both women reaped the benefits in publicity and lucrative personal appearance fees.[129]

The season remained very short even as the number of contests increased. Travel between the best-paying events was also expensive and few contestants were able to earn a living through their winnings. Rodeo couples like the Steeles and the Blancetts, who could share expenses and combine winnings, obviously had an advantage. Even for them, rodeo was seasonal work that did not pay enough to support the contestants in the off-season. Most athletes had to combine rodeo with some other occupation in order to make ends meet.

In 1914 Fannie and Bill Steele began a new business supplying stock to Montana rodeos. They also organized their own Wild West show, which originally included Fannie and Bill, along with a chuck wagon and string of outlaw horses captured on their ranch. They traveled from rodeo to rodeo, camping in the small towns along the way. Their posters advertising free exhibitions by "Fannie Sperry Steele, Champion Lady Bronc Rider of the World," attracted crowds, among whom they passed a hat for donations. Sometimes they also offered prize money to spectators who could successfully ride one of their outlaw horses.

During their first year of operation, Fannie won several bronc busting contests on the way to the Miles City Roundup. There she took the $400 first prize as the Montana State lady bucking horse champion, and also finished second in the relay.[130] The Steeles ended the season at the Pendleton Roundup, where Fannie took second in both the bronc riding and the relay. At year's end, the Wild West show had eliminated travel expenses and turned a profit of $956.[131]

Mulhall was also on the road almost year-round performing in either her Wild West show or her vaudeville act. She also advertised in the trade papers that "Lucille Mulhall, the Girl Ranger," would ensure the success of any fair, carnival, or other event. In addition to her roping exhibitions, she offered varied entertainment featuring any number of cattle, cowboys, cowgirls, and Indians.[132] Yet, like Baldwin and Blancett, she really thrived on competition and would have preferred to be a full-time athlete. Since that was not possible, she scheduled her performances so that she was able to enter several contests. In 1915, Mulhall arranged to play the vaudeville theater in Cheyenne during the Frontier Days celebration, where she competed during the day and performed at night.[133] Often, she simply took leave from her shows to participate in the contests, having some family member take her place.

In 1916 she solved the problem for good by organizing her own rodeo company, Lucille Mulhall's Round-Up. This was also a significant development for cowgirls, as Mulhall became the only female producer and established a number of new rodeos that offered competition and employment for women. Since no more than one-third of all rodeos included cowgirl contests, Lucille's entry into the business was welcome news indeed. Still, she was not the only producer to offer cowgirls very good purses and benefits in 1916. Several colorful figures decided on that year to

launch elaborate productions that featured almost every event known to
the rodeo business, including all of the cowgirl contests. Unfortunately,
the audiences did not yet exist for rodeo on such a grand scale, and many
of the ventures were disastrous for all involved.

On July 4, 1916, the most ambitious production in rodeo history, "The
Passing of the West," opened at Butte, Montana. Promoter-producer
Charles L. Harris intended his extravaganza to be a combination rodeo
and Wild West show, its cast a who's who of the business. McGinnis recalled that Harris offered her one hundred dollars a week plus expenses
to perform in the show. She could also compete for prizes in women's relays and both hobble and slick bronc riding. More important, her husband, Earl Simpson, could travel with the group, and compete in all of the
rodeos.[134] The cast and crew of 140, including McGinnis, Simpson, Mulhall and the Steeles, their livestock and a thirty-two-piece band, traveled
by special train. From all accounts, it was a good show. The crowds were
enthusiastic, but never reached the size Harris anticipated. Following the
close of their July 13–16 shows at Billings, the performers discovered that
Harris had become a bloomer, leaving them with no transportation, salaries, or prize monies.[135]

Following this debacle, the cast and crew scattered, although many
hoped to meet in August when two more major contests were scheduled
back-to-back. Weadick was holding his biggest Stampede to date at the
Sheepshead Bay Speedway, New York City. Buffalo Bill's Shan Kive and
Roundup was due to open at Chicago the following week. Cody's production was a variation of his touring Wild West show, whereas the Speedway
Corporation hired Weadick to promote and manage the Stampede.

Weadick quickly found that New York lacked the community support
that surrounded his Canadian ventures. There were no Stampede sales on
underwear, and no baseball games moved to morning to avoid conflicts.
Publicity was almost invisible. To make matter's worse, a crippling street-
car strike and a raging polio epidemic kept people at home.[136] The New
York papers gave minimal coverage to the Stampede in progress, and rarely commented on the performers or announced daily results. Long afterward, several individuals collected enough information to compile a list of
winners. Baldwin took the bronc riding championship, slick. LaDue once
more defeated Mulhall for the trick roping title, and retired as the unde-
feated world champion.[137] Among the new faces finishing in the money at
New York was eighteen-year-old bronc rider Eloise "Fox" Hastings. According to her own account, Hastings ran away from a convent school

when she was sixteen to marry rodeo cowboy Mike Hastings. He taught her to ride, to rodeo, and eventually to bulldog steers.[138] The New York Stampede was her first major contest.

Another interesting character was "Prairie Lillie" Allen, winner of the hobble bronc riding. Born Lillian Gray Little in Columbia, Tennessee, in the late 1880s, Lillie moved to Chicago in 1905. There a childhood visit to Dubrock's Wild West show at Riverside Park made an immediate impression. Determined to be a part of the exciting scene, she donned a mask to prevent her parents' discovering her and joined the show as a bronc rider. She subsequently worked for such obscure Wild West outfits as Broncho [sic] John Sullivan and Tiger Bill, and even headlined her own small show. Lillian earned a meager living in 1912, showing western films to tiny communities. She also offered to ride outlaw mules that locals brought to town to challenge all comers. While her situation seemed bleak, she persisted, honing her skills until women's competitive opportunities improved. In 1916, she won the cowgirl bronc riding at Garden City, Kansas, as well as at the New York rodeo.[139] Because of financial problems, the New York victory did not improve her income as she had hoped. In fact, it was only after relentless pressure from the press that backers finally paid contestants even a portion of the money they had won.[140] Still, Prairie Lillie Allen had finally established a name for herself as a top cowgirl, and enjoyed many successful seasons on the circuit.

The men and women who traveled from New York to Chicago found that Buffalo Bill's Chicago Shan Kive also suffered from poor publicity and offered much smaller purses than those originally promised at New York. On the other hand, Cody paid the winners after the last event each day, much to the relief of those New York veterans.[141] Mulhall was an active and enthusiastic participant at Chicago, snubbing broncs, hazing for the bulldoggers, and taking third in the cowboy steer roping. Sperry Steele, who had done poorly at New York, won the bronc riding title at Chicago, earning a total of $340 in prizes and day money. While that amount may seem small, it was greater than either of the New York Stampede bronc riding champions actually collected![142]

Following the Shan Kive, Mulhall hired a number of the New York and Chicago contestants for eleven performances at the Milwaukee State Fair, a successful endeavor that drew more than 10,000 spectators. Fannie recalled the event clearly: "I rode 42 bucking broncos in one week. We put on 11 shows a day in a side wall arena that was open to the sky. I rode in six bucking events every day for a solid week, but I loved every minute of it."[143] In October, Lucille's group moved on to the American Royal Horse Show and Frontier Contest at Kansas City, where Fannie again won the bronc riding competition.[144] The group then disbanded, and Fannie and Bill headed home to resume their Wild West show.

While the Steeles, Mulhall, Baldwin, and Allen explored new territories and pioneered exciting rodeo venues, many of their colleagues experienced neither the excitement nor the frustration of New York and Chicago. Travel expenses were a serious problem to many, and they often missed out on very lucrative contests simply because they were unable to get there. Sometimes, special trains carried stock, contractors, contestants, and others from one major contest to another, or from a community where many rodeo people gathered to a distant rodeo site. One such group went from the 1913 Los Angeles Rodeo to the Salt Lake City contest and beyond. It included the relay string owner who first hired Vera McGinnis, enabling her to inaugurate her career at some of the year's major events.[145]

In 1914, Vera married popular rodeo cowboy Earl Simpson, a member of the same group. The marriage finally assured her inclusion in the rodeo family, where she found acceptance from the women, and a sense of security and protection from both her husband and the other cowboys. The marriage also created its own set of problems, many of them financial. The couple spent the winters at Jackson Hole, Wyoming, barely making ends meet, and struggling against the elements. From that location they traveled to and from western rodeos on horseback or by wagon, sleeping in tents along the way. They packed to Billings, Montana, and Los Angeles, California, in 1915, and in 1916 set out by wagon to join the ill-fated "Passing of the West." An unfortunate mishap while crossing the Snake River en route to Butte ruined all of the new costumes that Vera had spent the winter designing and sewing. Although the exhausted couple finally did arrive at their destination, their problems were hardly over.[146]

When the show folded, they returned to Jackson Hole, and then in July left again for the Cheyenne Frontier Days, hoping their newly purchased horses would enable Vera to win the prestigious relay. Upon arrival they learned that the race was a mile and a half in length, requiring three horses, rather than the two that they owned. They purchased another thoroughbred and spent the next two weeks living in a tent and training their horses for the big contest, all to little avail. Even though she took day money several times, Vera won no major prizes at Cheyenne.[147] When the

Frontier Days closed, many of the participants left by special train for the New York Stampede, while McGinnis and Simpson went a different direction. Having invested virtually all of their money in relay horses, they decided their best hope lay in the Colorado county fair racing circuit. They pursued it for some time with mixed results.[148] Vera closed out the 1916 season at the War Bonnet Roundup in Idaho Falls, Idaho, where she took second in the cowgirl relay and defeated several men to win the trick riding competition.[149] Although they missed out on two prominent rodeos farther East, the couple fared no worse financially than the participants at the New York Stampede.

As she grew more successful, McGinnis found her marriage beginning to unravel. She was much more competitive than Simpson, and unwilling to give up the exciting rodeo life for a remote wilderness homestead. She never considered sacrificing her career in order to save her marriage and she and Earl eventually divorced. Whether married or single, Vera rarely got ahead financially, and sometimes found herself sleeping in the stalls alongside her horses. Nonetheless, she was determined to be a champion cowgirl, and pursued that goal until a near-fatal accident in 1934.[150]

Many other aspiring cowgirls lacked her gritty resolve, and more than half the women who participated in professional rodeo during this era dropped out after only one or two years on the circuit.[151] Some of the more persistent ones took winter jobs in western films, on ranches, or at riding stables, while others did manual labor or worked in restaurants. Sizable groups of cowboys and cowgirls began wintering together in Arizona, California, and Fort Worth, Texas, where some of them produced small rodeos. Eventually those off-season contests helped make rodeo more nearly a full-time occupation.[152]

Lucille Mulhall's joining the field as producer of shows and contests was also helpful. Lucille was particularly important because she was the best-known woman in the business, and had enjoyed tremendous success in every aspect of western entertainment. She had also been very helpful to female newcomers, and included contests for cowgirls in every event that she produced. She staged several round-ups at sites where no previous rodeo existed, and earlier in the year than most. For all of these reasons, it seemed likely that as her company grew and prospered, so would the number of contests available to women.

Lucille's company did begin 1917 on a promising note, producing the round-up at the annual Fort Worth Fat Stock Show. That 1917 round-up, held in the Fort Worth coliseum, was America's first indoor rodeo. Lucille won the cowgirl trick roping and Vera McGinnis the trick riding. Ruth Roach won the bronc riding, and took second in trick riding, with each winner getting a $100 prize.[153] The Fort Worth Round-Up marked the contest debut of Roach, who began her career by running away from home to join the 101 Ranch Wild West in 1912. Born Ruth Scantlin, she grew up in Excelsior Springs, Missouri, and learned to ride donkeys and Shetland ponies on her uncle's farm. Soon after she joined the show she married fellow performer Bryan Roach, and despite several subsequent divorces and marriages competed as Ruth Roach for the remainder of her long career.[154]

Two months after the Fort Worth contest, Lucille staged an equally successful round-up at San Antonio, where she also gave daily steer roping exhibitions.[155] In promoting and producing the San Antonio event, Mulhall and business partner Homer Wilson employed sophisticated public relations techniques, some of which remain in use today. For example, stores all over the Alamo City sold souvenir steer-head pins that entitled wearers to free admission to the round-up. This not only created advance sales for the contest, it involved a large segment of the community in the promotion. Modern production techniques were also in evidence. The San Antonio round-up was one of the first rodeos to use chutes, an innovation that did not reach Cheyenne or Calgary until 1919.[156]

The round-up received excellent press coverage, with feature stories and large photographs in almost every issue of the *Express*. Like the reporters at Winnipeg in 1913, the San Antonio writers often found the women's bronc riding to be the most thrilling event of the day. Among the women they covered were former Wild West show performer Mayme Stroud, who won the event, and the ever-colorful Prairie Rose Henderson, who finished second.[157]

World War I

World War I began to catch up to rodeo by mid-year, and Mulhall's company had no further business. Many cowboys were in the service, and remaining contestants tended to stay close to home. *The Wild Bunch*, a trade publication established in 1915 by Homer Wilson, gives clear evidence of the decline. The monthly increased steadily in size and readership during its first two years; but in 1917 available news diminished and the magazine grew smaller, ceasing publication with the July 1917 issue.[158] The next year cowgirls participated in only ten rodeos. Most of them were in small western towns like Tucumcari, New Mexico, and Garden City, Kansas. It was not until 1920 that the sport resumed full operations, and by that time dramatic changes had take place in American life as well as in the world of rodeo.

With the decline of rodeos and the death of Buffalo Bill in 1917, the only aspect of western entertainment to thrive during World War I was film. A new cowgirl star who began her movie career in 1917 was Mary Louise Cecilia "Texas" Guinan (also known as Mamie Guinan). Her life had taken several unusual turns since her 1884 birth on a ranch near Waco, Texas. While her parents, both Irish immigrants, encouraged their energetic daughter to develop her musical and academic talents, her interests lay elsewhere: "But it was the early cattle drives, Indian battles, and other exploits of McLennan County's pioneers that held Mamie's fascination. On her father's ranch she learned to ride, rope, and tame unruly broncs. She was a frequent visitor at the local shooting gallery . . . and was soon hitting targets with a six-shooter from the back of her running mount. At age fourteen she made an impromptu appearance at a frontier days celebration, where her equestrian and roping skills delighted an audience of thousands and won her the sobriquet 'Texas.'"[159]

Soon after, she won a competition of a different kind, a two-year Marshall Field scholarship to the American Conservatory of Music in Chicago. While there, she also studied in the School of Dramatic arts, and then returned home to graduate from the elite Hollins School for Girls. After an unsuccessful stint with a Waco theater company, Texas finally hit the road as a rodeo and Wild West show participant (4). Even there she never experienced the success that her earlier efforts might have indicated. Her name never appeared in the trade papers, and by 1906 she was in New York to try her hand at the musical stage (5).

In the absence of firsthand information, one can only guess at the cause of Guinan's failures. It is certainly likely that during her years at Chicago and with the touring company her rodeo skills eroded seriously. It is also likely that her educational and cultural background made her a poor fit in the rodeo family of the times. Her brief marriage to a journalist certainly suggests that she did not become one of the group. Even though she left the rodeo and turned down future offers to join the 101 Ranch Wild West, she maintained her interest things western.

Eventually, she found the perfect outlet for her talents in western movies. According to biographer Glenn Shirley, she starred in three westerns: *Get-Away Kate, Fuel of Life,* and *The Stainless Barrier,* between October and November of 1917. "Her image of self-reliant womanhood—a cowgirl in chaps with six-shooter in hand who could meet the bullying masculine world on its own terms—caught fire and was well promoted" (20). By 1919, when rodeo began to pick up, she had made another seven films, and signed a contract to make twenty-six more (21). Sometimes costarring with Tom Mix, Texas Guinan helped keep the image of the cowgirls alive during World War I.

When rodeos resumed full production after the war, women's place was firmly established in the sport. Pioneer cowgirls like Baldwin, Sperry Steele, Blancett, McGinnis, LaDue, and Mulhall, stars of the New York, Calgary, and Winnipeg Stampedes, helped make women's contests an integral part of professional rodeo. Before some of the largest crowds in rodeo history, they demonstrated that females were capable of far greater physical achievements than was generally believed possible. Through a combination of athletic ability, courage, determination, and showmanship, they won the support of audiences, media, and their fellow rodeo professionals. It was not an easy life, and many women did drop out due to lack of money or loss of desire. Those who remained reveled in the excitement of travel, bright lights, and the thrill of competition. Following the World War I hiatus, Guy Weadick and several other major promoters again gave cowgirl contests top billing and prizes at major rodeos. The most important was the 1922 Madison Square Garden rodeo, which set the stage for a new, more professional era for the sport.

Chapter Three

Champion Cowgirls in the Golden Age of Sport, 1919–29

Rodeo experienced tremendous growth during the twenties. The most significant development was the introduction of annual rodeos into major cities, with cowgirls leading the parades. Sites included St. Louis, Philadelphia, Chicago, and most important, Madison Square Garden in New York City. Women's popularity was due in great measure to the skills of promoter-producers like Tex Austin and Fred Beebe. Under their leadership, purses rose steadily throughout the decade, with some top cowboys and cowgirls having annual earnings six times the average per capita income. The 1929 death of bronc rider Bonnie McCarroll and the formation of the RAA paved the way for a new era in women's rodeo history. But before those crucial events occurred, many women joined the rodeo circuit, and cowgirls enjoyed new triumphs and breakthroughs in their sport.

The decade was also one of the most turbulent in American history, with rapid changes taking place in every aspect of life. Economic uncertainty and disillusionment about the peace negotiations followed swiftly after the initial euphoria that greeted the end of World War I. Seven years of prosperity then overshadowed all troubles until the 1929 crash set off the Great Depression. During the twenties, the numbers of radios, telephones, movie theaters, and automobiles increased significantly, altering patterns of communication, recreation, and life itself. The amount of money Americans spent on diversions rose by 30 percent, producing a boom for all manner of commercial amusements including rodeo.[1]

These factors helped create the "Golden Age of Sport." Fans for the first time could listen to the exploits of their heroes on the radio, and watch them in action on film. The media helped manufacture and popularize these heroes, and they in turn served a vital function in the rapidly changing society. As Benjamin Rader observed: "As society became more complicated and systematized and as success had to be won increasingly in bureaucracies, the need for heroes who leaped to fame and fortune outside the rules of the system grew. No longer were the heroes lone businessmen and statesmen, but the 'stars' of movies, television, and sports."[2] The best-known of these sport stars were Babe Ruth, Red Grange, Jack Dempsey, Bill Tilden, and Bobby Jones, but female athletes also enjoyed a golden age. In addition to channel swimmer Gertrude Ederle, the most successful and popular were tennis players Hazel Wightman and Helen Wills and aviatrix Amelia Earhart. All helped challenge the rigid gender divisions that had permeated society and change the image of the All-American Girl.[3]

The issue that had most united women during the prewar years was the suffrage. They had reason to celebrate when the Nineteenth Amendment finally passed in 1920, giving them the right to vote. Soon after that hard-won victory, the women's alliance began to unravel. Even though women's groups did coalesce behind social reforms and several unsuccessful efforts to obtain passage of the Equal Rights Amendment (ERA), they never achieved the solidarity that had characterized the suffrage battle.[4] They also realized that gaining the right to vote had not brought equality, as, for example, women's earnings remained no better than 55 percent of men's.[5]

Another problem was that many women of the younger generation seemed bored with politics.[6] For all of these and other reasons the quintessential female of the twenties was neither the Gibson girl nor the suffragist but the flapper. Her life-style was anathema to respectable middle-class women of previous generations. "Young, hedonistic, sexual, the flapper soon became the symbol of the age with her bobbed hair, powdered nose, rouged cheeks, and shorter skirts."[7]

Whether or not they adopted the ways of the flapper, all women benefited from the greater liberties that she introduced. The revolution in dress was particularly helpful to female athletes because it allowed much greater freedom of movement, which in turn enabled greater athletic skill and achievement. Coaches rightly observed that Ederle's channel swim could not have happened in earlier decades. Corsets and other heavy clothing would have made swimming impossible, and also have prevented the physical conditioning needed for endurance sports.[8] Even after women's clothing became conservative again during the thirties, forties, and fifties, their athletic attire continued the progress begun in the twenties.

Despite the popularity of sports, the best-known amusements of the period were the speakeasies. They were especially widespread in cities where more than half the population then resided, and are another unforgettable symbol of the jazz age. The proliferation of these illegal saloons must have been a bitter defeat for the women who had battled so long for passage of the Volstead Act. At the same time, they propelled to stardom the most famous cowgirl of the decade, Texas Guinan. After more than three hundred films, she quit Hollywood for New York in 1922. As hostess and entertainer at a series of illicit Broadway nightclubs, the former movie star became the toast of the town and a very wealthy woman. She gets credit for turning New York nightlife into "an essential and basic industry," while earning as much as $70,000 a month.[9]

During a phenomenal ten-year reign as one of Broadway's top entertainers, Guinan also toured the United States and Canada with her elaborate stage shows. Although she lived in a thirty-two-room flat, drove expensive cars, and dressed in designer clothes, diamonds, and furs, she never forgot her roots. A cowgirl to the end, Texas often included "Wild West" acts in her shows, and sometimes rode her favorite horse, Pieface, on stage.[10] Her acceptance by all strata of society proved that cowgirls could make it big in the entertainment world. The female stars of the Madison Square Garden rodeo probably benefited from Guinan's success, as they too achieved popularity and acceptance that transcended the sport itself. For rodeo cowgirls the twenties also meant the end of the trousers-taboo, something Guinan had never acknowledged. By mid-decade bloomers and divided skirts virtually disappeared from the contest arena.[11]

Cowgirls during the twenties won money in an average of eighteen rodeos a year. The press reported on an average of twenty-five female contestants annually, with the low being nineteen in 1920, and the high thirty-three in 1928. During that time, approximately one-third of all rodeos included contests for women, with the larger city rodeos being more likely to do so than smaller rural ones. Rodeos that held women's competitions usually scheduled two such events, with an average total purse of $4,735 per rodeo. The average prize per person per rodeo was $658 in 1925.[12]

By the end of World War I, significant changes had also occurred in western entertainment. The death of Buffalo Bill in 1917 brought an end to the heyday of Wild West shows as the premier western amusement. Even as rodeos surpassed Wild West shows in importance, they retained ties to the entertainment world. Many cowboys and cowgirls still performed on the Wild West and vaudeville stages and in western movies as well as in the rodeo arena. At the same time, rodeo producers sprinkled their programs with entertainment. Contests like Cheyenne, Pendleton, and Calgary featured Indian dances and ceremonials, as well as buffalo rides and events involving stagecoaches and chuck wagons. The husband and wife team of Powder River Jack and Miss Kitty Lee wandered the circuit from the turn of the century through the thirties performing such "old time favorite cowboy songs" as "Red River Valley" and "Trail of the Lonesome Pine."[13] All of these acts helped maintain rodeo's ties to the mythical nineteenth-century West.

Other daredevil entertainers presented a mixture of Old West and modern civilization. These men and women jumped their horses over cars and trucks, and sometimes bulldogged steers from the running boards of moving automobiles.[14] Their acts did not meet with the approval of everyone. Glen R. Vernam believed that bulldogging from automobiles and other mechanized events had no place in the arena, "For rodeo is the realm of the horse, the Old West." Vernam likened automobiles in rodeo to "entering a dummy in a dance contest."[15]

In indoor arenas and other places with limited space, popular contract acts included high school horses, educated steers, knife throwers, whip crackers, and sharpshooters. Some of the performers came from the ranks of rodeo contestants, while others were entertainers exclusively. With its exciting entertainment features and colorful outfits, rodeo was far ahead of other professional sports in recognizing and exploiting its place as popular entertainment. At the same time, show business connections blurred the lines between sport and theater, making it easier for dishonest operators to stay in business.[16]

With the decline of the Wild West shows, several former owners like California Frank Hafley and Col. Jim Eskew organized rodeo companies similar to Lucille Mulhall's Round-Up. This helped the contestants by providing salary as well as winnings.[17] Cowgirls' situation might have improved even more had there been some females in leadership positions. Mulhall had the experience and name recognition to become a real leader in the field. With her retirement, rodeo was left in the control of powerful independent male producer-promoters like Weadick, Hafley, Eskew, and Tex Austin, whose grandiose dreams soon transformed it into a more modern, urban sport.

Some Wild West show cowboys and cowgirls like Ruth and Bryan Roach and Mayme and Leonard Stroud had already turned their attention to rodeo by 1917. They launched their competitive careers with Lucille's company. Others stayed with the Wild West shows, often with disastrous results. None serves as a more dramatic example than Lulu Bell Parr, one of the first prominent cowgirl bronc riders. She had been an international headliner with Buffalo Bill, Pawnee Bill, and the 101 Ranch Wild West between 1910 and 1920. At Buenos Aires in 1914, former Argentine president José Figueroa Alcorta showered Lulu with gifts for her outstanding performance. She was also a top name on the vaudeville circuit, and with her reputation should have been able to succeed in the rodeo game. Unfortunately, Lulu stayed with the shows for the remainder of her career. Instead of entertaining the rich and famous, she appeared in ever smaller towns with such obscure outfits as Tatlinger's Tex Mex Wild West and Cook Bros. Texas Ranch 99. It was at best hand-to-mouth existence. Nearly destitute, Parr died at Dayton, Ohio, in January of 1955.[18]

Florence Hughes Randolph also began her career with the circus and Wild West shows. She joined the rodeo circuit in 1919, and her story had a much happier ending than Parr's. Born Cleo Alberta Holmes at Augusta, Georgia, in 1899, she used the name her father preferred to call her, Florence. As a child, she often rode mules on her grandfather's plantation, not learning to ride horseback until she was thirteen. Thrilled with the experience, she convinced her parents to apprentice her to a circus equestrian family. From 1913 to 1915, she was a trick and Roman rider and trick roper for Col. King's IXL Ranch Wild West. When that enterprise failed, she organized her own show, Princess Mohawk's Wild West Hippodrome. She toured with various Wild West shows and carnivals for four years until an accident brought financial ruin.[19] She was searching for a new livelihood when she learned of the rich purses being offered at the 1919 Calgary Stampede. Making her way to Canada, Princess Mohawk defeated eight men to win the three-mile Roman standing race. She won the Prince of Wales Trophy and a silver mounted saddle that she promptly sold for a much-needed $1,500.[20] It was the beginning of a phenomenal twenty-year career during which she competed in more than five hundred rodeos and earned a place in the National Rodeo Hall of Fame.[21] Only four feet six inches tall and weighing ninety pounds, Florence had the build of an elite gymnast of the 1990s, and was perfectly suited to the complicated riding tricks that made her famous.[22]

She began competing as Florence Holmes rather than Princess Mohawk soon after Calgary. Her rise to fame paralleled a time of turmoil in her personal life, including a five-year period of marriages, widowhood, and divorce. She competed as Florence Hughes, Florence King, and Florence Fenton before marrying cowboy Floyd Randolph in 1925. That union endured for the remainder of their lives, and she was best known as Florence Hughes Randolph.[23]

The 1919 season when Florence made her debut also marked the revival of rodeo, with almost twice as many cowgirl contests as in 1918. The season had begun with the annual Fort Worth Fat Stock Show and Rodeo, where women stole the show. The *Star Telegram* featured a half page of action shots of Ruth Roach. The caption read: "Of all the features at the Fat Stock Show and Rodeo, none is more thrilling than the riding of Ruth Roach, cowgirl."[24]

The biggest contest of 1919 was Weadick's Victory Stampede at Calgary. It was the scene of one of Vera McGinnis's major triumphs, as she won the cowgirl relay race. However, Vera was about the only familiar face in the competition. Most of the veterans of Weadick's earlier Stampedes were no longer active on the big-time circuit. Mulhall retired earlier that year when she married wealthy Texas rancher and rodeo aficionado Tom Burnette. While it appeared to be an ideal union, the two were at odds almost from the start. By 1922 Lucille was back home at the Mulhall ranch in Oklahoma, where she lived the remainder of her days.[25]

Bertha Blancett concluded her competitive career at the 1919 Pendleton Roundup, and thereafter worked for a time as a guide at Yosemite. She also continued her film career, made many guest appearances at rodeos, and invaded another male bastion, working as a rodeo pickup through the 1930s. In 1961, seventy-seven-year-old Bertha was the Grand Marshall at the Pendleton Roundup.[26] Fannie and Bill Steele began limiting their activities to the Montana area where they exhibited their Wild West show and she competed in local rodeos. She made her last professional appearance at the 1925 Bozeman, Montana, Roundup. The following year they quit both the show and the contest circuits and purchased a dude ranch. She continued to ride most of her life, and gave occasional bronc riding exhibitions into her fifties.[27]

The 1919 Stampede lacked both the stars and the widespread publicity and extensive local coverage of its predecessors. It drew a disappointing crowd of only fifty-seven thousand. Even Weadick himself admitted that the timing was poor, and that the Stampede should have been held a year later. Although the total purse was actually five thousand dollars larger than for the 1912 Stampede, it was worth far less due to postwar inflation. One major improvement made in 1919 was the introduction of chutes for the broncs. This did speed up the action, even though riders still had to continue until bucked off or in control of their horses.[28]

There was no cowgirl bronc riding competition at the 1919 Stampede, apparently because Weadick refused to sanction any more hobble riding, and there were not enough slick riders left to make a contest. There was an exhibition by headliner Tillie Baldwin, along with Prairie Lillie Allen, Marie Gibson, Fox Hastings, and several others.[29] Cowgirl trick roping was also absent from the program, although Florence LaDue did give daily exhibitions. The opening parade featured Baldwin and LaDue, but the Stampede really belonged to the next generation, women like Fox Hastings, Ruth Roach, and Lorena Trickey, who began their rodeo careers during the second decade of the twentieth century, and remained in the limelight during the twenties and thirties.[30]

Following the 1919 Stampede, Baldwin made a return visit to her native Norway and then played the New England fair circuit, giving exhibitions of bronc and trick riding and bulldogging. In 1925 she married William C. Slate. Thereafter she taught at a riding academy near their Connecticut home, and occasionally performed with visiting Wild West shows.[31] Rose Henderson also married in 1925, but remained active in contest rodeo through the thirties.[32] LaDue and Weadick continued to headline the vaudeville circuit for as long as it endured, even though she quit competitive rodeo in 1916.

Metropolitan contests during this era provided a tremendous challenge to the established western rodeos, and promoters of both attempted to gain additional publicity and credibility though commercially sponsored trophies and prizes. The earliest of these awards for women was the Denver Post Trophy awarded to the outstanding female rider at the Cheyenne Frontier Days since 1904. Nineteen-twenty saw the introduction of a new and more significant Cheyenne award, the McAlpin Trophy. Sponsored by the McAlpin Hotel, it went to the champion all-around cowgirl at the Frontier Days, and carried with it an all-expense-paid trip to New York City. *Ranch Romances,* a magazine that published rodeo news along with the love stories, awarded a valuable trophy to the champion cowgirl bronc rider at Madison Square Garden. A Juergens and Anderson Company trophy went to the all-around cowgirl at Tex Austin's Chicago Rodeos.

The most valuable and prestigious trophy of all was introduced in 1927, when the growing popularity of western films led Metro Goldwyn Mayer Studios (MGM) to commission Lambert Brothers Jewelers of New York to produce a $10,000 silver MGM Trophy. It honored the champion all-around cowgirl at the Madison Square Garden rodeo. It was a "tribute to the charm and courage of western womanhood."[33] Rules stipulated that when the same woman won it three years in succession, she retired the trophy.[34] Today the original MGM Trophy, first won by Florence Hughes (Randolph), is displayed at the National Rodeo Hall of Fame at Oklahoma City, donated by three-time winner Tad Lucas, who retired it in 1930.[35]

Although engravings clearly state that Lucas retired the original trophy in 1930, the *New York Times* in 1932 reported that she also won MGM trophies at Madison Square Garden in 1931 and 1932.[36] More intriguing, Randolph, 1927 winner of the original MGM Trophy at Madison Square Garden, reportedly won an MGM Trophy as the all-around cowgirl at rodeos produced by Fred Beebe in 1931 and 1932.[37] While only one MGM Trophy exists today, it is very possible that there were originally two or even three of them.

Whatever their numbers, the significance of such a valuable award for female athletes cannot be overlooked. Equally important was the interest Hollywood studios were taking in female rodeo stars. With huge purses, valuable publicity, and perhaps even motion picture contracts at stake, professionalism increased in the rodeo fraternity. Outstanding cowgirls, like great champions of any sport, were intensely competitive, willing to make extreme sacrifices, overcome serious injuries, and train long and hard to win and retain championships. It has generally been believed that women did not exhibit such grit and competitiveness until much more recently, but cowgirls dispel that myth.[38]

Florence Hughes Randolph was one dedicated professional. She recognized the significance of the Madison Square Garden rodeo, and left nothing to chance in preparing for that contest. She constructed at her ranch an exact replica of the Madison Square Garden arena in which to train and perfect her routines.[39] Vera McGinnis was also a determined athlete. She made this assessment: "I'd always aspired to be a champion cowgirl. At one time or another I'd won first in every big event that cowgirls can compete in, yet I didn't feel like a champion. . . . I knew I had to keep doing my best and, most of all, keep working."[40]

In addition to the hard work, these women were willing to accept the ultimate challenge, even if it posed considerable financial risk. When she received the invitation to Tex Austin's 1924 rodeo at Wembley Stadium in London, McGinnis also had an offer from a touring rodeo company. They would have paid her a flat salary to headline their events, and also allowed her to compete for cash prizes in their women's contests. To compete in England, she had to pay most of her own expenses. Against those costs there was no guarantee except whatever she could win competing against the best cowgirls in the business. Of course, competing against the best is the supreme goal of most athletes, and Vera accepted the challenge with little hesitation. Her decision proved to be a wise one, as she was the major female winner at Wembley.[41]

Along with the financial risks, cowgirls also faced considerable danger, including the possibility of career-ending injuries and even death. Yet the women took them in stride. In 1971, Randolph told an interviewer somewhat proudly: "I have been carried off for dead several times." She was actually pronounced dead in the arena in 1923. Following another rodeo accident several years later she was rushed to a hospital, where she awoke to hear the doctor say that if she lived, she would never walk again. Alarmed, she jumped from the bed and fled the building, clad only in a sheet.[42] With all their frequent and serious accidents, however, cowgirls like Randolph were rarely criticized for participating in dangerous events. Instead they were praised for their courage and tenacity. Even the few cowgirl fatalities, like those of cowboys, were taken in stride by both competitors and the press until 1929.

Many new names appeared among the cowgirl winners in the twenties, including Tad Lucas and Lorena Trickey. Lorena had captured the prestigious McAlpin Trophy in both 1920 and 1921.[43] This prize, with its well-publicized trip to New York, was quite a breakthrough for the Oregon cowgirl who had developed her skills out of economic necessity. When her parents died, Lorena and her two brothers took over management of the family ranch. She had earned respect as one of the top hands in the area before her Cheyenne victories and New York trips made her a top star.[44] A bronc, Roman, and relay rider, Trickey captured a third McAlpin Trophy in 1924. She also won the 1925 bronc riding title at Chicago and several championships at Pendleton.[45]

Tad Lucas was born Barbara Inez Barnes, on September 1, 1902, at Cody, Nebraska. One of twenty-four children of Lorenzo White Barnes, Tad began riding at a very young age.[46] She later told interviewers she had no memories of life before she could ride. She started helping her brothers break colts when she was seven, and along with her siblings competed in horseback races and contests against other ranch children and local Sioux Indians. She also rode calves for amusement, and made her professional debut in the steer riding competition at the Gordon, Nebraska, Fair in 1917.[47]

Tad Barnes (Lucas) made her rodeo debut riding a steer. Photo courtesy of ProRodeo Hall of Fame, Colorado Springs, Colorado.

Tad moved to Texas soon after, settling at Fort Worth with a brother. She rode broncs at rodeos in tiny communities like Spur, Texas, and moved on to bigger contests at Belle Fourche, South Dakota, and Fort Worth, becoming a full-time professional cowgirl in 1922.[48] The following year, she toured the United States and Mexico with the 101 Ranch Wild West, and took second in bronc riding at the Madison Square Garden rodeo.[49] Tad's fascination with female trick riders began in the Wild West show. With help from Reine Hafley, she started learning the event. In 1924, she was among the fortunate cowgirls invited to compete at Tex Austin's London rodeo. While in New York City awaiting departure for England in May, Tad married fellow professional Buck Lucas.[50] Their honeymoon was the voyage to London aboard the *Menomee*. In London, Tad first competed in trick riding, the event that would earn her greatest fame.[51]

Female athletes enjoyed greatly increased opportunities to compete both at home and abroad during the twenties and thirties. In tennis, Hazel Wightman and Helen Wills won the doubles at both the Olympic Games and the Wimbledon tournament in 1924, with Wills also taking the Olympic singles crown. Wills won eight Wimbledon singles titles between

1927 and 1938, and between 1927 and 1932 lost not one set in singles play.[52] At the 1920 Olympic Games, American women competed in swimming for the first time. Two years later, they also participated at the first annual Women's Olympic Games at Paris, France, under the auspices of the Fédération Sportive Féminine Internationale (FSFI). Those Paris games were a turning point in women's sport history, leading to the inclusion of women's track and field at the 1928 international Olympic Games. There, sixteen-year-old Elizabeth Robinson captured reporters' attention when she won the women's 100-meter race and became the youngest gold medalist in Olympic track and field history.[53] Both the Women's Games and women's track events in the Olympic Games unleashed a storm of protest from American physical education groups. They stressed recreational sports for the masses instead of highly publicized contests for the elite. In spite of their persistent opposition, the public generally supported American women who competed in international amateur contests.

Big City Rodeos: New York and London

Nineteen twenty-two opened a new era in rodeo history, as well as for cowgirls, with the first successful Madison Square Garden rodeo. Even though some rodeo hands remained bitter toward New York because of the financial disaster of the 1916 Stampede, it was probably inevitable that someone would produce a rodeo at Madison Square Garden. It was a Mecca for American sport, and indoor rodeo had already proved its viability at Fort Worth. These factors, as well as the increasing popularity of the sport itself, gave promoter-producer Tex Austin and his associates reason to be optimistic when they announced their rodeo for November 4–14.[54]

This first Garden rodeo did not initially get the publicity accorded its successors, and was virtually ignored by some New York papers.[55] Most of the early attention came only because of charitable activities. Austin had arranged for profits from the contest to go to the Argonne Association, an organization of Manhattan socialites who raised funds for French war orphans.[56] Publicity also focused on Mabel Strickland, who had already enjoyed a phenomenal year. By the time she reached New York, Strickland had traveled nearly ten thousand miles and won money in at least eight rodeos.[57] She succeeded Trickey as the top cowgirl at the Cheyenne Frontier Days, and roped against the cowboys at Pendleton. At the Ritzville, Washington, Roundup she roped and tied a steer in twenty-seven seconds, won day money against the top cowboys, and captured a gold medal as the champion all-around cowgirl.[58]

Tex Austin's 1922 World's Championship
COWBOY CONTESTS
Madison Square Garden
New York City
November 4-14

Grand Entry and Introduction
Bareback Bronk Riding
Fancy Roping
Cowgirls Bronk Riding
Calf Roping
Cowgirls Trick Riding
Cowboys Bronk Riding with Saddle
Exhibition High Jumping Horse Apollo
Bronk Riding, continued
Exhibition "Chief" Jumping over Chandler Automobile
Cowboys Trick and Fancy Riding
Steer Riding
Wild Horse Race

Contests in boldface type. Official program for November 4. From the Barker Texas History Center, Austin, Texas.

Strickland was born in Washington State in 1897, and grew up on a ranch near Walla Walla. She began her rodeo career in 1912 as Mabel DeLong, riding relay races for the famous Drumhellers. She soon added steer roping and trick riding to her career, and won championships in all three events. By the time of her 1917 marriage to bronc rider–steer roper Hugh Strickland, she had established a formidable reputation in the Northwest.[59] Because she had won the important McAlpin Trophy, the press covered Strickland's New York arrival and activities fairly well. Mrs. William P. Hamilton, chairman of the Argonne Association, had the trophy prominently displayed at a dinner she gave for rodeo participants.[60] Among the dinner guests was a reporter for the *New York Herald*. He wrote that Strickland along with Bonnie McCarroll and Fox Hastings, all clad in evening gowns, had succeeded in "utterly ruining all Eastern ideas concerning lady broncho [*sic*] busters."[61]

It was fortunate that women had already established their prominent role in rodeo by 1922. Austin realized that New York audiences would be unlikely to sit through day-long shows such as those staged in the West, or to be patient with the lengthy delays that often characterized outdoor contests. Consequently, he scheduled far fewer events at New York than were standard at the time. Although women's events are usually the first thing cut, Austin left the cowgirl contests intact and deleted other activities instead. His shorter program, along with arena director California Frank Hafley's ability to keep the program moving without delay, helped assure the success of the venture. This first Garden rodeo set a precedent that kept women in New York rodeo headlines for the next two decades.[62]

Reporters were not overly enthusiastic about either the men or the women at the first performances. One reporter for the *New York Times* observed that neither cowboys nor cowgirls were wild and woolly, but that the women's costumes "rivalled any circus lady who ever pirouetted on horseback."[63] Another journalist began with a somewhat negative attitude, then changed his opinion after interviewing the women. He reported: "We went behind the scenes expecting to interview half a dozen tomboys, but found ourselves in the presence of six mistresses of dignified deportment."[64] His article did give details of each woman's background, but he placed most emphasis on their professional careers, major championships, and significant athletic achievements.[65] His was the same kind of treatment that cowgirls received at Weadick's Canadian contests. It helped set the stage for their favorable coverage by the New York press in the years that followed.

Word-of-mouth publicity helped increase attendance steadily as the rodeo progressed. Thousands were actually turned away from the last three performances, as the *Billboard* reported "New York Is Rodeo Mad."[66] Fans were enthusiastic about the final Garden contests, in which many future stars earned headlines. Bonnie McCarroll took the bronc riding title, and $400, while Bonnie Jean Gray finished in a tie with Strickland for the trick riding championship. Each won $350, and a coin toss determined that Strickland would keep the trophy.[67] Other cowgirl contestants included Fox Hastings, Dot Vernon, Mayme Stroud, and eighteen-year-old Reine Hafley.[68]

Reine, the daughter of sharpshooter Mamie Francis, was born Elba Reine Skepper at Janesville, Wisconsin, in 1902. She made her vaudeville debut with her mother's act when she was three and a half, and was riding with the Pawnee Bill Wild West show a year later. When Mamie Francis married Wild West show promoter California Frank Hafley in 1909, Reine changed her last name to Hafley and joined Frank's show. She performed as a trick, bronc, and elephant rider, and oriental and flamenco dancer. Her competitive career began at age sixteen, when she placed second in trick riding at the Cheyenne Frontier Days and third at the Fort Worth rodeo.[69] By the time of her 1925 marriage to cowboy Dick Shelton, Reine was an established star of the contest circuit.[70]

The success of the Madison Square Garden rodeo was a major turning point in the development of the sport. It finally dispelled the idea that rodeo audiences had to come from the cattle country in order to appreciate the events.[71] Not only did it expand the potential audience, it gave the sport new credibility. As one insider had noted in 1916, playing in New York meant the big time, that rodeo had really arrived.[72] Succeeding at Madison Square Garden was really the big time, and the beginning of a new era. *The Billboard* rightly predicted that the Madison Square Garden contest would become an annual event.[73]

The contest even influenced cowgirl costumes. New York papers at the time of the rodeo were filled with ads for the upcoming Madison Square Garden Horse Show. There were many pictures of female riders wearing jodhpurs.[74] This seems to have been a watershed for cowgirls. Within two years, similar jodhpurs had become standard attire for trick and bronc riders. A 1923 photo showed "the most prominent cowgirls": Ruth Roach, Florence Hughes, Bonnie Gray, Bea Kirnan, Rose Smith, and Ruby Roberts, all wearing jodhpurs. Their accessories included cowboy [*sic*] boots, huge neckerchiefs, and enormous western hats. Three of the women also wore

Cowgirls in Houston wearing typical 1924 costumes. Left to right: Bea Kirnan, unknown, Mabel Strickland, Fox Hastings, Ruth Roach, and Florence Randolph. Photo courtesy of Marilyn Hansen, Ben Loma, California.

long flowing sashes around their waists.[75] Female participants at the 1923 Kansas City Rodeo and the 1924 London contest were similarly attired.[76]

Relay riders were the first cowgirls to adopt practical rather than decorative costumes because their events were decided by the stopwatch, not judges. Pictures through the years show that few of them bothered with fancy accessories or even personal appearance, and many wore riding breeches long before their fellow contestants dared to do so. They were rarely copied by women in rodeo events where victory depended on subjective opinions. This was particularly true for trick riding, as scoring actually included costume. Reputation also had a significant impact on judged events, since officials, like those in figure skating or gymnastics today, tended to favor established champions over exciting newcomers. It was therefore important look neat and attractive, and at the same time to stand out from the crowd, in order to attract good publicity and establish a winning tradition in trick and bronc riding. For all of these reasons, the bronc and trick riders were the last cowgirls to adopt trousers as their standard competition gear, but the change was swift and almost universal once it happened.

The transition was facilitated because most cowgirls still mastered the more traditional female skills like sewing, and were able to design and make all of their own costumes. Economic necessity also dictated this, since it was impossible to purchase appropriate attire "off the rack," and having costumes tailor made was prohibitively expensive. Cowgirls therefore remained highly individualistic, and continued to create distinctive outfits. Some rodeos awarded lucrative prizes to the best-dressed cowgirls, and a variety of styles became evident.[77] Some women wore skintight, knee-length trousers with brocade decorations, along with boots and accessories like those described above. For the London rodeo, Vera McGinnis created Spanish-influenced outfits featuring bell-bottom satin trousers and matching boleros, both trimmed with brocade. McGinnis's suits and Tad Lucas's 1924 innovation, wearing leather chaps for bronc riding, attracted many imitators.[78]

The significance of elaborate costuming did not become apparent to sisters Vaughn and Gene Krieg until after they joined the big-time rodeo circuit. Born in 1904 and 1909 respectively, the two grew up on a Colorado ranch. Both learned to ride before they were five, and like their counterparts of the nineteenth century, were soon helping their brothers break wild horses and pursue stray cattle. Unlike cowgirls of the earlier era, the Kriegs always wore overalls, even when competing at local rodeos like the Watermelon Days at Rocky Ford, Colorado.[79]

Sixteen-year-old Gene in 1925 became the youngest woman ever to win the bronc riding at Cheyenne Frontier Days. A slick rider of the old school, she so impressed impresario Verne Elliott that he hired her as a relay rider. He also wanted her to compete in bronc and trick riding at the upcoming Chicago and Pendleton rodeos. While Elliott tutored her in these events, he hired a seamstress to fashion more appropriate clothing than overalls. Elliott was a good teacher and judge of talent, and Gene won $1,200 at Chicago. During the next two decades, as Gene Krieg and later Gene Creed, she captured many titles in bronc and trick riding and racing. She rodeoed in all except two states, as well as in England, Australia, and Mexico. The 1925 visit to a seamstress was her last; thereafter Gene made all of her own costumes.[80]

The 1922 rodeo was so successful that New York was treated to two western contests the following year, one at Yankee Stadium and a second at the Garden. Both featured all-star casts, yet only two women, Strickland and Gray, participated in both. The Yankee Stadium rodeo offered women the biggest purse to date, $8,200 for trick riding, bronc riding, and relay racing.[81] Ringling's Madison Square Garden contest attracted greater publicity than the Yankee Stadium event, but awarded women a total purse of only $6,175. McGinnis collected $675 by winning the best-dressed cowgirl contest and finishing in a tie with Gray for second in the trick riding. Rose Smith, wife of legendary cowboy Oklahoma Curly Roberts, took $960, including the $600 first prize in bronc riding, $185 day money, and $175 in the costume event. At Yankee Stadium, Bonnie McCarroll won the bronc riding, and Donna Glover the relay. The biggest New York winner of all was Strickland. She won the trick riding at both Yankee Stadium and Madison Square Garden to collect more than $2,000 in prize money.[82]

Mabel repeated her triumph at Madison Square Garden in 1924, where Reine Hafley took the bronc riding championship, with McGinnis, McCarroll, Stroud, Hastings, Lucas, and Smith also participating.[83] Within a few years, the Madison Square Garden event had become the most important rodeo in the United States. Held in late October or November, it was the culmination of the season, and the place where the mythical world's championships were really won. The success and popularity of this event led to an increase in both the number of contests and the size of purses nationwide, hastening the day when the top cowboys and cowgirls could earn a living through their sport.

Perhaps because of the enormous success of his venture, Tex Austin was unable to maintain his role as producer of the Garden rodeo. He lost out to John Ringling in 1923, and had to be content with producing the Yankee Stadium contest. He returned to the Garden in 1924, for his last New York rodeo. Austin also featured cowgirls at rodeos he produced at Chicago Stadium from 1921 through 1929; in London in 1924 and 1934; and in Los Angeles in 1935. Fred Beebe was another important producer. He staged the 1926 and 1927 Madison Square Garden rodeos, as well as major contests in St. Louis, Philadelphia, and Kansas City in the late twenties and thirties. All offered excellent prizes for women.[84]

The rodeo Austin produced at Wembley Stadium was his most ambitious venture. His cast included Ruth Roach and new husband Notowa Slim Richardson, Tad and Buck Lucas, Bonnie and Frank McCarroll, Bea and Tommy Kirnan, Vera McGinnis, Marie Gibson, Florence Randolph, Bryan Roach, and Rube Roberts.[85] Bonnie McCarroll won the bronc riding title at Wembley, where Tad Lucas made her trick riding debut. The most successful cowgirl of the group was McGinnis, who took both the relay and trick riding titles, and was actually in contention in the bronc riding when she was bucked off for only the second time in her career.[86]

Many of these stars remained in Europe for several months for rodeos and exhibitions. McGinnis's twin victories at Wembley made her the star during stops at Paris, Brussels, and Dublin. She returned home to compete in the 1924 Madison Square Garden rodeo, and then left the country once more. During 1925–26, she signed to headline a "Wembley Rodeo" tour of the Orient. Although she was the only actual Wembley participant in the company, the tour was the fulfillment of dreams Vera had since early childhood.[87]

The entourage stopped at Hawaii, Japan, the Malay States, and Singapore, where the sultan of Johore was in the audience. He so enjoyed Vera's performance he invited her to the royal box to discuss her most difficult trick riding feat, going under the belly of her speeding horse. He also invited her to lunch at his palace, an event that remained the highlight of her life.[88] His friendship was most helpful later on, as the rodeo company fell behind in their payments to her. When the show arrived at his domain of Johore, Vera contacted the sultan. He made it plain to the owners that if they wished to avoid severe penalties from his government, they should pay her promptly, and they did. Even then, she did not have enough money to ship her horse back home, and had to sell him to the management.[89]

Vera had two exciting years visiting places most Americans of her time could hardly imagine. Although it was a great adventure, the travel kept her out of the spotlight, and out of the running for the increasingly lucrative prizes being awarded at American rodeos. She spent her best years touring the world, and was never able to capitalize on her London fame back in the United States. She returned home with wonderful memories but little else, and immediately had to purchase and train a new horse in order to resume her career. Although she did enjoy some success on the western circuit, Vera never again competed east of the Mississippi.[90]

While rodeo's major stars were enjoying their triumph at Wembley in June of 1924, some contestants who remained at home were much less fortunate. A Knights of Columbus rodeo went bankrupt in Brooklyn, leaving more than 150 cowboys and cowgirls "temporarily discommoded" and resentful of the money they had lost. The Knights of Columbus organization claimed that the problems were a result of bad faith by their partners, U.S. Championship Rodeo, Inc., and the Knights did pay the contestants a portion of the prizes owed them. This was only one example of the ongoing problems associated with dishonest operators, shoestring promoters, and unscrupulous producers who harmed the business.[91]

Even the London rodeo had its controversy. Pressure from the humane societies forced cancellation of the steer roping as a public contest. Austin and his London partners planned to continue the competition in private so the participants would not lose out on prize money, but this too was halted.[92] Nonetheless, most considered the rodeo a major triumph, and it received extensive publicity in the United States as well as in Europe. The success of the sport abroad helped increase the popularity and prestige of rodeo and its participants back home. The *Detroit News* used the women's foreign accomplishments and acclaim to criticize their treatment by American press and producers. An elaborately illustrated article detailed the skills and achievements of several cowgirls, and described events at the 1924 Pendleton Roundup. There, Mabel Strickland, Fox Hastings, Lorena Trickey, and Rose Henderson had requested permission to compete in the same contests as cowboys, and thereby vie for the all-around cowboy prize. The Pendleton Roundup Association denied their request, exhibiting an attitude that showed quite a contrast to the earlier years when women like Bertha Blancett had regularly challenged the men and given them a run for the all-around title. Despite the controversy, Strickland remained a favorite at Pendleton. In 1927 she set a steer roping record there, and was also named the Roundup queen.[93]

Triumphs and Tragedies

Through all of this progress, there still existed no central rodeo organization to maintain records on its members, and results of most contests never appeared in print. Consequently, it is extremely difficult to ascertain exactly how much money an individual earned in any year, or how many contests she may have entered. It is evident though, that Strickland's 1923 prizes at New York were not an anomaly. Purses in the big-city rodeos remained quite large. The best cowgirls, including Tad Lucas, Reine Shelton, Gene Creed, and Velda Tindall collected winnings of $1,500 to $2,000 in just two or three contests. In 1926, Florence Randolph won $6,000 at the Sesquicentennial Rodeo at Philadelphia, where she took the trick and bronc riding and all-around cowgirl title.[94] These women enhanced their incomes with money won at a myriad of lesser-known rodeos, as well as their salaries for contract performances. Since stars commanded top dollars for their exhibition work, some made sizable incomes.[95]

Of course, for every Lucas, Shelton, Creed, Randolph, or Tindall, there were countless others who did not fare nearly so well. A little over half of the 190 women who competed during this period had careers of three years or longer. The average career for that group was fifteen years. The

Eloise "Fox" Hastings, the most famous cowgirl bulldogger of the twenties and thir-ties, exhibiting her skills in the twenties. Photo courtesy of the National Rodeo Hall of Fame at the National Cowboy Hall of Fame, Oklahoma City, Oklahoma.

most obvious difference between those women and the ones who quit the business after one or two seasons was their versatility. Cowgirls with long-er careers competed in an average of 2.4 different events, and more than 70 percent of them were performers as well as contestants. Conversely, the women with careers of one to two years competed in an average of only one event, and only two of them were performers.[96] The significance of this latter figure cannot be overlooked, since contract work often paid travel expenses, leaving all prize money as profit. (See table A.4.)

One cowgirl whose fame as a contract performer totally eclipsed her contest activities was Fox Hastings, who made her debut as an exhibition bulldogger at the 1924 Fort Worth rodeo. She repeated the feat at the Houston Cattlemen's convention rodeo, and was called the outstanding act of the entire event.[97] Overcoming several injuries, Hastings bull-dogged at more than a dozen rodeos as well as the revived 101 Ranch Wild West that year.[98] She was already a well-known trick and bronc rider when she took up bulldogging, having learned the event from her husband, Mike Hastings.

The couple gained considerable fame as husband and wife bulldoggers, although much of Fox's notoriety came from her manager, Foghorn

Clancy. A flamboyant rodeo announcer and publicity man, he made her the most photographed and interviewed cowgirl of the late twenties. He also created the myth that she was the first woman bulldogger, an error that has been repeated ever since.[99] Yet Clancy did not do it all. Fox was very good at her event, establishing a record time of seventeen seconds in 1924. She was also a charismatic performer, who could smile at the cameras while lying in the mud, still clinging to the neck of a freshly thrown steer.[100] When participating in trick and bronc riding, she was a flashy dresser, sporting bold colors and enormous bows in her red hair. Her bulldogging attire was quite a contrast. It copied cowboy steer wrestlers, and included boots laced to the knees, knickers, turtleneck sweaters, and sometimes football helmets instead of hair ribbons.[101] Although the press had traditionally been most respectful of cowgirl athletes, Hastings's masculine attire and participation in a rough, traditionally male event caused reporters to stress her domestic side. The following is an example: "To the rodeo crowd she is Fox Hastings, cowgirl extraordinary. To neighbors she is Mrs. Mike Hastings, a good cook and tidy housekeeper."[102]

Fox continued to earn headlines for the next several years, as she rode broncs and bulldogged at rodeos from New York to Los Angeles. Just prior to the 1927 Madison Square Garden rodeo, this announcement brought her even greater fame: "A new contest in the history of western sports will be fought out in the garden . . . for the first time by Claire Belcher, cowgirl of Ponca City, Oklahoma, and Fox Hastings, of Iowa Park, Texas, who will engage in a special steer-wrestling contest for a prize of $5,000 offered by Beebe. Fox has never had a rival as a steer wrestler."[103]

The contest never took place. The judges canceled it, claiming that both women violated the rules. However *The Billboard* was enthusiastic about the exhibition that replaced it, reporting that "Claire Belcher won the admiration of everyone when she bulldogged a ferocious Brahama [*sic*] Steer without even disarranging her golden curls."[104] Both women also competed in bronc riding, and Claire participated in trick riding as well, but the glory in those events went to others. Florence Randolph won the trick riding and took second in bronc riding to collect more than $1,300, the all-around title, and the new MGM trophy. The $600 bronc riding prize went to Marie Gibson.

Thereafter Fox and Claire shared the cowgirl bulldogging headlines. Both suffered a variety of serious injuries, and Belcher was nearly killed when a steer fell on her at a Tampa, Florida, rodeo. By 1929, cowgirl bulldogging contests were illegal at most places, though exhibitions were still permitted.[105] While bulldogging was just as dangerous for males as for females, there was never any mention of banning cowboy bulldogging. This was a classic case of males making rules that limited the athletic opportunities of females. Similar regulations had affected women in other sports for years, while rodeo had initially been much more liberal. Even without the competition, the two stars continued to enjoy performing their feat for several years thereafter, and several more cowgirls joined in.

The careers and lives of Claire and Fox had many parallels. Claire had also entered the rodeo business with her first husband, bulldogger Bob Belcher, in 1926. She too was a bronc and trick rider and relay racer who learned bulldogging from her husband. In 1927, she starred with the 101 Ranch Wild West and during the next two years won many titles and gained sensational publicity nationwide.[106] Her marriage to Belcher did not survive those heady days, and by the end of 1929 Claire had a new husband, bulldogger Jack "Red" Thompson.[107] Fox's success also put a strain on her marriage. By 1929, she had divorced Mike Hastings and married another cowboy, Chuck Wilson. She continued bulldogging through the thirties, when she and Wilson purchased a guest ranch in Arizona.[108]

While some women like Fox and Claire enjoyed great success, others experienced personal problems that damaged or ended their rodeo careers. Effie Griffey, also known as Montana Belle, was a multitalented roper and rider and Wild West show impresario hailed as the "Queen of the Arena."[109] In May of 1923, Effie turned herself in to the Kennett, Missouri, sheriff, stating that she had killed her assistant manager, William Smith.[110] Although authorities released Griffey after her preliminary hearing, her show opened under new management on May 22, and her name vanished from the trade papers.[111]

On November 7, 1927, Lorena Trickey faced first degree murder charges in Lakeview, Oregon. She stood accused of stabbing to death her common-law husband, J. P. "Slim" Harris, during an argument on September 2.[112] Her fellow professionals packed the courtroom for the trial of the popular cowgirl, who pleaded self-defense. With the announcement that she had been found not guilty, a wild demonstration erupted among her colleagues in the audience.[113]

After that trauma, Lorena never again enjoyed the competitive success that had characterized her earlier career, when she defeated both men and women at contests large and small throughout the United States. After a brief return to competition, Lorena married cowboy Magnus Peterson in 1928. They both retired from rodeo the following year, and moved to Nevada, where she attended the School of Mines and Magnus worked for the state. They also did some ranching before purchasing a quicksilver mine where they lived and worked until Lorena's death in 1961.[114]

Despite these tragedies, the popularity of the sport continued to attract new faces. Among the women joining the circuit in the late twenties were sisters Alice and Margie Greenough, who grew up on a Montana ranch with several brothers. Margie claims that "Rodeo was born in us. We learned to ride horses before we could walk. Dad would give us a bucking horse and expect us to make a good horse out of him. If we bucked off, we better find him and bring him back home."[115] Both women were excellent athletes, with Alice a figure skating champion. At a community rodeo at Forsyth, Montana, cowboys convinced Alice to enter her first public bronc riding contest. Thereafter the sisters competed in a variety of events including races and relays. They earned their greatest fame in bronc riding, which both found more exciting than racing.

Alice and Margie were allowed to finish school through the eighth grade before being put to work under the stern direction of their father, Packsaddle Ben Greenough. By 1929, two of the Greenough brothers were already on the big-time rodeo circuit, while the sisters worked around Red Lodge, Montana, awaiting their opportunity to become professional cowgirls. In March, they answered an advertisement in *The Billboard* that Alice remembers as saying "bronc riders wanted." They soon received a wire from the producer inviting them to join his company in Ohio. Their mother expressed dismay at their decision, while Ben Greenough eventually gave them his blessing.[116]

Although Alice and Margie had left home "to join the rodeo," their first employer, King Bros. Wild West Rodeo and Hippodrome Racing Unit,[117] was not really a rodeo company at all but one of the last big Wild West shows. In addition to riding broncs and exhibiting their cowgirl skills, the sisters had to ride buffalo and perform in skits where they wore funny clothing and ran screaming from burning buildings. Neither enjoyed this part of the job, although they now agree it was a good experience. When the season closed at Des Moines, Iowa, they had nothing to show for their efforts except a can of tomato soup, which tells something about the economics of the Wild West show business. One of their fellow cast members was pioneer bronc rider Lulu Belle Parr. Then fifty-three years old, she should have retired years before, but since she had no other means of support, she continued to work. The King show lacked prestige, and performing there indicated the decline of the former superstar, while for Alice and Margie it was the first step in their rise to the big time. Still, they had no money to travel home, and spent the winter working in Des

Margie Greenough Henson claimed rodeo was born in her. Here she exhibits the skill which led to her long, successful career and induction into two rodeo halls of fame. Photo courtesy of Margie Greenough Henson, Tucson, Arizona.

Bonnie McCarroll, thrown from Silver, 1915. This photo is often mistakenly captioned as Bonnie's fatal ride of 1929, but it appeared on a magazine cover in 1915. Also note that Bonnie was riding slick, and is thrown free and clear of the horse, whereas in 1929 she rode hobbled and got tangled up in the stirrups. Photo courtesy of the National Rodeo Hall of Fame at the National Cowboy Hall of Fame, Oklahoma City, Oklahoma.

Moines. Their experience with the show had not improved their financial situation, but the sisters had made the contacts necessary to launch their real rodeo careers the following season. Margie had also met her future husband, bulldogger Heavy Henson, another fellow performer.[118]

The Greenoughs had joined the Wild West show in a year forever etched in the public memory for the stock market crash that set off the Great Depression. Even if the market had not done anything unusual, the year would have been a notable one in the history of rodeo cowgirls. The tragic death of bronc rider Bonnie McCarroll and the formation of the RAA combined to change the basic structure of the sport and women's position in it.

Bonnie McCarroll was thrown and fatally trampled at the Pendleton Roundup, when she got tangled up in her hobbles and could not escape the pounding hoofs.[119] The incident created a furor that would not abate, and for the first time a rodeo fatality had a dramatic and lasting impact on the sport. There are many reasons for this change in attitude. First of all, cowgirls were involved in three other serious, though not fatal, accidents at Pendleton that year, and the management was very sensitive to grow- ing negative publicity. Bonnie was an extremely popular member of the rodeo family, and adding to the tragedy was the fact that Pendleton was to be her last rodeo. After seventeen years on the road, Bonnie and her husband had already announced they would retire, and she had hoped her winnings would help pay for decorations in their Boise new home.[120]

During the eleven days when Bonnie clung to life in a Pendleton hos- pital, the media had ample time to dramatize her life story and the cruel irony of her accident.[121] Daughter of an Idaho rancher, Bonnie Treadwell had ridden horseback all her life, and joined the rodeo circuit as a slick bronc rider when she married bulldogger Frank McCarroll in 1912. Pendleton had been the scene of her first major bronc riding title three years later. Exactly when or why she made the fatal switch to hobble riding is unknown, but Bonnie was a daredevil. She competed in trick riding, and her contract repertoire included three extremely dangerous events: steer riding, bulldogging, and automobile jumps.[122]

The Rodeo Association of America

Immediately after Bonnie's death, the Pendleton Roundup committee dropped cowgirl bronc riding from their programs.[123] Thereafter, the de- bate continued throughout the profession. Some individuals and organizations supported outright bans of cowgirl bronc riding, while others advocated a change in the rules. One group that could have provided invaluable assistance in the matter was the fledgling RAA, also formed in 1929. Unfortunately, that organization of rodeo producers consistently ignored pleas that they sanction women's bronc riding and issue rules ensuring the safety of participants. Had they acted, they might well have increased the popularity of the event and also helped prevent several cowgirl fatalities in the ensuing years. They might also have garnered more support from contestants, who felt the RAA was insensitive to their needs.[124]

The reason for the RAA's opposition to women's contests may never be known, as all of their records are lost. Their action does not necessarily indicate the existence of widespread opposition to cowgirl contests. During the RAA's formative years, San Francisco attorney Maxwell McNutt dominated the organization. Experiences in other sports suggest that one individual can prevent the inclusion of women's events. Just as James Sullivan's power within the AAU kept American women from AAU-sanctioned sports, and from swimming at the 1912 Olympic Games, McNutt may well have been responsible for the RAA's stance on the matter of cowgirl contests.[125]

The RAA did not actually prohibit members holding women's contests, but RAA-sanctioned rodeos had to include four specific events. Soon the organization's award structure expanded to recognize eight contests, and many member rodeos began including them all, usually at the expense of locally popular contests and events for women.[126] The RAA grew slowly, never enrolling more than one hundred rodeos, but its most vocal members represented such major western contests as Cheyenne Frontier Days and the Calgary Stampede. While it remained controversial through most of its existence, the RAA did have the effect of standardizing rodeo events, and in that regard its influence spread well beyond the membership itself.[127] The mere fact of its existence as the first centralized agency in the sport gave it a certain prestige and helped solidify control in a traditional patriarchy. Since there were no female producers, women had no way to join the organization and make their voices heard.

The RAA's impact was felt in other ways as well. The organization in 1929 selected the magazine *Hoofs and Horns* as its official publication. The magazine publicized RAA activities, advised members of rules and upcoming events, and helped contestants keep abreast of standings. This benefited both the RAA and the new periodical tremendously, while further obscuring women's achievements. Even though *Hoofs and Horns* did cover cowgirl activities, with columnists like Foghorn Clancy writing many features about them, neither the RAA standings nor photos of finalists and national champions included women.

With the fallout from the McCarroll accident and the opposition of the RAA, cowgirl bronc riding became increasingly rare in the West. At the same time, it gained popularity at big eastern rodeos controlled by powerful independent producers with no interest in or need for joining the RAA. Cowgirl relay racing, meanwhile, retained its popularity at western contests, despite the fact that it too could be quite dangerous. There are several possible reasons for the continued inclusion of cowgirl relay racing. One was certainly its regional popularity, another the fact that relay races were part of a larger circuit that included county fairs and other events besides rodeos. The power and influence of the relay string owners, usually wealthy stock contractors on whom rodeos depended for their existence, were also important. Whatever the reasons, the subject of women's relay races never came up at RAA meetings, and discussions of it rarely appeared in the press like bronc riding.

Unfortunately for the women who competed in them, relay races were possible only at rodeos held at race tracks or specially built arenas such as the one at Cheyenne. They could not be conducted indoors, and consequently were never a part of the major eastern circuit that grew increasingly popular in the wake of the Madison Square Garden success. Cowgirls soon found themselves in the peculiar position of having few contests other than relay races open to them in the West, and only bronc riding and trick riding in the East.

Many other changes occurred following the first Madison Square Garden rodeo in 1922. In addition to the radical alteration in styles of women's costumes had come a revolution in travel. While special trains were still used for major contests like Madison Square Garden and Cheyenne, pack trips gradually ceased. By the late twenties, rodeo performers began purchasing automobiles and trailers to transport themselves and their stock. McGinnis bought her first rig in 1927, and spent most of the season traversing the highways from California to Washington for trick riding and relay events.[128] With her horse in an open trailer, she bumped along dirt roads, and like others in the business, sometimes slept in tent cities along the way to the next rodeo.[129]

The most popular and famous cowgirl of the decade was certainly Tad Lucas, owner of most of the major titles and trophies offered professional

Tad Lucas, premier cowgirl of the twenties and thirties, riding Juarez early in her career. Photo courtesy of the National Rodeo Hall of Fame at the National Cowboy Hall of Fame, Oklahoma City, Oklahoma.

cowgirls. Lucas was singled out for stardom from her earliest appearances in 1922 and 1923 at Belle Fourche, South Dakota; Pittsburgh, Kansas; and Fort Worth, Texas. She hit the big time at the 1923 Madison Square Garden rodeo where she took second in bronc riding and third in the best-dressed competition for a total of $475.[130] After mastering trick riding for the 1924 London rodeo, she really hit her stride. Tad won four trick riding titles at Fort Worth between 1926 and 1933, as well as at Philadelphia in 1926 and Boston in 1931. At Cheyenne, she took the trick riding title in 1925 and 1927, and won the relay in 1930, 1931, and 1932. At Chicago between 1925 and 1929 she captured three trick riding titles, two relay titles and two all-around titles, collecting trophies donated by Montgomery Ward, the Chicago Association of Commerce, and Juergens and Anderson Company.[131] Lucas's greatest triumphs came at Madison Square Garden. There she won the trick riding title in 1925, 1926, and 1928 through 1932, winning the all-around cowgirl title in 1926 and again in 1928 through 1932. This brought her the *Ranch Romance* Trophy in 1926, and the MGM trophies from 1928 through 1932.[132]

Although she began her career as a bronc rider, and competed in that event throughout her career, Tad's greatest success came in trick riding. She never won a major bronc riding title until 1940, when she captured the crown in an invitational contest at the Cheyenne Frontier Days,[133] but through the years, she rarely finished out of the money in bronc riding. In fact she usually ranked high enough in the event to ensure that if she won the trick riding championship, the all-around title would also be hers. Tad's biggest challengers were her close friends Florence Randolph and Reine Shelton. The intense rivalries between the three friends added interest to their contests, while their superb professionalism set a standard for younger cowgirls to emulate. Still, neither Shelton, Randolph, nor the talented newcomers ever achieved the recognition and admiration accorded Lucas, truly the quintessential cowgirl of the twenties. One journalist summarized her career this way: "Tad has always been admired by everyone who had the good fortune to meet her. She is right at home in the saddle and makes a marvelous picture on a horse. She is considered the world's greatest woman rider."[134]

Tad and her colleagues experienced substantial progress and won many honors during the twenties, while the real impact of the pivotal 1929 events was not immediately apparent. As the decade came to a close, few women could have guessed what lay ahead. Although the women of rodeo never became household names like Gertrude Ederle and Helen Wills, many cowgirls enjoyed unprecedented prosperity and stardom in the Golden Age of Sport.

Chapter Four

Home on the Range, 1930–47

Americans experienced a dizzying array of changes between 1920 and 1946, as the euphoria of the Roaring Twenties crashed with the stock market, plunging the nation's collective psyche into a depression as severe as that suffered by the economy. With up to 25 percent of the work force unemployed, and many others suffering greatly reduced standards of living, this period remains vivid in the minds of those who experienced it. Although the economy did begin a gradual improvement at mid-decade, it did not approach pre-Depression levels until 1941, by which time the nation was involved in World War II, another tragedy of major proportions. In addition to facing separation from and even loss of loved ones, Americans on the home front also experienced new deprivations brought about by wartime shortages and rationing.

All through these decades, women entered the work force in record numbers. Although public sentiment overwhelmingly opposed married women working outside the home, wives made up a growing portion of female employees. By 1944, married women outnumbered single women in the work force for the first time.[1] Along with their increased role as wage earners, women also bore the brunt of holding families together during the crises.[2]

Throughout the Depression and the war, popular culture and entertainment played a key role in distracting the public from their problems. During the thirties, Babe Ruth, Lou Gehrig, Bobby Jones, and Helen Wills continued to reign supreme in their sports and in the hearts of their fans, while radio became a major entertainment form for the first time. The thirties and forties were also the peak years of influence for Hollywood films, which attracted an average audience of eighty-five million weekly. As Susan Ware observed: "By providing cheap family entertainment and reinforcing traditional ideals, movies made an important contribution to the 1930s."[3] This influence continued through World War II.

Big-time rodeo also thrived during the Depression. While the economic crisis did have an effect, forcing many marginal operations into bankruptcy and depriving lower-echelon contestants of opportunities, the name stars and contests had few problems.[4] Throughout the economic crisis, prizes at major rodeos continued to increase, and contestants' incomes rose proportionately. Cowgirls were much more fortunate than other working women at the time. Although the number of married women in the work force did rise from 12 to 15 percent during the Depression, as late as 1940, only 11 percent of married couples both worked.[5] During the Depression, many employers had rules or at least practices specifying that when both husband and wife worked for the same firm, it was the wife who had to be dismissed if personnel reductions were needed; others simply refused to hire married women.[6] With no such rules in rodeo, many cowgirls fared quite well and some rodeo couples earned record amounts.

The first big money winner among cowboys was Bob Crosby, whose 1928 income was $25,000, much of it probably collected in matched roping contests.[7] By 1935, the average rodeo cowboy earned an estimated $2,000 per year, compared with $2,391 for a dentist, and $1,227 for a teacher.[8] Although exact figures are not available, it appears from the RAA records that the champion all-around cowboy won more than $9,000 in prizes and bonuses in 1936.[9] By 1937, the average income was $3,000, and at least thirty top hands earned between $8,000 and $9,000.[10]

Far less money was available to women because purses for their events were usually no more than 60 to 70 percent of the purses for equivalent men's contests, and rodeos had only one to three events for women, versus eight to ten for men. Data collected for this book indicates that during the thirties, cowgirls participated in an average of eighteen rodeos annually, competing for purses of $4,000 per rodeo, or $2,000 per event. The average prize per woman per rodeo was $270 in 1936, making the average annual earnings around $4,000 per woman.[11] Of course, several made much more; Tad Lucas, for example, reported income of $12,000 in 1935.[12] While some money did come from contract work, she was a big winner as well.[13]

Cowgirls were also able to enhance their incomes through commercial endorsements, something few women athletes then enjoyed. Alice Greenough endorsed a variety of Australian products from saddles to re-frigerators when she won the cowgirls "buck jumping" championships in Melborne in 1934 and 1939. After she captured the 1940 bronc riding ti-tle at Madison Square Garden, she received several lucrative offers, in-cluding one for cigarettes. Although an adamant nonsmoker, Greenough did not hesitate to sign the contract. In addition to the financial rewards, publication of the ads also helped reaffirm and promote her status as the world champion.[14]

Unlike Lucas and Greenough, most cowgirls had far lower earnings than the average cowboys because of fewer events and lower purses. Of course their situation relative to the men was not unusual, but typical in American society at the time. Women were almost always paid much less than men, even for the same jobs, with the highest-paid women in many organizations making less than the lowest-paid men.[15] Even today, Amer-ican women earn only 70 percent of the salaries made by men.[16]

Cowgirls also participated briefly in the movie boom, and a group of them from Los Angeles, Hollywood, and Burbank formed the Association of Film Equestriennes, with backing from the Riding Actors Association.[17] Vera McGinnis and Mabel Strickland, two of the directors of the associa-tion, performed in the 1936 Bing Crosby movie, *Rhythm on the Range,* along with Paris Williams.[18] By the forties, however, western films had undergone radical changes, with the roles of women altered so there was no further need for rodeo cowgirls.

International rodeos also flourished during the thirties, with successful contests staged in London, Dublin, and Melbourne, as well as in Cuba and Mexico. In addition to providing international exposure for rodeo and its participants, the international contests increased the publicity at home. Most of the major international events paid huge prizes, with promoters sometimes paying all or part of the contestants' travel expenses. Interna-tional contests, along with those staged in major American cities, helped fuel the steady increase in cowgirls' earnings. At the same time, the im-pact of the McCarroll fatality and the RAA began to change the environ-ment for women. Subsequently, the formation of the CTA and the entry of Gene Autry into the rodeo profession left women with few options.

Theirs was a situation all too familiar to American women in interna-tional sports. Physical educators renewed their opposition when the Olympic Games came to Los Angeles in 1932, but could not stop wom-en's progress. Mildred Ella "Babe" Didrikson was the outstanding female athlete of those games, winning two gold medals and one silver in track and field. Still, Didrikson did not achieve the enduring popularity of her predecessors. The same might be said for the American women who competed at the Berlin Olympics in 1936. Although they took five of six medals in diving, and upset the favored German women in the 4 x 100-meter track relay, none of the female athletes really captured the public imagination. Neither double gold medalist Helen Stephens, who anchored the winning relay team, nor Dorothy Poynton Hill, who took gold in platform and bronze in springboard diving, became superstars like Gertrude Ederle, and both are practically forgotten today.[19] The impact of the physical educators was felt most strongly among women of the middle class, who found few opportunities and no encouragement to develop their athletic skills. Olympic and world class female athletes were often held up as negative examples of unfeminine behavior and hence undesirable women.

One noticeable change for women in the thirties was fashion. In contrast to the flapper styles of the twenties, skirts fell again to within a foot of the floor, and severe, tailored suits with huge shoulder pads became the standard.[20] In spite of these changes, cowgirls did not retreat from the progress begun in the twenties. During the thirties, women on the big-time rodeo circuit usually made fifteen to twenty new costumes a year. Several innovative designs appeared including sailor suits; blouses with huge, flowing sleeves; trousers with matching capes; and elaborate western suits of leather and buckskin.[21] The women often purchased supplies for the coming season while in New York for the Madison Square Garden rodeo.[22] Alice and Margie Greenough told me they found it impossible to wear western clothing while shopping in New York, because local crowds would begin following them around town. Whether this was because of the novelty of seeing people in western gear, or the attractiveness of their particular costumes, is uncertain. It did create a problem for women who usually lived and worked in western attire. At the same time, they found that the wonderful array of available materials made shopping in New York worth the extra effort.[23]

Even though automobile sales fell markedly during the Depression, there were more cars on the ever-improving streets and highways in 1937 than there had been in 1929.[24] Rodeo cowboys and cowgirls benefited greatly from these improvements, as modes of transportation and life on the road gradually improved. Following their 1931 marriage, Gene and Shorty Creed carried their horses in an open trailer, and put boxes on the sides of the car to carry clothing, kitchen utensils, and gear, so that they could use the trunk as a manger to feed the stock. They camped out along the way with fellow participants until hotels and motels replaced camping and tent cities. By the mid-thirties, most contestants were carrying their animals in enclosed trailers and their own belongings in the automobile trunks.[25] Individuals who participated in bronc riding or rode for relay string owners had fewer expenses than ropers and trick riders because they did not have to worry about transporting and feeding animals. Women like Alice Greenough, who owned automobiles and hauled no animals, often made extra income transporting less-fortunate colleagues to the next rodeo. As is always the case, progress bypassed those struggling to make ends meet. One was Vera McGinnis. She was convinced the only way to make money at relay racing was to own her own string, yet the costs involved always seemed to exceed her winnings.

Along with the progress and success, cowgirls soon experienced big changes in their position, even as rodeo itself grew in popularity. This chapter covers the years from 1930, when the impact of Bonnie McCarroll's death and the formation of the RAA began to affect women, to 1946, the last year before cowgirls began their own efforts at independence within the sport. In the years between, rodeo women were significantly affected by two events. The first was the 1936 formation of the Cowboys Turtle Association (CTA), which in concert with the RAA established centralized patriarchal control over the sport. The second was the emergence of Hollywood star Gene Autry as the premier producer of big-time rodeos. These events, along with World War II, forever changed the status of women in the sport.

One big change following the formation of the RAA and Bonnie McCarroll's death was that women had mostly relay contests open to them in the West, and trick and bronc riding in the East. Their opportunities diminished even more in the mid-thirties, when major rodeos began to alter the format of their trick roping and riding events. In order to speed up the proceedings, many changed these events to contract acts, while others limited the number of participants by inviting a only a few expert practitioners of each event. Those select individuals received a flat fee for exhibiting their skills at the rodeos. They were also judged, with winners collecting sizable prizes. This practice of holding "invitational" contests in trick roping and riding led to claims of fraud and dishonesty, as well as some very public disputes as to who had actually won the events at certain rodeos.[26] Even though both cowboy and cowgirl contests were affected, the changes were much more devastating to women, since they had fewer contests.

One result of these developments was that many women who excelled at racing began restricting their activities to the western circuit, while those for whom bronc riding was the premier contest concentrated on the growing number of eastern rodeos. Only a few exceptionally versatile athletes competed throughout the country. One of them was Tad Lucas, who began the 1932 season at the Fort Worth rodeo in March, and finished the year in November at Boston Garden. Before she arrived home, she had traveled more than nine thousand miles. She also won money at Cheyenne, Wyoming; Sheridan, Oregon; Burwell, Nebraska; Chicago; and New York City, successfully participating in relay racing, trick riding, and bronc riding.[27] Others who traversed the continent were Florence Randolph, Rose Davis, and Alice Greenough. Many more, including headliners like Paris Williams, Vera McGinnis, and Bonnie Jean Gray, restricted their activities to the West.

In addition to her competitive activities, Bonnie Gray had become famous as a contract entertainer who jumped her horse, King Tut, over automobiles. Her 1930 marriage to Donald Harris was one of the most elaborate in the history of the sport. The wedding took place on a California ranch, with Gray astride King Tut, and all other participants, including the minister, on horseback. Following the ceremony, Bonnie Jean jumped King Tut over an open car in which her new husband and the maid of honor were seated.[28]

Even highly skilled and flamboyant women like Gray never attained the fame and media attention accorded those who regularly appeared at Madison Square Garden and the other eastern city rodeos. This lowered their earning potential as contract performers, and made it less likely that they would ever again appear on the big-time circuit. The effective splitting of the country for cowgirl contests had a much more devastating financial impact on some contestants than did the Depression.

Col. William Thomas Johnson

Cowgirls who participated in the big eastern rodeos were greatly helped by Texas ranching millionaire Col. W. T. Johnson, who in 1931 took over the Madison Square Garden rodeo and introduced the first cowboy contest at the Boston Garden, thereby becoming the most powerful man in the sport.[29] Johnson began his rodeo career in October of 1928, when he produced a San Antonio rodeo to entertain visitors to the national American Legion convention. His cowgirl contests included trick riding, bronc riding, and Roman racing.[30] Unfortunately, the legionnaires were much

Florence Hughes Randolph, one of the greatest trick riders of the twenties and thirties. Photo courtesy of the National Rodeo Hall of Fame at the National Cowboy Hall of Fame, Oklahoma City, Oklahoma.

Vera McGinnis at the famous Agua Caliente racetrack, where cowgirls often won money as jockeys during the rodeo off-season. Photo courtesy of the National Rodeo Hall of Fame at the National Cowboy Hall of Fame, Oklahoma City, Oklahoma.

more interested in the bullfights and other "exotic" fare offered in nearby Mexico than in the rodeo, and Johnson lost more than $40,000. He had purchased so much stock and equipment that he decided the only way to recover his investment was to remain in the business. The following year he produced a spring rodeo at El Paso, Texas, as well as the Texas State Fair rodeo at Dallas, where he entertained a number of officials from Madison Square Garden. Johnson himself was much in evidence at New York during the 1929 and 1930 rodeos, before taking over the Madison Square Garden contest in 1931.[31] That same year, his inaugural Boston Garden rodeo was the most successful event ever held there. His 1931 Chicago, New York, and Boston successes helped rodeo attract greater crowds than any other branch of indoor or outdoor amusement, leading to speculation that several more big indoor rodeos could succeed during the upcoming winter season.[32] By 1934 Johnson had rodeos at Detroit, Michigan; Philadelphia, Pennsylvania; Indianapolis, Indiana; Dallas, Texas; Kansas City and Sedalia, Missouri; and Chicago. His contests grossed several million dollars, more than any others in rodeo history,[33] and earned big profits for arenas as well. Boston Garden management, which had originally offered to rent Johnson their facility in 1931, was by 1936 paying him more than $80,000 up front to produce the rodeo.[34]

Johnson was a perfectionist and hands-on manager who expected everything to be first class. His entire operation was carried out by men who were his full-time employees, and he used his own high quality stock in the rodeos. The most important factor in his success was probably Johnson's own flamboyant ability to attract attention. A huge man, more than six feet and two hundred pounds, he always rode at the head of downtown parades, waving his enormous hat to the crowds. He also led the grand entries into the rodeo arena, sometimes accompanied by a fanfare of trumpets and waving of banners. His first arena director, Bryan Roach, was responsible for an innovation which greatly increased rodeo's appeal to big-city audiences. Instead of directing the rodeos on horseback in the arena, he set up a booth and handled matters by telephone. This speeded up the proceedings beyond the wildest dreams of men like Weadick, Austin, or Beebe.[35]

While those men had regularly given women top billing and lucrative purses at rodeos in the United States, Canada, and Great Britain, Johnson outdid them all. Photographs of Johnson surrounded by a bevy of cowgirls were always featured in the advance publicity for his rodeos, and the women themselves were and are loyal supporters. At a time when health and accident insurance was nonexistent in the dangerous business, Johnson financed the medical treatment of women injured at his rodeos, visited them in the hospital, and paid for their transportation home when they were released.[36]

Johnson also scouted the country for young talent, and was often responsible for bringing cowgirls onto the big-time circuit, a transition not easily accomplished without sponsorship. This was especially true following the demise of the Wild West shows, which had been an important avenue by which women moved into the profession and eventually the top contest circuit. Small local rodeos that had once offered women their first competitive opportunities were also less likely to do so in the thirties. Thus Johnson provided ambitious cowgirls an important link to the big time, which he himself had made more lucrative for women.

Part of the secret to his achievements was the same business acumen which enabled him to become a millionaire. Other significant factors included his promotional abilities and the outstanding quality of his bucking stock. Johnson was always on the lookout for new contract acts to provide variety and keep audiences coming back. Several helped maintain rodeo's connection to the Old West. The Cowboy Band from Simmons University in Abilene, Texas, first performed for Johnson in 1932. They were so popular that he signed them to play at all of his rodeos for the next five years.[37] In 1932 he brought Powder River Jack and Miss Kitty Lee to Boston and New York. They had entertained western rodeo audiences with traditional songs for many decades, but the eastern appearance revived their careers. Radio performances in New York provided new outlets and audiences for their talents. One of Johnson's most popular attractions bore no relationship to the traditional West. It was a basketball game on horseback, directed by Tom Johnson, Jr.[38]

Some cowboys and cowgirls in the early thirties avoided the grueling travel from contest to contest by performing with circuses and Wild West shows that transported them and their animals for most of the season. They limited their competitive activities to Col. Johnson's eastern rodeos, where purses were high and travel between contests short. One bright star who burst upon the scene in this manner was Lucyle Richards, generally recognized as the most beautiful of all the professional cowgirls. She first earned headlines as the wife and Wild West show partner of cowboy star Oklahoma Curly Roberts, and was known professionally as Lucyle Roberts. Their activities both in and out of the arena were regularly described in the trade papers until 1933, when the two apparently parted company.[39]

Official Program
World Series Rodeo—1935
Madison Square Garden
New York City

Col. W.T. Johnson, San Antonio, Texas—Director
Grand Entry of Cowboys & Cowgirls, Introduction of Special
   Personalities
Horseback Quadrille
Bareback Bronk Riding Contest
Cowboys' Trick and Fancy Roping Exhibition
Cowgirls' Bronk Riding Contest
Mounted Basketball Game
Cowboys' Calf Roping Contest
Col. W.T. Johnson Presents—"Going Back to Texas,"
   with his midget mules, old time chuck wagon and Texas Long
   Horn Steer. An exhibition of the World's greatest cutting horse.
   Trained and Ridden by Bob Crosby.
Cowboys' Bronk Riding Contest
An Exhibition of the World's Greatest Liberty High Schooled
   Horse "Buck," trained and ridden by Hardy Murphy, Owned by
   Col. W.T. Johnson.
Cowboys' Steer Wrestling Contest
Exhibition by World's Championship Horseshoe Pitcher Ted Allen
Cowgirls' Trick And Fancy Riding Exhibition
Cowboys' Steer Riding Contest
Jimmy Nesbitt Driving "Our Sheik" to a Chariot

Contests in boldface type. Official program, October 11. From the ProRodeo Hall of
Fame, Colorado Springs, Colorado.

While her striking appearance and famous husband certainly helped launch her career, it was athletic ability that made Lucyle a rodeo star. She hit the big time at Johnson's 1929 Dallas rodeo, and in 1930 attracted headlines for her skill and beauty. She was especially successful at Chicago, where she competed in trick and bronc riding and also exhibited bulldogging from an auto.[40] During the next decade Lucyle was a headliner and top money winner at major rodeos throughout the United States and abroad.

A 1934 article called her both the prettiest and best dressed of all the cowgirls, adding that her combination of beauty and skill had brought the Madison Square Garden crowd of 18,000 to its feet.[41] She won the bronc riding and all-around titles at Boston in 1934, when she also competed at Tex Austin's 1934 London rodeo, and then along with Alice Greenough and Pauline Nesbitt participated in the Wild Australian Stampede in Melbourne.[42] Lucyle was often selected for publicity stunts and photos, but her personal problems and failed marriages eventually took their toll, preventing her from fully enjoying her rodeo success.

At the time when Lucyle's career was at its peak, some of the stars of earlier years were closing out their careers. Ruth Roach's last major title was the 1932 bronc riding championship at Madison Square Garden, although she continued to rodeo through 1938, when she married wealthy Texas rancher Fred Salmon.[43] Marie Gibson, winner of the 1927 and 1931 New York bronc riding titles, died after a bronc threw her at Idaho Falls in 1933.[44] Vera McGinnis nearly died as a result of injuries suffered when her horse fell and trampled her during a relay race at Livermore, California, in June of 1934. She sustained a broken neck, broken hip, collapsed lung, and five fractured vertebrae, and while she was on horseback again within three months, she did not fully recover for three years. She did perform in films and with Ken Maynard's Diamond K Ranch Wild West, Circus and Indian Congress, but she never competed again.[45]

In 1934, at the G Bar B Dude Ranch in Stamford, Connecticut, the legendary Prairie Lillie Allen rode her last bronc, "just to show she still could."[46] Through the late forties, Allen was a regular guest at the Madison Square Garden rodeos where she was treated royally by rodeo officials.[47] Lucille Mulhall gave her last trick roping exhibition at the second annual Knox-Mulhall Rodeo at Knox Ranch, Oklahoma, in 1934, and made her final bow at a public entertainment during the '89ers Celebration at Guthrie, Oklahoma, the next year. She said it would be her last appearance, although she intended to keep riding horses "as long as I can get a leg across."[48] After a long struggle with financial and alcohol problems, she died in an auto accident in 1940.[49]

Tad Lucas's career nearly ended after a 1933 Chicago rodeo accident. While attempting to go under the belly of her speeding horse in the trick riding, she lost her grip and fell under the horse's feet. Her left arm was so badly crushed that it required six operations, including several bone grafts. Doctors feared she would lose the arm, and it did remain in a cast for three years afterward. However, within a year she was back on the circuit as a contract performer, limiting her tricks to those requiring the use of only one arm.[50]

Reva Gray, one of the top relay racers of the thirties, was caught during a horse change and killed at the 1938 Cheyenne Frontier Days.[51] Gray was a well-known figure in the western states, and had been called by the *Los Angeles Times* the most famous cowgirl in America, yet her death did not cause the outcry that had accompanied Bonnie McCarroll's fatal ride nine years earlier.[52]

Reine and Dick Shelton, veterans of many of the biggest rodeos of the twenties and thirties, decided in 1938, "at the height of their careers," to retire to a Texas ranch to raise their son Tommy. Although literally born on the rodeo circuit, Tommy left all that behind with his parents, and today is a school superintendent.[53] Chuck Henson, son of Margie Greenough and Heavy Henson, was also raised on the tour in obvious delight. Since his parents remained on the rodeo circuit through the fifties, he learned the sport from the inside. He participated in college rodeo before launching his professional career as a rodeo clown. In 1978 he won PRCA Clown of the Year honors.[54] On the other hand, Alice Greenough's two sons were never involved with the rodeo business, and indeed had little role in their mother's busy, active life.[55]

By the time the Sheltons retired, a virtual revolution had taken place in the world of rodeo. It began when sixty-one cowboys went on strike against Col. Johnson at the 1936 Boston Garden rodeo. They demanded that he double the $6,400 purse, stating that prizes were too low for even the winners to meet expenses. When Johnson refused, they walked out. The strike was not a last minute decision but one which had been carefully planned well in advance. Johnson was determined to break the strike, and attempted to continue the rodeo using grooms and stable hands for cowboys. They were a dismal failure and after a chorus of boos greeted their efforts at calf roping, Boston Garden manager George V. Brown closed the show and refunded the admission. Hours of negotiating followed, with Johnson finally agreeing to double the purse and compensate the men who had missed the first day's competition. Funds came from entry fees, the Boston Garden, and Johnson's pocket. To assure no further disruption, he required all participants to sign a contract that they would cause no more agitation. The rodeo went on as scheduled, with crowds exceeding the previous year's attendance.[56]

Exactly why the cowboys selected Johnson as their target is not absolutely certain, for his were not the only rodeos with small purses. His honesty and integrity had never been questioned. The same could not be said of producers like Milt Hinkle, who was still operating, but had never been subject to a strike. Although power and visibility played a part, the evidence suggests that the cowboys (unlike the cowgirls) did not like Johnson, who was perceived as an outsider getting rich at their expense. There was certainly a basis for this belief. Unlike most of his peers, Johnson had never been a rodeo cowboy. A former banker, he was a fifty-three-year-old millionaire when he entered the business. On the other hand, men like Weadick and Austin had come up the hard way and become producers as salaried employees attempting to make money for their backers, rather than wealthy individuals enhancing their own financial positions.

Another difference was that Johnson had no rodeo hands in his family, and apparently did not want any. When in the mid-twenties his beloved daughter Ora Lee fell in love with Lee Robinson, then one of rodeo's premier calf ropers, Col. Johnson was violently opposed. He felt that she was too young to marry. He was also convinced that being a rodeo cowboy, Robinson would never amount to much, and was unworthy of his daughter. Johnson sent Ora Lee from boarding school to boarding school, with Robinson in pursuit, and was prepared to send her to Europe under the watchful eye of her maiden aunt Ora when the couple eloped. Johnson was furious, and the family was not reconciled until three years later when his two-year-old granddaughter Mary won the colonel's heart.[57] The story ended tragically just a year later, in 1927, when Ora Lee, Lee, and Mary died in a fiery automobile crash.[58] Even after the reconciliation, Johnson's long-standing opposition to Robinson was bound to have had a lasting impact on the close-knit rodeo fraternity. Cowboys could hardly avoid feeling that he saw them as "other," a source of income but not good enough to be a part of his family. The fact that he seemed to accord cowgirls preferential treatment could only exacerbate the alienation.

The strike convinced Johnson that he had had enough of the rodeo business. Soon after the Boston contest he sold his rodeo company, which

Sixth Annual
World's Championship Rodeo
Boston Garden, Boston, Mass.
November 1936

Grand Entry of Cowboys and Cowgirls, with Introduction of
Special Personalities
Horseback Quadrille
Cowboys' Bareback Bronk Riding
Cowboys' Trick and Fancy Roping Exhibition
Juvenile Trick Roping
Cowgirls' Bronk Riding Contest
Mounted Basketball Game
Cowboys' Calf Roping Contest
Jimmie Nesbitt and Jasbo Fulkerson and their Educated Mules
Cowboys' Steer Wrestling Contest
Wild Cow Milking Contest
Cowboys' and Cowgirls' Trick and Fancy Riding Exhibition
Steer Riding Contest

Contests in boldface type. Program for November 11. From the National Rodeo Hall
of Fame at the National Cowboy Hall of Fame, Oklahoma City, Oklahoma.

included more than six hundred head of cattle and horses, and a staff of one hundred and fifty, for $150,000, and retired to his Texas ranch. While the new owners, Everett Colburn and M. T. and W. J. Clemens, had reaped a bonanza, the cowgirls had lost their greatest ally.[59]

The cowboys, flush with success after bringing down the most powerful rodeo producer in America, formed a permanent organization, the Cowboys Turtle Association, now the PRCA. The Turtles were by no means an overnight success. They struggled for many years before gaining acceptance and the power to regulate the sport. The CTA would probably not have lasted very long had not the cowboys been able to forge an early agreement with their old nemesis, the RAA. The pact stipulated that Turtle rules would be in effect at all RAA-sanctioned rodeos. The combined power of the two patriarchies ensured the survival of both, but it left the cowgirls in a very vulnerable position.[60] For them, rodeo was never the same after 1936.

Col. Johnson had very little competition when he established his dominance in eastern rodeo. One of the few other companies active in that part of the country was Eskew's J. E. rodeo company, which also played some of the larger indoor arenas. Others, including the Leo J. Creamer and George Adams rodeo companies, also earned respect, while never challenging for the big eastern contests. Since the RAA controlled most western rodeos, and Johnson and Eskew concentrated on eastern cities, hundreds of tiny local rodeos in Texas and the Southwest still operated as community celebrations, with neither national affiliation nor professional producers. It was at these small contests that several new activities for cowgirls were begun in the thirties. Some held great promise, while others represented a major setback for women.

Sponsor Girls

One momentous change was the introduction of sponsor contests, which originated at the Stamford, Texas, Cowboy Reunion in 1931. These contests were not primarily athletic, and were a major factor in moving traditional cowgirl contests out of the mainstream of American rodeo. From the beginning, women in sponsor contests were seen primarily as decorations. As a Stamford historian noted:

> The western atmosphere of the Texas Cowboy Reunion was accompanied with a touch of femininity in 1931 when Warren B. Toyman, Chairman of the committee in charge of the parade asked the businesses and Chambers of Commerce of the surrounding areas to send a girl to sponsor the area she was from.

The young ladies, sixteen years or older, led the opening day parade, participated in special features of the rodeo, and took part in local social events
planned for them. The main purpose of the sponsors was to add a little charm
and glamor to the previously masculine rodeo.

Prizes were given to the girl who had the best mount, the most attractive
riding outfit, and showed the best horsemanship. Horsemanship was decided
by the judges as the girls rode their mounts in a figure eight fashion around
barrels.[61]

The Stamford idea spread rapidly across Texas and the Southwest, with
each local rodeo adding its own particular touches. Most required contestants to ride around barrels set in various patterns such as figure eight or
cloverleaf. Sometimes the women had to compete in another cowgirl
event such as a flag race, cutting contest, or even a roping competition.
Regardless of the skills involved, costume, pulchritude, and bloodline
were much more important than athletic ability in determining the final
winners of sponsor contests.[62]

The introduction of sponsor contests was a major setback to women, as
they represented all of the things that female athletes had struggled to
overcome, such as the emphasis on beauty and attire instead of athletic
skill and the concept that females are really mere props or decorations,
not legitimate athletes. It was particularly startling in rodeo, where cowgirls had long held their own as serious contestants, often competing as
equals against men. At the same time, it also presaged the neo-Victorian
attitudes of the forties and fifties when American women were pressured
to become cheerleaders and enthusiastic supporters of male athletes,
rather than sports contestants.[63] Rodeo was once again a leader in wom-
en's sports, this time in a very negative direction.

It has been suggested that the women who participated in sponsor contests could "barely ride," but this is an error. Like all ranch women of their
time, they could certainly ride horseback quite well. Some could also do
cutting, roping, and racing, but these skills were not the primary qualifications of winners. Consequently, real cowgirl athletes from the working
class who excelled at those events usually finished far behind the rich and
the beautiful in the sponsor contests.[64] Isora Young, who represented the
Reeves County Sheriff's Department in countless sponsor contests, recalled one in which the women attempted to rope five calves at each performance. Young nabbed all fifteen without a miss, yet finished a poor
second to the lovely daughter of a millionaire rancher, who never roped a
calf during the entire three days of the rodeo.[65]

Significantly, skilled cowgirls like Fern Sawyer, Nancy Binford, and
Thena Mae Farr, who also possessed the requisite wealth and beauty to

be popular winners, resented the fact that their skills were not the primary reason for their victories. They also sensed the unfairness with which
many of the contests were conducted. Like their contemporaries, they
watched judges moving barrels about during the competition, and changing the rules of the contest from day to day. Those and similar actions have
led some women to maintain that sponsor contests were crooked.[66] Even
when conducted fairly, sponsor contests were not contests in the true
sense of the word, and presented only frustration to women who wanted
a legitimate opportunity to compete.[67] Fortunately, other developments
such as the growth of cowgirl calf roping contests were more positive.

Women had competed in steer roping since the earliest days of rodeo,
with Mulhall, Blancett, and Strickland earning considerable fame roping
steers against the cowboys. However, steer roping was always controversial. As Elizabeth Atwood Lawrence explained: "Steer roping . . . calls for
a perfect partnership between a contestant and his horse, as the roper
aims to tie down a big steer singlehandedly against time. Some states do
not allow this event to be held at all because of the rough treatment of
steers that it entails. . . . and even some western stockmen who are inured
to the work of the range indicated they are critical of the event because
many steers are injured and killed during its performance."[68] For these
reasons, many states banned steer roping, and calf roping became the
popular replacement.[69] When that happened, women quickly showed
great interest and ability. Like their foremothers, they were sometimes
able to compete against cowboys in the calf roping, especially at small local rodeos.

Cowgirl calf roping was also popular as a special jackpot or challenge
contest in connection with professional rodeos before becoming a regular event at prominent contests from Texas to California.[70] These activities soon caught the eye of Col. Johnson, who invited Isora to rope at
Madison Square Garden. She was unable to take advantage of what
seemed like the chance of a lifetime. Her employer, the Reeves County
Sheriff's Department, would not allow her time off to go to New York,
despite allowing her to represent them at sponsor contests almost every
weekend. A young single parent in the depths of the Depression, she was
unwilling to give up her secure position, even for a chance at the big
time.[71]

One of Isora's frequent rivals was Jewel Duncan, the daughter of a trail
driver, who also grew up on a west Texas ranch. She began roping against
men in local rodeos in the twenties, and in 1929 became the first woman

Mabel Strickland, one of the premier cowgirl steer ropers, competing at Pendleton, Oregon, in 1932. Photo courtesy of the National Rodeo Hall of Fame at the National Cowboy Hall of Fame, Oklahoma City, Oklahoma.

roper at the legendary Pecos, Texas, rodeo. She was elected Queen of the Pecos contest in 1935, largely on the basis of her skill and popularity as a roper.[72] Her achievements were nationally publicized when rodeo columnist Tex Sherman made Jewel the centerpiece of an article advocating that the RAA sanction women's roping contests. Sherman predicted in 1937 that with RAA support, cowgirl calf roping competition would attract thousands of entries annually.[73]

By 1936 cowgirl roping contests were included at several important rodeos. The most lucrative was held at Sidney, Iowa, where 157 women including Isora competed for $6,000 in prizes, with Duncan the winner.[74] Isora returned to win the Sidney contest in 1937 and 1938. By that time she too had established a fine reputation, winning several contests including rodeos at Midland and Pecos, Texas, and the Pendleton Roundup.[75]

Jewel and Isora teamed up in 1937, advertising in *Hoofs and Horns* as "Roping Cowgirls Jewel Duncan and Isora De Racy: Brand New Attraction in the Rodeo Game. Exhibition and Contest Roping."[76] They traveled hundreds of miles competing and exhibiting as independent contractors. The two were such a hit at the Indianapolis rodeo that they were signed for the remainder of the season, and again in 1938, by Milt Hinkle's Texas Ranger rodeo. They got excellent write-ups wherever they appeared with the Rangers, and were sometimes accorded star treatment.[77] Isora found the notorious Hinkle "a real character." Although it took persistence, she always collected her paycheck from him.[78] Isora and Jewel worked together and competed against one another until 1939, when Isora married cowboy I. W. Young. The couple then joined Eskew's company, where Isora was among the featured performers at the annual Duquesne Garden rodeo at Pittsburgh.[79] Jewel, meanwhile, continued to make headlines at various Texas contests.[80] Other women earning recognition as ropers during these years included Ora Quigg, Josephine Proctor, Sydna Yokley, Ann Webb, Marjorie Stewart, and Sally Taylor.[81]

As cowgirl roping grew in popularity, some major rodeos in the Southwest added it to their programs. Sally Taylor won the cowgirl calf roping at the 1939 Houston Fat Stock Show and Rodeo, where Isora Young took second, and was also a contract performer. Tad Lucas was a timer at Houston, but did not compete.[82] Later that summer, a crowd of more than 20,000 saw Mrs. Christine Northcutt take the women's calf roping title from a field of thirty at the famous Stamford, Texas, Cowboy's Reunion, where the sponsor contests had begun eight years earlier.[83]

Cowgirls had high hopes in November of 1940, when T. E. Robertson's

All American Rodeo at Fort Worth offered handsome prizes for women in both bronc riding and calf roping. Among the women competing in calf roping were Nancy Binford and Fern Sawyer, two locally known young cowgirls who would later be instrumental in forming the WPRA. The roping field also included Sally Taylor, Ann Webb, and Mecca and Sue Savage, while Madison Square Garden veterans Alice and Margie Greenough, Alice Adams, and Vaughn Krieg collected day money in the bronc riding.[84] After a promising start, the contest was closed down by a Turtle strike, and forced into bankruptcy. The final winners were never announced, and the remainder of the series was cancelled.[85] Although the exact reasons for the strike are uncertain, it is known that the Turtles continued their opposition to Robertson for several years. In 1942, they again forced him into bankruptcy, still owing salaries and prize monies to such future hall of fame honorees as Chester Byers, Junior Eskew, Tad Lucas, Alice and Margie Greenough, and Vivian White. That year, Robertson's associate producer was the notorious Milt Hinkle, so the Turtles had good reason to doubt his credibility.[86]

Unfortunately the cowgirls soon learned that the 1940 strike was not an isolated incident. It was one of a variety of actions instigated by more radical elements within the CTA, which were detrimental to the organization and to the sport. The last-minute strikes not only placed a hardship on contestants, they caused chaos and financial disasters for rodeo committees. As a result, many rodeos, including such eminent contests as the Pendleton Roundup, dropped out of the RAA and barred Turtles from entering their contests.[87]

Women were nonvoting members of the Turtles, and had elected representatives to the organization, fully expecting to benefit from their membership. Unfortunately, cowboys rarely acted on the cowgirls' behalf, having declared in 1938 that the women were "on their own." Cowboys did actually threaten to walk out of the 1939 Fort Worth rodeo because cowgirl bronc riding competition had been dropped in favor of "Ranch Girls" (sponsor girls). The leader of that strike was Huey Long, whose wife Peggy Long was cowgirl bronc riding representative to the CTA. After making their bold stand, the cowboys called off the strike when management agreed to include a two-woman bronc riding exhibition at one performance. Obviously, allowing two cowgirls to give one exhibition did nothing for the other bronc riders who were put out of work, or for the inclusion of women's contests at future Fort Worth rodeos.[88]

Several cowgirls attempted unsuccessfully to negotiate individually with rodeo committees.[89] With the very future of their organization and their sport at stake, it is perhaps not surprising that the Turtles had little interest in women's issues. The women could not do much to alter the situation because they were such a minority. While there had always been fewer women than men in rodeo, the disparity had increased as the sport grew. Even had all of the cowgirls, along with all of the cowboys who were married to cowgirls, voted as a bloc, they would not have been able to outvote the single men and those cowboys whose wives did not compete in rodeo.

Of all the strikes called by the Turtles, the one at the 1940 Fort Worth rodeo had the greatest impact on women. Entering the rodeo, many had hoped that cowgirl calf roping was on its way to becoming a standard rodeo event. Even with the strike, that might have happened had Col. Johnson remained in the business. The strike shattered the women's dreams, and they had to wait almost a decade for another similar opportunity.

Given these conditions, it is logical to ask why the cowgirls did not form their own organization. There were several reasons. One was that women joined the Turtles fully expecting to benefit from their membership, and many felt that they were helped. Even though the Turtles did little for cowgirls' unique problems, they vastly improved conditions for all rodeo contestants. Of particular importance were the elimination of dishonest promoters and the equitable allocation of prize money. Women like Tad Lucas and Alice and Margie Greenough did resent having to pay dues to an organization in which they had no vote. At the same time they realized that in some ways the improvements overshadowed the disadvantages, and perhaps even the attitude of some of the Turtles toward women's contests.[90]

It would be easy to suggest that the women should have formed their own organization, but it is doubtful if many cowgirls would have been willing to defy their husbands to do so. Even though they had enjoyed much greater freedom and autonomy than many women elsewhere, their lives had ultimately been controlled by males. The West, like the rodeo business, was a patriarchy, and most of the cowgirls had been raised under the stern control of their fathers. Although they had been treated as virtual equals with their male siblings when it came to chores, they had also been told by their fathers when and where to work and when to terminate their education. It was partly to escape those conditions that many joined the rodeo, sometimes running away from home or disregarding their parents' wishes in order to do so. The rodeo business had given these women a much freer and more exciting life-style, yet their fate still rested with powerful males: promoters, producers, judges, rodeo committees, husbands, and now the CTA-RAA. The women who eventually did take matters into their own hands and organize the GRA after World War II had far different backgrounds and educational levels from the cowgirls of the mid-thirties.

Even with all of the turmoil, the Madison Square Garden rodeo remained relatively unchanged during the first two years after Johnson left. Everett Colburn and the other men who replaced him lacked the charisma and imagination of their predecessor, and reporters frequently noted the absence of the flair that had been provided by the big Texan. Then in 1939, Colburn decided to bring a group of Texas sponsor girls to New York as a publicity gimmick. He chose women from local sponsor contests, all of whom were young and attractive daughters of wealthy Texas ranchers. Only one member of the group, Fern Sawyer, subsequently competed in professional rodeo. She later described that first New York sponsor contest as "silly," while most of her peers were enthusiastic.[91]

In publicizing these women, the promoters revealed something of a double standard, as well as an obvious effort to appeal to well-heeled New Yorkers. Upper-class Americans still found amateur sports much more socially acceptable than professional competition, and took a particularly dim view of female professional athletes. Hence, the *Madison Square Garden Magazine* assured readers that the sponsor girls were strictly amateurs, and "never appear in the regular prize money contests with older cowboy and cowgirl competitors. These youthful beauties are called 'Sponsor Girls' because they are sponsored socially and otherwise by the localities they represent."[92] The girls realized they were in New York primarily to publicize the rodeo, and enjoyed seeing the sights and helping attract attention to the event.[93] They made a variety of promotional appearances, including a tour of the Empire State Building with Alfred E. Smith, all of which seemed to accomplish their intended purpose. Journalists reported that "They took New York by storm . . . and New York showered them with attention, admiration, and applause."[94]

While the publicity appearances were successful, their actual rodeo performance was a total flop. The sponsors were required to exhibit their equestrian skills by mounting and dismounting, and riding around several barrels. Judges rated them on horsemanship (50 percent), personal appearance (25 percent), and the appearance of their mount (25 percent).[95] *The Billboard* reported the event as follows: "A definite letdown, in view of the advance notices, and an outright drawback in performance is the 'exhibition of horsemanship by the Texas Ranch Sponsor Girls' . . . the routine does the show more harm than good and it would be wise to shelve it quietly."[96]

This negative press did not seem to deter Colburn, who invited another group of young lovelies, billed as the "Ranch Glamor Girls," to appear at both Madison Square Garden and Boston Garden the following year. The 1940 Ranch Glamor Girls participated in cutting contests instead of riding around barrels and were better received by the media than their predecessors, beginning a tradition that lasted for decades.[97] Still, they were not treated like the old-style competitive cowgirls, who got the same type of press coverage as the cowboys. Glamor girls and sponsor girls were seen as mere objects, not legitimate athletes, leading reporters to make comments like this: "Best of the new features are the six Ranch Girls, billed as amateur riding daughters of wealthy ranch owners. . . . They are all young and attractive and won't have any trouble scoring."[98] Apparently, such remarks bothered neither the girls nor the producers, as the contests and the promotions remained essentially the same for years. From the beginning, the adjectives used most frequently in connection with these women were "rich" and "beautiful."[99]

By 1939, sponsor contests had also made their way into the big Texas events like the annual Fort Worth Rodeo, where the competition was actually legitimate, not based on beauty, costume, and bloodline. The talented cowgirl who won the 1940 Fort Worth Ranch Girl Contest was Margaret Owens (Montgomery), an outstanding roper and later first president of the GRA.[100] Because of her success, she was invited to join the Madison Square Garden Ranch Girls later that year, but for unknown reasons never appeared at the New York rodeo.[101]

Another Texas cowgirl who aspired to compete at Madison Square Garden was Mary Ellen "Dude" Barton. She was born in Matador, Texas, in 1924, and began riding as soon as she was old enough to sit up. By age two she was riding behind her dad on his fastest cutting horses. He also tied her onto a saddle so that she could accompany him when he drove cattle from Flomot to Matador. She mastered all of the ranching and rodeo skills of her nine siblings and followed them into rodeo, often competing against men in local rodeos. She once defeated fifty-six men in ribbon roping at a county meet.[102] Although they were little challenge to her skills, she participated in many sponsor contests because they were usually the only rodeo events open to women. In 1942, she was a basketball star at Flomot High School, the football sweetheart, and winner of the Musical Chairs, official contest for the Fort Worth "Ranch Girl Honor Guests."[103] Although Dude won eight of the nineteen go-rounds at Fort Worth, and was considered a cinch to take the title even before the last night of the rodeo, she never got the Madison Square Garden invitation she had hoped for.[104] One of the women Dude had soundly defeated, Nita Mae Boyd of Sweetwater, was a 1943 Madison Square Garden ranch girl. Unfortunately, Barton's experience was not unusual, and performing at Madison Square Garden remained an unfulfilled dream for most working-class, athletic cowgirls.[105]

One cowgirl whose New York dreams did come true was calf roper Sydna Yokley, whom Colburn invited to perform along with the first sponsor girls in 1939. Unlike DeRacy, Yokley had no financial worries, as she was wealthy and beautiful like the sponsor girls. With her outstanding athletic skills, Yokley attracted much more favorable publicity than they did. She was featured in the New York press and in *Time Magazine*.[106] Her acceptance by the audience and national media suggests that even without the help of Johnson, cowgirl ropers might well have became a standard attraction at future eastern contests had not another 1939 event changed the course of rodeo history forever.

Gene Autry, the "Singing Cowboy"

Hollywood singing cowboy Gene Autry was a spectator at one performance of the Madison Square Garden rodeo that year, and management asked him to perform for the crowd.[107] Although he was the country's top western film star, Autry was still an unknown in New York City.[108] The rodeo changed all that, and the enthusiastic response to his impromptu appearance led several producers to invite Autry to star at their rodeos the following year. In 1940 he starred in shows for Eskew's company at several cities including Pittsburgh and Philadelphia.[109] Autry also headlined Colburn's Madison Square Garden and Boston Garden rodeos, where ranch glamor girls rode around while he sang "Home on the Range" and put Champion through his routine.[110] Autry broke attendance records everywhere he appeared, and the trade papers covered him relentlessly. Suddenly, he was the focus of most rodeo articles appearing in *Hoofs and Horns* and *The Billboard*, and all of his publicity was positive. Autry himself benefited greatly, as attendance at his movies increased after he began appearing at rodeos, while the popularity of his films brought new fans to the sport.[111]

Autry was not the first western singer to perform at a rodeo, far from it.

Alice and Margie Greenough with singing cowboy Gene Autry, behind the chutes at the Madison Square Garden rodeo, two years before he took it over. Photo courtesy of Alice Greenough Orr, Tucson, Arizona.

Cowgirls on horseback at Madison Square Garden, 1940. Left to right: Iva Dell Draksler, Alice Greenough, Margie Greenough, Pauline Nesbitt, Tad Lucas. Note Draksler applying makeup. Photographers often required female athletes to pose in this manner, although it was rare for cowgirls. Photo courtesy of the National Rodeo Hall of Fame at the National Cowboy Hall of Fame, Oklahoma City, Oklahoma.

Johnson had brought old-time singers Powder River Jack and Miss Kitty Lee to New York and Boston,[112] and in the thirties Eskew had paid Tex Ritter $25 per day to perform at some of his rodeos.[113] But these singers were merely contract entertainers, no more nor less important than ones who added variety to the proceedings by exhibiting high jumping horses or trained steers. Autry, on the other hand, was the main attraction, better paid and much better publicized than the contestants themselves. Rodeo was never the same.

In 1941, Autry was featured at four eastern cities with Eskew's company. He also performed at the Madison Square Garden and Boston Garden rodeos, where Colburn paid him the highest daily salary ever drawn by a film star for personal appearances. Once again, all of his appearances broke attendance records, and he still holds the all-time record for Madison Square Garden.[114] Producers who could not afford Autry scrambled to sign other Hollywood cowboys, making a big star of Roy Rogers and reviving the careers of Ken Maynard and Hoot Gibson.[115]

Autry's first film appearance was a brief singing role in a 1934 Maynard movie, and he made his first feature film the following year. He was also a regular performer on the "National Barn Dance" radio program and his own successful stage shows. In 1939 he launched his Melody Ranch radio show, which ran through the early fifties. Between 1937 and 1942, when military service interrupted his career, he was the number one western entertainer in the country.[116]

Autry's impact on western film was dramatic. At the time of his debut, the standard formula westerns were losing fans. Autry's personal appeal and the singing cowboy concept revived the genre.[117] He also changed the basic format of the westerns. Unlike their predecessors, Autry's films were not set in the mythic nineteenth-century West, but in contemporary America, where a cowboy hero named Gene Autry traveled far and wide to assist ordinary citizens in their struggles with big business, high-handed villains, and special interests. Modern inventions like cars, trucks, recording devices, and even television were central to the plots, setting trends his many imitators followed closely.[118] One journalist described his films this way: "Those who have not seen a Western in ten or fifteen years are greatly surprised when they take in an Autry film. The old frontier is pretty well settled now. . . . There are more dude ranches than cattle ranches in the new Westerns. Rustlers, horse thieves, desperadoes, halfbreeds and greasers are almost extinct; the villains are mainly businessmen. Gene's life is spent not in outshooting bad hombres but in outwitting capitalists. He is a combination of Sherlock Holmes in a ten-gallon hat, Don Quixote, and Bing Crosby on Horseback."[119]

In his relentless quest for quality and innovation, Autry wrote or commissioned a whole set of new songs for each film. This not only helped the films, it changed the course of country music.[120] His formula also included decent stories, and a little romance played "against the sweep of desert scenery, mountains, and untamed land and an ocean of sky."[121] Although Autry was something of an anachronism in his own films, he always emerged a hero, in part because as he himself observed: "There wasn't a Repo truck or wood-paneled station wagon on the road that my horse Champion couldn't outrun."[122]

Autry's new westerns attracted huge crowds, and had a noticeable impact on the public perception of the American West. Clearly it was a very different place from the West popularized by Buffalo Bill Cody and his imitators, not only because of the setting and mechanization but also because of the changed status of women. No longer the competent, roping, riding, heroines of yore, women in singing cowboy movies were merely decorations, to be rescued by the heroic cowboys and then won over by their songs.[123] Scholars have concluded that real cowboys had a deep admiration for women who could manage to be simultaneously feminine and rugged, but women in cowboy B epics were usually not too bright, and always helpless.[124] William Savage described such women this way: "Regardless of what she is or how she got that way, the cowboy hero rides to the rescue, she realizes that he is the man for whom she has waited ever since she was old enough to know she ought to wait, and the story ends with the cowboy having the option of kissing her or his horse."[125]

Most of the women in Autry's films were not only vapid, they were essentially anonymous, portrayed by actresses who could neither rope nor ride. Roy Rogers did manage to give his female star, Dale Evans, an identity, but in their early films she played an eastern "city slicker" who sometimes fell from her horse or got lost in the desert. Alice Greenough recalled attempting to teach Evans to ride for an early film, and finding that Dale had never been on a horse. Following her 1947 marriage to Rogers, Evans's film roles became more westernized, but Greenough still insists that "she's no cowgirl!"[126] This would come as a great surprise to the generation of Americans who grew up watching Evans in B westerns, for to them she remains the quintessential cowgirl. The relentless parade of such helpless heroines altered the public image of western women and paved the way for acceptance of different women in rodeo, which increasingly mirrored the West of Autry's films.

This radical change was profoundly influenced by changing attitudes of American society. Just as westerns wrestled with contemporary social issues, they depicted and also reinforced prevailing ideals of woman, whose place was securely tied to the domestic sphere. American women of the thirties were advised to limit their aspirations to husband, family, and domesticity, and were strongly discouraged from working outside the home, especially if they were married.[127] In the mid-thirties, home, husband, and beauty were still believed to be women's primary goals. It was widely suggested that by leaving home, working women had weakened the moral fiber of the nation, and created a crisis of spirit. Not surprisingly, a 1936 Gallup poll showed that four of five Americans, and 75 percent of women, believed that women should not work outside the home if their husbands were employed.[128]

Already evident in society and in western film, these attitudes soon impacted western sport, and women like Dale Evans did replace the real cowgirls of the rodeo. Another reason for this change was that big-time rodeo was no longer designed for the ranching culture which spawned it but for sophisticated audiences in eastern cities. Even though real western women had changed very little, rodeo had lost touch with its roots. The evolution became a revolution in 1941 when Gene Autry decided to add rodeo to his growing entertainment empire and began purchasing stock and organizing a production company.[129] He entered the business at a difficult time, as World War II soon brought drastic changes to every aspect of life.

RAA and Turtle officials were concerned that rodeo might become a victim of the war, and as early as 1941, 28 percent of rodeos connected with fairs were cancelled. By 1942 rodeos on the West Coast from Canada to the Mexican border and inland as far as New Mexico were also called off for security reasons.[130] In spite of assurances that eastern rodeos would be allowed to continue, several, including those at Pittsburgh and Cleveland, were force to cancel their 1943 contests after initially getting the go-ahead from Washington. This was particularly unfortunate for Pittsburgh, where it had taken eight years to build an audience for the sport.[131]

At the same time, cowboys joined the service in growing numbers, so fewer and fewer contestants were still active.[132] To keep the sport alive, RAA officials encouraged producers and local committees to stress patriotic themes and to pitch their advertisements only to the local areas because of gasoline and tire rationing. With more than one hundred members in the military, Turtles eased eligibility requirements so local cowboys could take their places. Other gestures included donating rodeo proceeds to war relief, giving war bonds as prizes, and holding rodeos for military personnel.[133]

Rodeo was not the only sport affected or threatened by the war. Two major international competitions in which American women had earned fame, the Olympic Games and the Wimbledon tennis tournament, were both discontinued. There were no Olympics between 1936 and 1948, and many top athletes missed their chance in the spotlight. Alice Marble became the last American woman to star at Wimbledon before that tournament was suspended from 1940 to 1945. Marble won three titles: women's singles, women's doubles with Mrs. Sarah Palfrey Fabyan, and mixed doubles with Bobby Riggs, but she never had the opportunity to enjoy the glory of her predecessor, Helen Wills.[134]

Closer to home, Phil Wrigley, owner of the Chicago Cubs baseball team, decided to establish an alternative to major league baseball, threatened by a predicted manpower crisis. In 1942, he created the All American Girl's Professional Softball League, that became the All American Girl's Professional Baseball League (AAGPBL) in 1943. The women were never needed at Yankee Stadium or Wrigley Field, and by 1944 it was obvious to Wrigley himself that the threat to major league baseball had ended, so he sold the league to one of his advertising agents. Although far from the big cities, the AAGPBL did find appreciative audiences in the Midwest, where games drew good crowds and a generally favorable press through 1949. Thereafter, its popularity began to decline, leading to its 1954 abolition.[135] The league's demise paralleled the decline of minor league baseball generally, and the enormous growth of television, which brought live major league action into the homes of former minor league and women's league fans. The AAGPBL was an innovative idea and showed the potential for women's athletics, but did not itself lead to enhanced professional sports opportunities for females. Still, the women proved that American audiences would support female athletes, even in traditionally male bastions such as the national pastime.

Wrigley was not the only one to consider using female athletes to replace males. Even before he had formed his league, several individuals had organized all-girl rodeos. Columnist Tex Sherman reported that Jack Christie, publisher of the *Equestrian Magazine of Hollywood,* produced such a contest at the Riverside Drive Breakfast Club of Glendale, California. Frances Griffin, leading actress in the film *Tombstone* was reportedly among the contestants, with veteran announcers and standard rodeo stock used for the contest.[136] In the summer and fall of 1942, several all-girl rodeos were staged in Texas to entertain the troops and give cowgirls a chance to continue their profession.

The first of these was organized by Fay Kirkwood at the Fannin County Fair Grounds in Bonham, Texas, from June 26 to 29, 1942.[137] Kirkwood was a well-known Fort Worth equestrienne and society figure who had on several occasions traveled the state with Tad Lucas and the Fort Worth Boosters to promote the Fort Worth Fat Stock Show and Rodeo.[138] She began as organizer, promoter, and producer of the Bonham contest. Finding all of the tasks too much to handle, she sought more experienced hands to assist. Fred Alvord took over most of the production work, and Alice and Pete Adams served as arena secretary and announcer respectively, while Fay continued to handle the promotions and publicity.[139]

Citizens and civic groups of Bonham gave tremendous support and publicity, but advertising was at first extremely sexist, some of the worst I have seen for any cowgirl event. The first major ad for the rodeo depicted an Indian maiden in shorts and halter top astride a raring horse, stating: "Yip-E-E-E!!, Bonham Presents Fay Kirkwood's All Girl Rodeo."[140] Apparently the ad did not please Kirkwood, for the next day a cowgirl dressed in typical western attire, sitting astride a rocket, replaced the Indian.[141] At least she was female. Among forty illustrated ads for the rodeo, only four depicted women; two showed them wearing swimsuits, and two showed actual cowgirl gear. Twenty-nine depicted males.[142]

Kirkwood's program included a number of contract acts, as well as standard contests such as bulldogging, calf roping, and bronc riding. These attracted a sizable contingent of Madison Square Garden veterans including Tad Lucas, Alice Adams, Vaughn Krieg, Vivian White, and Claire Thompson. There were also sponsor contests for the local amateurs.[143] Kirkwood was unaware that many local cowgirls really wanted to compete in the professional contests, apparently assuming that they were satisfied with the sponsor contests. Some of them must have discussed this with her, because her later rodeo included more contests, with the professional events open to all who wished to participate.

Local support was reminiscent of Calgary in 1912, with special rodeo sections in the newspaper, "go western" days, and the other kinds of community involvement that had been essential to the success of many rodeos over the years. Huge crowds turned out and newspaper coverage was extensive and favorable.[144] The *Bonham Daily Favorite* on June 28 head-

lined: "Rodeo Success, Crowds Pleased, Its O.K. Fay!!!" (p. 6). Her promotional efforts were compared to those of nationally known Foghorn
Clancy, and judged superior.[145]

Fay was as pleased as the community, and immediately set about planning additional contests, including one at Wichita Falls, Texas, the weekend of July 28–August 2. Although still heavy on exhibitions, eleven of
them and only eight contests, this rodeo still offered greater opportunities for local women than the Bonham event. The program included four
"professional" contests: calf roping, bronc riding, steer riding, and bulldogging, and four amateur (sponsor) contests: musical chairs, flag race,
reining, and cutting.[146] At least two local cowgirls, Dude Barton and Sally
Taylor, entered the professional calf roping contest as well as all four sponsor events.[147] Dude won the sponsor's musical chairs and flag races,
finished second to Josephine Proctor in the professional calf roping, and
took third in both cutting and reining, while Taylor won the reining and
took third in the roping.[148]

Thena Mae Farr won the cutting and took second in reining. Another
excellent athlete and familiar figure in sponsor contests, Farr was then
serving the second of her four terms as "Miss Seymour," and was also cap-
tain of the Seymour High School girls basketball team.[149] Both Farr and
Barton turned in outstanding performances, but most of the headlines
and coverage went to Tad Lucas and Dixie Lee Reger (Mosley). The
Wichita Falls Record News reported that Lucas, while "starring in every
contest . . . staged one of the most colorful events of the show when she
presented her educated horse, White Wing."[150] Eleven-year-old Dixie,
who made her debut as Suzy the Clown, was probably the last of the cowgirls to be born into the old-time rodeo business. She was the daughter of
rodeo producer, announcer, and contract performer Monte Reger. In
1931, when Dixie was only one year old, she and her older brother and
sister toured with their parents, exhibiting a trained longhorn named Bobby Twister. After a difficult first year, the act did catch on and was scheduled at fairs, rodeos, and even on vaudeville before the Reger troupe
joined Eskew's J. E. Ranch rodeo in 1935. There, at age five, Dixie made
her trick riding debut on a Shetland pony and began learning trick roping
from the now legendary Junior Eskew.[151] In 1940, Monte Reger organized
a Wild West show. The family troupe also worked rodeos with Monte announcing and the three children exhibiting trick roping and riding and
automobile jumps. Dixie became America's first juvenile professional ro-

deo clown during the family engagement with Kirkwood's Wichita Falls rodeo.[152]

Even though her rodeos were successful, Kirkwood was disillusioned. She had scheduled the Wichita Falls contest after meeting the commander of a nearby military base who had assured her that his men would enjoy and support the rodeo. When she arrived at Wichita Falls for the contest, this officer invited Fay to dinner at his home. He ruined the evening by making a pass at her, whereupon she rebuffed him. He retaliated by declaring her rodeo off-limits to the very service men it was designed to entertain. Fay's reaction was swift and final. "That broke me! I decided that if that was what I had to deal with, it wasn't worth it! I just canceled the rest of my rodeos."[153]

Another producer of all-girl rodeos was Vaughn Krieg, the 1934 Madison Square Garden bronc riding champion and herself a contestant in Kirkwood's events. Unlike her sister Gene, Vaughn had not joined the rodeo as a teenager, for by age eighteen she was married to Tom McKinney and the mother of two sons. They eked out a living as farmers near Mesa de Maya, Colorado, for several years. In 1926, she cut those ties and joined the rodeo, quickly becoming one of the top bronc riders in the business. By 1932, as Vaughn Johnson, she was also a bulldogger and trick rider of note.[154]

After several failed marriages, Vaughn found the right cowboy in Lynn Huskey, and the two were wed in 1933. She later told a reporter that she married Huskey so she could be sure of always being a cowgirl.[155] Both continued their successful careers, and soon purchased a ranch near Towson, Oklahoma, that they named the "Flying V" after Vaughn. There they built a rodeo arena and also constructed a clubhouse to display their trophies, photos, and her Madison Square Garden saddle.[156] The two began producing annual Flying V Rodeos in 1937, attracting excellent crowds to the contests, to which many of their colleagues from the major rodeo circuit came to compete.[157]

With six years' experience as a producer, she formed Vaughn Krieg's Flying V All Cow-Girl Rodeo Company in 1942. Since she was planning to entertain at military bases, Vaughn organized the rodeo around patriotic themes, with the Flying V standing for victory. The show opened at the Lamar County Fair Grounds near Paris, Texas, in September of 1942, with twenty-five rodeo queens among the participants.[158] Krieg's program was much more competitive than Kirkwood's, as it featured three contract acts, one sponsor contest, and six events for professionals. An all-star cast of rodeo hands competed in calf roping, wild cow milking, bronc riding, bulldogging, cutting, and steer riding. Among the participants were Marjorie Roberts, Ruth Roach, Lucas, and Krieg herself, who competed in bulldogging, bronc riding, calf roping, and steer riding.[159]

Like Kirkwood's production, Krieg's rodeo attracted its share of sexist publicity, while the actual write-ups were quite good. The coverage was unbiased and matter-of-fact, though lacking interviews, photos, or a final wrap-up. Timing probably contributed here, as high school football was hogging most of the sports pages. Still, Vaughn lacked Fay's theatrical flair and ability to attract reporters to her every move.[160] It is therefore interesting to speculate what might have occurred had Krieg and Kirkwood combined forces. With Fay's skill at public relations and Vaughn's arena know-how, they should have made a dynamic team. The headlines and crowds that both attracted certainly indicated that an audience did exist for all-girl rodeos, but their extent was never known. Vaughn had intended to take her rodeo to other parts of the country, but I found no evidence of additional Flying V All Cow-Girl Rodeos.[161] It is likely that tire and gasoline rationing, which intensified during 1942, made expansion impossible. Therefore, even with their excellent receptions and financial success, the contests did not survive World War II.

The same was true for other promising developments of the early forties. Cowgirls in Texas and Florida competed in legitimate, timed flag races and barrel races instead of sponsor events in rodeos held at Beaumont, Liberty, Kirbyville, and Waco, Texas, and Largo, Florida. A series of "Buckskin Rodeos" at Beaumont sometimes featured flag races, barrel races, and cutting contests for women. In November of 1943, Maxine Maier won all three contests at the last Buckskin Rodeo of the season, "overshadowing some good performances by the cowboys."[162]

At the Pinella County Fair in Florida, flag races attracted veteran cowgirls like Peggy Murray and Faye Blackstone. Blackstone, who had been a professional contract performer since 1937, remained active in rodeo until 1951, with the flag and later barrel racing circuits providing a second career to the former trick rider.[163] She was unusual in this, as most of the Madison Square Garden veterans found flag and barrel races boring. For many, local contests could not replace the major rodeos from which they were excluded, or the thrill and glory of appearing at Madison Square Garden.[164] Like the all-girl rodeos, the races and the small rodeos that sponsored them seemed to die out as World War II intensified.

Flying V
All Cowgirl Rodeo
Paris, Texas
September 1942

Grand entry of guests and review of all cowgirl performers,
    forming a Texas star in the arena.
Presentation of flags and introduction of stars and special guests.
Calf roping contest
High school horses shown by Vaughn Krieg Huskey, Margie
    Roberts and the Pratt sisters.
Trick and fancy riding by Glorianne and Darlene Tyndall, world's
    youngest cowgirl
Bronk riding contest
Review and inspection of sponsor girls from surrounding towns
Miss Lillie Lyons and her trained steer, Texas
Bronk riding contest, second section
All-girl rodeo mascot, Kaytricia Ann Pope and her horse, Tony
Sponsor girls' flag race—against time
Bulldogging contest
Cutting horse contest
Sensational jump on two horses over auto, Alice Sisty
Steer riding contest
Speciality number
Wild cow milking contest
Trick and fancy riding
Finale, "V" for Victory formation.

Contests in boldface type. Program for September 3, 4, and 5. From the National Rodeo Hall of Fame at the National Cowboy Hall of Fame, Oklahoma City, Oklahoma.

Gene Autry's Flying A Rodeo Company also began in 1942. Unlike the other new events, it had the fame, fortune, and prime locations to become a major success story. The Flying A Rodeo that premiered at Houston in February of 1942 was the prototype of all the rodeos which followed. As promised, it was very streamlined, and included only five cowboy contests. While in keeping with the wartime suggestions of the RAA, it was also a lavish, Hollywood-style show. Parades and production numbers employed special effects like black light and fluorescent costumes. Women were consigned to peripheral roles as parade riders and square dance participants. The emphasis was overwhelmingly patriotic, reaching its thrilling climax in the finale, "Cavalcade of the Men Who Made America." Cowboys representing heroes like George Washington, Davy Crockett, and Teddy Roosevelt rode into the arena on beautiful horses while their eulogies were read over the loudspeaker. When the last arrived, a huge American flag was lowered, and all of the other rodeo participants rode in to form a huge V for Victory around the heroes.[165] The Houston audience responded with great enthusiasm, as did the crowds at all future Flying A rodeos.

To launch his company, Autry had outbid Eskew for all of the big rodeos the J. E. Company previously produced. This virtually ruined Eskew, who remained thereafter a minor player in the rodeo game.[166] Autry staged a series of Flying A Rodeo Stampedes at these cities, all short distances from one another, on successive dates in April and May. All were held indoors and sanctioned by the RAA.[167] The arrangement ensured that contestants would not have far to travel between rodeos, and that sizable audiences would be available in the immediate vicinity, in line with the RAA proposals to limit travel.

Purses at the Flying A Rodeos ranged from $5,000 to $9,000, with an added incentive for individuals who competed in all of them. The contestant with the highest total earnings for the entire series in each of the five events won bonus money ranging from $250 to $750.[168] This plan, revolutionary at the time, was the prototype for the current bonus system. Top money winners at rodeo series sponsored by companies like Dodge Truck, Wrangler Jeans, and Sharp Electronics earn as much as $9,000 in addition to official prize monies.

In addition to performing in his own productions, Autry also signed on to star for Colburn's Lightening C Rodeo Company at Madison Square Garden and Boston Garden. He then joined the armed forces, at considerable risk to his lucrative career, because it seemed the right thing to do.

Autry sent Roy Rogers to fill his engagements at Boston and New York, and then appeared at Madison Square Garden wearing his military uniform. He got a thunderous ovation.[169] Besides his military duties, Autry remained actively involved in his business. In September of 1942, "The Greatest Announcement in Rodeo History" proclaimed that the Flying A Ranch and Lightening C Ranch rodeos were combined to form "Gene Autry's World Championship Rodeo Company, Madison Square Garden, New York, and Boston Garden, Boston, Everett Colburn, Manager and Arena Director."[170] Now head of the largest and most powerful company in the history of the sport, Autry also produced the New York and Boston rodeos. He apparently accomplished this feat by buying out one of Colburn's partners.[171]

Having already eliminated Eskew from the competition, Autry enjoyed a virtual monopoly over big-time rodeo. At Boston and New York, ranch glamor girls rode while Rogers sang "Home on the Range," just as they had done with Autry the previous year. In 1942, for the first time, there was no cowgirl bronc riding competition at either Boston or New York, a permanent change with a lasting and devastating impact on women.[172] By year's end it was obvious that whether produced by the Flying A or Lightening C, all of Autry's rodeos were very much alike, and that none included contests for cowgirls.[173] In 1943, the picture was complete as the "Cavalcade of Men Who Made America" became part of the Madison Square Garden rodeo.

Unlike Wild West shows and early rodeos that had attracted fans by evoking images of a romantic West that never was, Autry's contests reflected domestic values which were being rapidly eroded, and provided popular escape fare. Even though a majority of Americans continued to support the belief that women should remain at home, women were actually joining the work force in record numbers, often in positions once reserved exclusively for men. At a time when the epitome of masculinity was the soldier defending his country, this placed some civilian males in a demoralizing situation. Not only were they left out of the battlefield heroics, with so many females taking wartime factory jobs, "many suffered additional ignomiyy of doing work that even women could do."[174] In contrast, Autry's shows symbolized more traditional values and more acceptable, if stereotyped, gender roles.

The rodeos not only emphasized patriotism, they left all of the heroics to the cowboys, while women's limited activities reflected a male perspective that stressed "feminine" traits.[175] Although the cowgirls in Autry's ro-

1943 Official Program
World's Championship Rodeo
Madison Square Garden
New York City

Music Furnished by James Cimmeron's Cowboy Band
"Tumbling Tumbleweeds"
Bob Nolan and "Sons of the Pioneers"
Grand Entry and Introduction of Officials
Cowboys' Bareback Bronc Riding Contest
Horseback Quadrille
ROY ROGERS AND TRIGGER
Cowboys' Calf Roping
Cowboys' Trick and Fancy Roping Exhibition
Cowboys' Saddle Bronc Riding Contest
"Home on the Range" Starring ROY ROGERS with the
    Ranch Girls
Cowboys' Steer Wrestling Contest
Ken Boen and "The Old Grey Mare"
Cowboys' Wild Cow Milking Contest
Cowboys' and Cowgirls' Trick and Fancy Riding Exhibition
Introduction and Presentation of Trophies to the 1943 Champions
Cowboys' Wild Brahama Bull Riding Contest
Cavalcade of Men Who Made America

Contests in boldface type. Program for October 31. From the ProRodeo Hall of Fame, Colorado Springs, Colorado.

deos rode quite well, they remained passive, gentle, and ultimately dependent on the cowboys for their success, just like the women in his films.
Sponsor girls, unlike the old-time cowgirls, presented no real threat to the
cowboy heroes. They did nothing that replicated "man's work," nor did
they attempt to conquer or subdue unruly beasts. Because of their youth
and the continued emphasis on their amateurism, sponsor girls did not
appear to be working women. They therefore reinforced the stereotype
that woman's place was in the home, whether in the city or on the range.

This formula became the national standard, and spelled the final doom
for cowgirl competition in major rodeos, as Autry controlled them all. By
1946, he produced both the eastern circuit and the Houston, Los Angeles, Shreveport, and Toronto contests as well.[176] Since his rodeos were the
models that other contests followed, cowgirls soon had few places to compete. The last time that Autry participated in a rodeo where professional
cowgirls competed was Boston Garden in 1941. Thereafter, all rodeos
with which he was involved as producer or performer relegated women
to peripheral roles in parades, square dances, and "Home on the Range."
Like the women in his western films, rodeo cowgirls changed from genuine participants to mere props, whose primary purpose was to make the
cowboys look good.

The End of an Era

Autry's leadership and the impact of World War II had a drastic effect on
women's role in professional rodeo. Between 1930 and 1941, the average
number of professional cowgirls active annually had been fifty, with thirty-six of them winning money each year. Cowgirl contests took place at
rodeos in at least eighteen states, as well as four Canadian provinces and
several cities in Australia.[177] Among the biggest purses offered women
were the $6,800 awarded at both Fort Worth and London in 1934. The
figures for 1942, after Autry formed his company and the cutbacks intensified, appear at first glance to be similar to the previous years, as twenty-
eight women did win money in rodeos that year. However, the figures are
deceiving, as twenty-seven of the twenty-eight won their prizes either in
all-girl rodeos or in Texas or Florida flag and barrel races. The one exception was Danetta Burns of Alamosa, Colorado, who won the Denver Post
relay race at Cheyenne Frontier Days.[178] Contract work was also in short
supply and grew more difficult to obtain in the years that followed.

Consequently, all aspects of female participation decreased significantly between 1943 and 1946. An average of just twelve women per year were active in professional rodeo, and their roles consisted primarily of serving as contract performers or timekeepers for Gene Autry's company. The remainder competed in isolated rodeos from Wyoming to Florida. Rodeos holding cowgirl contests were far apart, and few had the same events for women, so that it was impossible for women to make a living from contest winnings.[179] Although cowgirls had for many years been far ahead of other American female athletes, that was no longer the case by the end of World War II.

Marjorie Roberts is one cowgirl whose life story might well have been different without the combined impact of World War II and Gene Autry. Her story also demonstrates both continuity and change in the saga of rodeo cowgirls. The eldest of six children, Marge was born at Chalk community, Kansas, in 1916. Her father E. C. began sitting her on the back of his saddle horse when she was six months old, and by the time she started school she rode like she was born on a horse. Like Alice and Margie Greenough and their brothers in Montana, the Roberts youngsters all worked in the family business. Since one of E. C.'s businesses was breaking horses, Marge began helping with this task. Like her brothers, and like the Greenoughs, she always rode slick, one of the last women to do so in big-time rodeo.[180]

Like her foremothers and peers, Marge began competing in local amateur and pasture rodeos by the time she was thirteen, riding both broncs and steers. She also took on the outlaw broncs that were sometimes brought to town to challenge the locals. On at least one occasion she conquered the worst bronc in the lot to collect her five dollars. Like the Greenough sisters, Marge began her professional career with a Wild West show, but there the similarities end. During the summer of 1932, she hitchhiked to Sidney, Iowa, and earned a spot in the Clyde Miller Wild West Show as a ten dollar per week bronc rider. When Mrs. Miller learned of Marge's age, she insisted upon obtaining her parents' permission. This was granted with the stipulation that Marge perform only in the summer, returning home each fall to attend high school until she graduated.[181] By contrast, Ben Greenough allowed Margie and Alice to attend school only through the eighth grade, whereupon they had to begin working full time.

During four summers with the Miller show, Marge Roberts gained valuable experience as a performer. In 1934 she graduated from high school, the only member of her family to do so. This placed her far ahead of her rodeo peers, but she was the leading edge of change, as high school and even college graduates joined the rodeo ranks following World War

II. Soon after graduation, Marge married fellow performer Eddie Boyson, and they quit the show to join the competitive rodeo circuit.[182]

In 1941, Marge won the invitational cowgirl bronc riding at the Cheyenne Frontier Days. That feat would normally have catapulted her to the top of the profession, a superstar of Madison Square and Boston gardens. But by that time competitive rodeo had become a dead end street for women. Marge earned her greatest fame, and hall of fame honors, as an innovative and exciting contract trick rider, not a contest winner.

About the same time her competitive career hit a dead end, her marriage also fell apart. Soon after, she married another cowboy, George "Kid" Roberts. During the forties, they wintered at Tucson, Arizona, working at dude ranches. This led Marge to a much more secure job. From 1952 until 1962, she ran the horseback riding concession at Lake of the Ozarks State Park in Missouri. By then her second marriage was over and she was back with Boyson, although they never remarried.[183]

Vivian White, winner of the last cowgirl bronc riding at Madison Square Garden in 1941, was another high school graduate who saw her rodeo career derailed by Autry and World War II. Vivian joined the rodeo when she was fifteen years old, but stayed in school, intending to go to college. In the end, rodeo won out over higher education. She achieved her first big victories in 1938, taking the trick riding at Cheyenne and the bronc riding at Madison Square Garden.[184] By the time she won her second New York title, she was a fourteen-year veteran of the circuit.[185] It was her last major victory. She had very few opportunities other than contract work during the war, but when the GRA came into being, she resumed her competitive career.

Most other cowgirl stars also had to make radical changes in their lives. Many went to work in totally new fields, often war-related industries. Some like Marge Roberts were able to use their equestrian skills in new ways. A few were able to continue in the rodeo business. Tad Lucas and Nancy Bragg became featured trick riders for many of the Gene Autry rodeos throughout the forties, with Lucas serving as an official timer at the contests. Florence Randolph retired in 1939 to become the producer of the annual rodeo at her adopted hometown in Ardmore, Oklahoma.[186] Alice Greenough and her lifelong friend, cowboy Joe Orr, retired from competition to form the Greenough-Orr Rodeo Company. They produced rodeos in the Northwest through the fifties, with Alice handling the bookkeeping and contracting and also giving bronc riding exhibitions at all of the rodeos.[187] The couple later married.

Things did not go so well for other stars of the Golden Age, especially three who had earned fame as steer bulldoggers: Lucyle Roberts, Claire Thompson, and Fox Hastings Wilson. In the forties, Fox developed tuberculosis, an illness not uncommon among rodeo and livestock professionals of those times. Her second husband Chuck was by her side through several agonizing years of treatment, but the joy of learning that that the disease was in remission was short-lived.[188] On August 2, 1948, Chuck Wilson died of a heart attack. Two weeks later at the Adams Hotel in Phoenix, Arizona, the fifty-year-old cowgirl died of self-inflicted gunshot wounds to the head and stomach. She left the following note to her employer: "I didn't want to live without my husband."[189] Unlike Wilson, both Richards and Thompson lived to rodeo in the fifties after experiencing some very hard times.

Claire began the thirties with great success, and won the bronc riding title and $1,000 at Tex Austin's 1934 rodeo in London.[190] Tragedy struck two years later at Madison Square Garden, where Claire broke a leg, while her husband Red was ripped open by a steer, leaving the couple with no source of income. With no insurance, the two faced a monumental struggle, for while Claire quickly overcame her injury, Red never recovered.[191] Claire supported her husband and son with her rodeo winnings, and remained very active in the business for several years. She wrote a column entitled "Cowgirl Comments," for *Hoofs and Horns*, and was one of the women responsible for forming an organization of cowgirl bronc riders during the 1938 Fort Worth rodeo.[192] When World War II began curtailing national opportunities, she and Richard Akarman produced weekly rodeos at the Bar C Ranch near Fort Worth. She also assisted the Marines in recruiting volunteers.[193] By that time, Red was blind and bedridden, and his care consumed most of her time. In 1943, after selling virtually all of their possessions to pay medical bills, Claire still could not afford the hospitalization that he needed. In a final attempt to secure financing, she advertised in *Hoofs and Horns* that she would sell the only remaining item of value, her trick riding horse.[194] Whether she ever sold the horse is not known. The following year, both Claire and Red were baptized, with Red carried into the church on a stretcher, followed by his pony.[195] Their struggle did not end until Red Thompson's death in 1949.[196]

Lucyle's problems began in the summer of 1938 when she became romantically involved with wealthy Houston lumberman and rodeo producer Frank Y. Dew. According to sworn testimony, Dew carried more than fifteen thousand dollars worth of insurance on her life, and had promised to marry her when she divorced third husband J. T. Richards.[197] That divorce became final on March 7, 1939, but no marriage to Dew followed.[198] Their stormy and sometimes violent affair did continue until April 24, 1941, when the two quarreled at Dew's River Oaks apartment.[199] He was fatally shot soon after.

The following morning, headlines in the *Houston Post* screamed: "Rodeo Cowgirl Shoots Ft. Bend Rancher Dead Here," and "Frank Y Dew is slain by Lucyle Roberts."[200] Lucyle was arrested and charged with murder, spending several days in jail before her attorney posted her bond.[201] Following her indictment on first-degree murder charges, she entered a plea of self-defense, while the state sought the death penalty. Throughout the April and May preliminaries, and the actual trial that ran from December 2 to December 5, the prosecution managed to drag up sordid details of her personal life: marriages, divorces, and drinking sprees. They revealed that Richards had been married to two different men between October of 1940 and March of 1941, which she explained as a combination of excessive drinking and failed efforts to get away from Dew. Her problems were not limited to the courtroom. Her father, who was supposed to testify in her behalf, was mysteriously run over by a truck and unable to appear. Lucyle herself sustained serious injuries in a plane crash just three months before the December trial.[202]

While attorneys for the state continued to smear her character, Lucyle tenaciously maintained that Dew had been physically abusive and that she had shot him in self-defense only after he had beaten her and pushed her down a flight of stairs.[203] Apparently the jury believed her, for after twenty-one hours of deliberation, they announced a verdict of not guilty.[204] Despite the trauma of the trial and the embarrassment of having her personal problems discussed on the front pages of the local papers for months, Roberts forged ahead with her usual flair. She married two more times, and also spent many years in rodeo. Lucyle noted on a biographical data sheet that she had been married so many times (seven) that she had lost touch with all her many friends from rodeo days.[205] Perhaps typically, one of the items that she donated to the National Cowgirl Hall of Fame following her 1987 induction was a clipping with the headline: "Cowgirl Coming to Trial as Slayer of Lover Who Turned Cool." It began: "Dark-eyed, beauteous Lucyle Roberts, whose white buckskin-clad figure has thrilled thousands at the top rodeo arenas of the nation, goes on trial here Monday for the killing of Frank Dew, wealthy Houston Lumberman."[206]

Lucyle and Claire both got their lives back on track, and attempted to resume their careers. The rodeo world to which they returned was quite different from the one they had left. Instead of the glamor of major eastern contests, both found opportunities in all-girl rodeos sponsored by the GRA.

Cowgirls lost their place in the rodeo spotlight for many reasons, but Johnson and Autry played the critical roles. The departure of Johnson was a major blow, since he truly believed that women belonged in professional rodeo and made every effort to keep them in the spotlight. It appears relatively certain that had Johnson remained in the business, cowgirl calf roping would have have become a part of his rodeos, either in addition to or in place of cowgirl bronc riding. Johnson's successors did take note of the growing popularity of roping, inviting Sydna Yokley to perform at Madison Square Garden in 1939. It seems reasonable to conclude that had Autry not intervened and totally remodeled the sport, cowgirl calf roping would have become *the* women's contest during the forties and probably have remained an integral part of rodeo.

It is interesting to speculate on exactly what Autry's role might have been had Johnson remained active in the field, since both were determined to be the best in the business. Johnson did retire, and Autry ultimately became the most influential single individual, other than Buffalo Bill himself, in the history of rodeo. He eliminated all his competition, while the cutbacks caused by World War II prevented any new threats to his domination.

Autry's popularity, professionalism, and financial security helped rodeo survive the war. He brought in new fans and kept their interest through his myriad of other entertainment projects. He also provided the innovative leadership lacking since Johnson's departure. Once in control, Autry maintained his hegemony for many years. In 1952, Guy Weadick, creator of the Calgary Stampede, suggested: "western rodeos should be organized on a historic instead of a Hollywood theme."[207]

As Weadick implied, all of Autry's changes were not for the best. From his first featured appearance at a rodeo, Autry was the star, not the athletes. Soon rodeos large and small began booking cowboy singers and movie stars, reviving the careers of former greats and giving opportunities to young hopefuls. By 1947, producers found that they could not stage successful rodeos in major cities without cowboy movie stars as the headliners.[208] When singing cowboys rode into the Hollywood sunset, western singers, and finally country singers, took their places. Although rodeo had always been tied to the entertainment world, competition was the premier element. Suddenly, entertainment became the main event. Still today, rodeo advertisements promote entertainment by singers like Garth Brooks, George Strait, or Clint Black, not the contests between top cowboys. Surely rodeo is the only professional sport in the world in which the athletes are not the stars. In the final analysis, Autry remodeled the sport itself to reflect the times: relatively few actual contests, elaborate production numbers, strong patriotic themes, and women in their place, at home on the range.

Chapter Five

Back to the Big Time, 1948–67

Rodeo cowgirls during the late forties and early fifties overcame the setbacks of World War II as well as the cultural forces that opposed them and began a renaissance that continues today. A small group of Texas women succeeded in establishing a circuit of all-girl rodeos, organizing the Girls Rodeo Association, and having GRA-sanctioned barrel races included at a majority of rodeos throughout the United States. As a result, more than 160 women won money in professional rodeo between 1947 and 1955. More than one-third of them remained active for three years or longer, approximately the same portion as found in the entire sample used for this book. More than half of the total group competed in barrel racing, while roping and bronc riding attracted approximately one-fourth. Relay racing, trick riding, and steer riding had practically disappeared by the late forties, but flag racing continued to grow, although more slowly than barrel racing.[1] (See table A.6.) Within two decades of the GRA's founding, cowgirls had also gotten their barrel racing championship into the world's richest rodeo, the National Finals Rodeo. These achievements would have been exceptional in any case, but were especially significant during the postwar years. Women at that time received little encouragement to develop their athletic or career aptitudes, and no one had even given voice to the concept of gender equity in sport. Kate Weigand described the era this way: "In the United States the years immediately following World War II were generally marked by increasing social and political conservatism. One important aspect of this conservatism was the revival of a traditional ideal of femininity and domesticity for women after nearly two decades of relative flexibility in conventional gender roles. . . . Women were expected to be passive, emotional, and incapable of making major decisions; they were not supposed to be concerned with issues outside the home, political or otherwise."[2]

Despite these beliefs, women joined the work force in record numbers. They also faced severe discrimination on the job. Critics castigated working women for taking jobs away from returning veterans and contributing to society's ills by abandoning their duties as wives and mothers.[3] Although more women did enter college than in the previous decades, only 37 percent finished, and the numbers of women taking advanced degrees declined.[4]

Clothing soon came to reflect the new ideology. Attire had been almost mannish during the war, featuring simple, economic styles. Soon afterward, French designer Christian Dior attempted to dress all women in his "New Look," of long skirts, pinched waists, and flat bosoms. Dior's creation again placed women in clothing that distorted their bodies and restricted their movements.[5] Thanks to his influence, women's fashion became more restrictive and confining than at any time since the Victorian period.[6]

Society and the media reinforced the stereotype that the only roles for women were sex object or homebody.[7] The belief remained that athleticism made women somehow less feminine and less attractive as wives. With increased emphasis on femininity, the old stereotype that equated female athleticism with lesbianism experienced a resurgence. McCarthyism, another dominant feature of the era, intensified this problem. In addition to making feminist activities suspect, McCarthyism exacerbated homophobia. This made the threat of being labeled lesbians by participating in highly competitive sport especially frightening to women. Since parents were usually more sensitive to these issues than youngsters, athletic girls and women had almost no encouragement to develop their gifts.[8]

The fundamental social changes went far beyond even these issues. A new civil rights law and the 1954 Supreme Court ruling in *Brown v. Board of Education of Topeka, Kansas,* led to racial unrest and demonstrations. The fifties also marked the rise of rock 'n' roll music. The new sound was immensely was popular with teenagers, but adults denounced it as immoral.[9] The extraordinary technological changes that helped accelerate the growth of rock music also altered the nature and fabric of everyday life. Television, virtually unknown before the war, reached more than 90 percent of homes by the mid-sixties.[10] From 1950 to 1955, the percentage of

American homes with television sets rose from 9 to 67, and by 1960 had reached 86 percent. Two of the most popular programs of the fifties were westerns: "Gunsmoke" and "Have Gun Will Travel."[11] These programs helped increase audiences for western events like rodeo. Television westerns also spelled doom for Republic Pictures, the company that had made stars of Gene Autry, Roy Rogers, and John Wayne. While Rogers and Autry developed their own television shows and Wayne starred for other studios, the 1959 demise of Republic marked the end of an era in western entertainment.[12] Like the Republic films, the television series did nothing to enhance the image of competent, athletic women. Instead they reinforced the prevailing stereotypes of domesticity and compliance.

The same was true of the 1948 Broadway hit *Annie Get Your Gun.* Its authors and lyricists ignored the accomplishments of the real Annie Oakley, who defeated Frank Butler at sharpshooting and went on to become his wife and lifelong companion. In the musical, Annie lamented that "You Can't Get a Man with a Gun," and lost the match to win Butler. The message was unmistakable.

Under these conditions, it would certainly be reasonable to expect similar developments in women's rodeo. The logical evolution should have been a continued expansion of sponsor contests, and the disappearance of the few remaining cowgirl events. Yet even though Gene Autry still dominated rodeo, that never happened. Cowgirls in 1947 initiated their turnaround. That year is recognized as a sports history landmark for a different reason—the end of racial segregation in major league baseball.[13] Both professional baseball and racially integrated sports experienced a rocky road in Texas, while women's professional rodeo soon thrived.

Far west Texas was still cattle country in the late forties, and did not slavishly follow the dictates of eastern fashions or ideas. The same western ranching culture that had spawned rodeo and produced the original female rodeo stars remained unique in many ways. The women who revolutionized rodeo in the forties and fifties still shared many experiences with cowgirls of the prewar era. In the old cattle frontier practically all women still rode horseback and performed ranch chores. Athletic, competent women enjoyed widespread adulation.

At the same time, the postwar group differed from the cowgirls of previous generations in several significant ways. Whereas their predecessors rarely finished more than the eighth grade, virtually all the women in the forties and fifties graduated from high school and many attended colleges. Most were also proficient at a variety of sports. Several were high school basketball stars, and a few majored in physical education in college.[14] Rodeo was still their first love, and they used their considerable talents and energies to ensure themselves a place in the sport.

In the mid-forties the rodeo profession itself began to modernize. In 1945, the Cowboys Turtle Association changed their name to the Rodeo Cowboys Association (RCA) and established their first permanent headquarters at Fort Worth. They then appointed Earl Lindsey, formerly with the Gene Autry organization, as the first full-time employee. He served the RCA as business manager, public relations director, and the cowboys' representative in negotiations with rodeo committees.[15]

By 1947, the RCA sanctioned more than one thousand rodeos annually, and cowboys competed for the richest purse ever, $155,400. Approximately one-half of all professional cowboys made a profit, while about 75 percent were injured each year.[16] Roy Rogers, Dale Evans, and of course, Gene Autry, remained the superstars. Therefore opportunities for women in the big time were still sponsor girl or glamor girl events, and an occasional bronc riding exhibition. Finally that began to change.[17]

One helpful organization was the Cowboys Amateur Association (CAA). It originated in California in 1940 to allow young amateurs to compete against one another and gain experience and an opportunity for the RCA tour. Unlike more traditional amateur groups such as the AAU, the CAA did not prohibit members' winning money in rodeo. Instead, they required them to progress to the CTA/RCA when their winnings reached $500.[18] At a time when neither the Turtles nor the RAA exhibited any interest in cowgirl events, the CAA included women's roping contests at their rodeos. Starting in 1945, these took place at approximately twenty-five contests in California alone.[19] One of the perennial winners was a transplanted Texan, Wilma Standard. In 1947 she attempted to expand women's opportunities by producing the first California all-girl rodeo. Veterans at the Sawtelle Government Hospital gave her contest an enthusiastic reception, and she held several additional shows locally. Like Vaughn Krieg in 1942, Wilma never found the financial support needed for a traveling company. In 1950, she moved home to Texas to compete in roping and develop a contract act with her four-horse Roman team.[20]

Several rodeos also held barrel races in 1946, and by 1947 the contests offered prizes ranging from $50 at Boerne and Hillsboro, Texas, to $350 at Wichita, Kansas.[21] By 1944, a few rodeos had also begun holding women's cutting horse competitions, often in addition to sponsor contests or barrel races. L. A. Worthington, owner of the West Fork Ranch at Jacksboro, Texas, produced competitive women's events in 1944 and 1945. At his rodeos, cowgirls participated in cutting contests and timed barrel races, with no points for beauty, costume, and so on. Worthington had good reason to promote the rodeos, as his three daughters, Jackie, Mary, and Ada, were all skilled equestriennes. Jackie often won the sponsor contests and gave exhibitions of bronc and bull riding.[22]

Jackie Worthington was born in Jack County, Texas, in 1924, and literally raised in the saddle on the family's ten thousand acre ranch. Although only 4 feet 8 inches tall and weighing under 100 pounds, she helped her father with all phases of ranch work, raising and breaking horses, branding, vaccinating, and dehorning cattle. Before World War II interfered, she and her sisters traveled to many rodeos in their Ford pickup, while their father's contests filled the gap for the duration.[23] Jackie was an all-around athlete who won trophies in many sports, and an accomplished musician often invited to entertain at local civic events. She was also a licensed pilot, and by 1949 had graduated from Texas State College for Women (TSCW) with a bachelor's degree in physical education.[24]

Jackie had a significant impact on women's rodeo, but only after Thena Mae Farr and Nancy Binford, two other west Texas women, made it all possible. Nancy and Thena Mae were also gifted athletes and well-known beauty queens who had won many sponsor contests during their lives. Yet these events were far from satisfying. Not only were wealth and beauty more important than skill in winning sponsor events, many of the so-called contests had no written rules. Women often complained that the judges put the barrels anywhere they wanted to any time they wanted to during the progress of the competition.[25] Binford and Farr hoped to provide an alternative to the sponsor contests, enabling women to test their skills against top athletes in traditional rodeo contests of roping and rough stock riding. To achieve this goal, they decided to produce their own all-girl rodeo, which took place at Amarillo, Texas, September 23–26, 1947.

The two women had known one another for at least seven years before launching their historic rodeo. Both participated in the ill-fated 1940 All American Rodeo at Fort Worth. In 1947, the twenty-five-year-old Binford owned Anchor Sporting Goods in Amarillo. While it was unusual then for a woman to own her own business, Nancy had an excellent role model. Her mother, Kathryn Cabot Binford, owned and managed the family ranch after the 1934 death of her husband. She drove wagons through the snow, fed cattle, and mended fences, while also raising her daughter.[26] Nancy had helped operate the ranch since the age of thirteen. She also completed her education, graduating from Texas Tech University in 1943. She taught in Lubbock in 1943–44, before opening her business. Nancy was a versatile athlete, roper, and equestrienne, and a noted beauty. Since 1939 she had been the Sweetheart of the Range Riders Club of Amarillo, traveling with them to rodeos and horse shows all over the United States.[27] Thena Mae, then age eighteen, had been a high school basketball star and 1945 winner of the celebrated Stamford Sponsor Contest. Following graduation from Seymour high school, Farr attended TSCW for one year. She then returned to join the family ranching operation, where she already owned several head of cattle.[28]

With their background and experience, it was not surprising that the two were able to plan their rodeo in every detail. The more difficult task might have been selling the idea to the promoters of the Tri-State Fair, an annual Amarillo event that for many years hosted a CTA/RCA rodeo. However, the women were equally skilled at public relations, having traveled far and wide as "Miss Seymour" and the Range Riders' Sweetheart. Rodeo was dead in Amarillo in 1947, and the fair committee needed an event that would fill the grandstand and provide much-needed entertainment. Though they had some doubters, the cowgirls attracted sufficient support to get the project off the ground. They continued their public relations efforts as they went up and down Polk Street in Amarillo inviting sponsors to purchase ads in the program, donate prizes for the winners, or both.[29] They also publicized the event throughout the Southwest, and succeeded in enlisting seventy-five contestants from twenty-five communities in Texas, New Mexico, Oklahoma, and Missouri. Participants paid entry fees ranging from $5 to 15 per event to compete for $1,260 in prize and mount money, and, for the all-around champion, a horse trailer.[30]

Contests for prize money included bareback bronc riding, calf roping, sponsor contest (barrel race), cutting contest, and team tying. Participants paid no entry fees in saddle bronc and steer riding, where winners received only mount money.[31] The sponsor and calf roping contests attracted the most entries, while bulldogging failed to make and became an exhibition by Pat McClain, the sole entry.[32] Beutler Bros. collected $1,600 for the standard rodeo stock used in the contest. The backbone of the operation was the Reger family, who received $750 for their varied talents. Monte Reger served as rodeo announcer and clerk, his daughters Dixie and Virginia performed trick roping, trick riding, and automobile jumps. Dixie was also the rodeo clown, and Virginia the official typist.[33]

Dixie, a future Hall of Famer, was as determined as anyone to see the project succeed. In addition to performing her contract acts, she entered every contest, even though Amarillo was her first competitive experience.[34] By the time she arrived for that historic rodeo, Dixie had graduated from Woodward, Oklahoma, high school. This was a major achievement. She had been a rodeo professional all her life, and spent most of her time on the road. She completed elementary school through correspondence courses, and tolerant officials at Woodward allowed her to miss the first and last six weeks of high school each year.[35] Binford still believes that Dixie and her family provided the key to success, keeping the rodeo moving and maintaining the interest of the audience.[36]

Advance publicity for the event included pictures and biographical data on some of the leading participants as well as the two producers. Photographers spent a day snapping Binford and Farr at a variety of locations. Many of the images appeared in the press during the next several years. In all the photos the two dressed identically in jeans, boots, and matching western shirts.[37] Fortunately, one picture that papers rarely used showed the two wearing aprons over their rodeo gear, and cooking in a kitchen.

Photographers were on hand when Worthington flew her plane to Amarillo for the rodeo.[38] Fern Sawyer, a 1939 Madison Square Garden sponsor girl, also attracted reporters' attention. Described as a "Double Tough Cowgirl Rider" and "prize winner from way back,"[39] the twenty-year-old already had a formidable reputation in cutting contests. She had defeated a field of twenty men to take the 1943 Pecos contest, and beaten the great Bob Crosby at a special matched competition in May of that year.[40] Both Fern and Jackie lived up to their advance billing, winning three of the events.

The local press covered the rodeo extensively, with most of the reporting unbiased and positive, never mentioning the cooking or sewing abilities of the contestants. There were a few unpleasant surprises, like the headline "Amazons of the Arena ready for today's semi-finals."[41] Most write-ups were more like this one: "If yesterday afternoon's semi-finals are any indication, rodeo fans are in for some super chills and spills tonight when the cowgirls compete in the finals of the Tri-State Fair All-Girl Rodeo."[42]

The rodeo was a rousing success. It played to standing room only, and drew the biggest crowd ever to witness an arena event at the fairgrounds.[43] One enthusiastic reporter observed: "The Girl's rodeo is a knock-out. The two promoters have a great opportunity. No reason why they shouldn't break into Madison Square Garden within the next winter or two."[44] Another observed that "There are sufficient girl stars to put

Nancy Binford and Thena Mae Farr, publicity photo for the Tri-State All-Girl Rodeo they produced at Amarillo, Texas, in 1947. This natural pose of the two cowgirls in their working attire presented a marked contrast to the cheesecake poses often forced on female athletes. Photo courtesy of the National Cowgirl Hall of Fame and Western Heritage Center, Hereford, Texas.

Fern Sawyer, GRA pioneer and honoree in two rodeo halls of fame, riding a bull in a forties all-girl rodeo. Photo courtesy of the National Cowgirl Hall of Fame and Western Heritage Center, Hereford, Texas.

Blanche Altizer Smith, GRA charter member, competing in an all-girl matched roping contest at Coleman, Texas, in the early fifties. Photo courtesy of the National Cowgirl Hall of Fame and Western Heritage Center, Hereford, Texas.

Dixie Reger (Mosley), the first female rodeo clown, performing at an all-girl rodeo in the early fifties. Photo courtesy of Dixie Reger Mosley, Amarillo, Texas.

on a rodeo as exciting as the men's and so much more colorful and breathtaking. When a pretty girl takes a spill, people gasp."[45] Even though feminists might take exception to the latter, the contestants and promoters found it quite complimentary.

Sawyer won the team tying, took second in cutting, and third in both calf roping and barrel racing to capture the coveted all-around title. In the bareback bronc and bull riding, "small but potent Jackie [Worthington] gave the fair-visiting crowd an outstanding exhibition," winning both of those events.[46] Dude Barton won the sponsor contest as well as the calf roping, and finished third behind Margaret Montgomery in competition for the all-around title. Jerry Ann Portwood took the cutting championship.[47] All the winners, as well as Farr and Binford, have since been inducted into the National Cowgirl Hall of Fame.

Many other participants went beyond the expected in hopes of making their dream of a professional rodeo career come true. Among them were Blanch Altizer (Smith), Isora Young, Rae Beach, Judy Hays, Sally Taylor, Dora Waldrop, and Vivian White. Delighted with their venture, Nancy and Thena Mae incorporated Tri-State All Girl Rodeo to produce additional contests in the years ahead.[48] They hoped to continue the tradition of having all aspects of the rodeos handled by women. Other than Monte Reger, the only males involved in the 1947 contests were the judges for the cutting horse competition and I. W. Young, Isora's husband, who helped with the chutes.[49]

The Girls Rodeo Association

The spirit of camaraderie that developed among the contestants lasted long after the final performance of the 1947 rodeo. They wanted to ensure future opportunities to compete in legitimate rodeo contests, and made plans to form a permanent organization of rodeo cowgirls to achieve that goal. On February 28, 1948, thirty-eight women, many veterans of the Tri-State All Girl Rodeo, gathered at the San Angelus hotel in San Angelo, Texas. There they formed the Girls Rodeo Association (GRA),[50] which is today's WPRA.

While their foremothers had apparently never even considered such a radical move, it was not unusual for this more educated group. Several of the women had majored in physical education in college, where they received extensive leadership training. Physical education departments were usually separated by sex, even in coeducational institutions, and women had numerous opportunities to work in student organizations, hold a variety of offices, and interact with female faculty members who were often national leaders in the field. At TSCW, which both Thena Mae and Jackie attended, women held all elective offices, ran all student organizations, wrote, produced, and directed elaborate stage plays, and conducted events for community and school groups. For these cowgirls, neither forming their own organization nor staging their own rodeos seemed unusual. Rather, they were the logical solutions to the problems that the cowgirls faced. Women's physical education departments also stressed dressing appropriately and good public relations as the means by which women could achieve their goals. The GRA also incorporated these ideas.

The local papers covered the meeting in detail,[51] while the publicity director, Sug Owens, made sure the fledgling organization received national recognition. Her first article appeared in the May issue of *Hoofs and Horns*.[52] These newspaper and magazine articles described a significant event in the history of women's sport that has rarely been reported accurately since. In *The Cowgirls*, Joyce Roach states that the GRA was formed in 1949,[53] and in the afterword to her second edition, Elmer Kelton accentuates her error: "Mrs. Roach speaks of the organization of the Girls' Rodeo Association . . . in 1949. I can vouch for that."[54] In *Cowgirls*, Theresa Jordon correctly states that the GRA was formed in 1948, but errs in claiming that the charter meeting occurred during Binford and Farr's first all-girl rodeo. Of course, that rodeo took place in 1947.[55]

The initial meeting did take place in 1948, and the women present elected Margaret Owens Montgomery as president; Dude Barton, vice president; and Mrs. Sid Pearson, secretary. Montgomery, who served two terms as president, was born on an Ozona, Texas, ranch. An outstanding roper, she won the sponsor contest at the 1940 Fort Worth rodeo, and was among the first women to compete in roping at Pecos, Texas. During the first four years of GRA competition, Margaret won thirteen buckles and five saddles at sanctioned all-girl rodeos, and was the 1948 all-around champion. She remained a top competitor and GRA board member until 1955, when the thirty-three-year-old died in an automobile accident.[56] The original board of directors included young cowgirls like Dixie Reger, Jackie Worthington, and Blanche Altizer, and Madison Square Garden champion Vivian White.[57]

Their primary aim was to provide women with legitimate opportunities to compete both in all-girl rodeos and in RCA rodeos. From the outset they planned to work within the system, use good public relations, and to sell

Margaret Montgomery, the first GRA president and 1948 all-around champion, was best known as an outstanding roper. Here she competes in a roping match shortly before her death in 1955. Photo courtesy of the National Cowgirl Hall of Fame and Western Heritage Center, Hereford, Texas.

women's rodeo to the public.[58] This philosophy has served the organization well ever since. The founders drafted rules of membership and regulations pertaining to several aspects of rodeo, including all-girl rodeos. A system patterned after the RCA's gave one point for each dollar earned at a sanctioned contest. The woman with the highest point total in each event at year's end was the national champion, with the woman earning the highest number of points in two or more events the all-around cowgirl. The final winners were to be determined at the last all-girl rodeo of each season.[59] Membership was open to women of all ages, who were also allowed to compete in high school rodeos but not in amateur or nonsanctioned rodeos.[60] The rules for all-girl rodeos included structure of entry fees and prizes, approval of promoters and producers, and rules of competition. The twelve events originally sanctioned included three each in roping and rough stock riding, four races, wild cow milking, and cutting.[61]

For many, the most important changes related to the sponsor contests, where the objective was to eliminate competitions based on beauty, costume, and arbitrary rules and replace them with standard, timed events.

Realizing that cowgirls were already popular with audiences and rodeo committees, the women sought to make GRA contests even more appealing and help promote women's rodeo in the process. Therefore, rules stipulated that women participating in GRA-sanctioned contests at RCA rodeos had to ride in the opening parades and always be dressed in colorful cowgirl attire when they appeared in the arena.[62] Rules also prohibited members smoking or drinking in the arena.[63] Critics argue that the women were offering to be objects or to be treated differently than the cowboys, but that is not really the case.

The RCA also enforced a strict dress code which required cowboys to wear jeans, boots, hats, and long-sleeved cowboy shirts both in the arena and in publicity and program photos. The rules until recently also prohibited release of photographs of any cowboy association member wearing short-sleeved shirts or glasses.[64] Almost all professional sports in which uniforms are not worn enforce some kind of dress code and, uniforms or not, attempt to make the athletes appealing to the public. Colorful costumes had been a cowgirl trademark since the nineteenth century. The GRA members asked not to be judged on their appearance or attire, but nonetheless agreed to dress attractively and continue the proud tradition. They also felt that always being attractively and appropriately dressed, even when not actively competing, was important to their overall goal of popularizing women's rodeo.

The women's desire to create a good impression extended beyond the confines of the arena and the grandstand. A journalist covering the GRA meeting held during 1948 Tri-State Fair week in Amarillo reported on the "array of beautiful, bright colored, well-tailored and eye-catching riding outfits that were to be seen parading into the meeting." She described the women's western suits in some detail:

> Mrs. Margaret Montgomery president of GRA, . . . was absolutely stunning in her all-white flannel outfit and fuscha neck scarf. Her white Stetson and brown alligator boots set off the ensemble beautifully.
> Miss Thena Mae Farr, . . . looked very elegant in her green gabardine outfit, white hat and blouse, and light green scarf.
> But honestly, it was a real sight to see that many (about 50) ladies dressed so magnificently, and so Western.[65]

Cowgirls from that era dress much the same today as in the forties and fifties when attending events like Hall of Fame induction ceremonies and dinners. Several are critical of the careless attire exhibited by some contemporary all-girl rodeo participants.

When their rules took effect in May 1948, GRA board members were already working with rodeo producers and committees. They hoped to persuade them to conduct women's contests according to GRA rules. It was not a hard sell! This was the GRA's greatest triumph. Although rodeo committees could choose from several events, barrel racing quickly became the most popular, and its growth has been phenomenal.

One of the first renowned rodeos to make the change from sponsor contests to sanctioned barrel races was the venerable Stamford, Texas, Cowboy Reunion, where the sponsor contest had originated in 1932.[66] From that date through 1948, clothing had remained the main feature of the contest. In 1949, they changed the scoring, and judged the women solely on their times in a cloverleaf barrel race.[67] Perhaps Stamford helped set the pace, as barrel racing replaced sponsor contests at small local rodeos and spread quickly to major contests. Within a very short time, rodeos all over the United States included GRA barrel races.

The first important indoor barrel race took place at the Houston Fat Stock Show and Rodeo in 1950. Most of the front page headlines and photos went to stars Roy Rogers and Dale Evans, and the sixty-seven women competing in the first rodeo queen competition. Still, the local papers published most of the daily barrel race results. Barrel racers got secondary headlines and several paragraphs on two dates, and the winners' names appeared with the other champions of the rodeo. At least nineteen different women won some money in the contest, with ten-year-old LaTonne Sewalt, 1950 and 1954 GRA champion, the final winner. GRA leaders June Probst, Blanche Altizer, and Thena Mae Farr finished second, third, and fourth respectively. Sewalt collected $130 for her efforts, compared to $1,230 for the cowboy calf roping champion.[68] Rogers and Evans were also on hand when barrel racing achieved the ultimate success, inclusion in the 1954 Madison Square Garden rodeo. There too, movie stars and the rodeo queen contestants outshone the barrel racers. Unlike Houston, the New York papers never even mentioned their results.[69]

With the rise of barrel racing competition in the fifties, rodeo queen contests often replaced the discredited sponsor contests. Almost as old as the sport itself, they were a problem only to the extent that they eclipsed or replaced actual cowgirl competition. The ways in which queens were selected varied enormously over the years. Sometimes local beauties vied for the title, and other times rodeo committees appointed them. Occasionally the committees paid top professionals like Vera McGinnis, Mabel Strickland, or Margie Greenough to be the queen and star of a rodeo.

As the GRA gained national prominence, publicity became less of a problem and rodeo queen contests and WPRA barrel races coexisted peacefully. Many women participate in both. Today, the ultimate rodeo queen is "Miss Rodeo America," a title WPRA vice president Pam Minick won in 1973.[70]

In 1958, the GRA sanctioned barrel races in twenty-one states and Havana, Cuba, with purses totaling $27,924.[71] Having so many barrel races to choose from, women were able to compete throughout the season, and their winnings soon exceeded all expectations.[72] The GRA itself experienced immediate growth as well. Whereas in 1948 seventy-four GRA charter members participated in sixty events, by July of 1950 there were more than one hundred members representing eleven states and one Canadian province. Most of them were single women between the ages of twenty-one and twenty-seven, with the actual range being from twelve to forty-five. By that date, the new GRA magazine, *Powder Puff and Spurs*, had 622 subscribers in thirty-one states and Canada.[73] The GRA obtained some important recognition and publicity through a regular column in *Hoofs and Horns*. A major annual publication of the times, Fog Horn Clancy's *Rodeo Histories and Records*, also published GRA event winners and all-around champions.[74] This information subsequently appeared in RCA publications *The Buckboard* and *Rodeo Sports News*.

Against all odds, the GRA had succeeded. They triumphed because of the members' indomitable spirit and determination. The women certainly had few role models, and little knowledge of the successful cowgirls of the prewar period. Western comic books were about the only aspect of popular culture where female heroines were presented as independent and athletic, and certainly the only one featuring realistic cowgirls. During the forties and fifties, cowgirl comic heroines like Prairie Kate, Buffalo Belle, K-Bar-Kate, and Buckskin Belle rode the range alongside the cowboys. More than any others, they provided a glimpse of the character and experience of early-day rodeo stars. Jack Shadoian, a specialist in media studies, described the women this way: "Tough, astute, violent, accomplished, eroticized, they perished with the Comics Code. But they had their moments of glory, and are worth considering now as unusual models of female competence. They were the commercial media's last sustained vision of females who could give the most redblooded males a run for their money on their terms. It was an era capable of producing the ultimate praise: 'Yuh're as good as two men!'"[75]

Shadoian admits that these exceptional women were part of the glamorized West that long fascinated Americans. Like the fictional western men, they were invariably "white, unmarried, high-spirited, physically superior individuals."[76] He also readily admits that the stories were aimed at a male audience, with the Belles and Kates designed to trigger sexual fantasies. Still, he feels that the women of western comics represent an ideal rarely presented to the American public: "They relish their manly skills and show no inclination toward shedding them for more appropriately feminine endeavors."[77] The same could apply to the pioneers who created the GRA.

With all of its successes, the GRA also faced problems. By 1949 it was already obvious that the GRA barrel racing circuit at RCA rodeos was far more lucrative and attractive for many cowgirls than the all-girl rodeo circuit. That year, fourteen-year-old Amy McGilvray traveled more than 25,000 miles to compete in twenty-two barrel races, winning $2,671.02. At the Fort Stockton, Texas, all-girl rodeo she took second in bull riding to qualify for the all-around title. She won easily at the finals in Corpus Christi, Texas, with total earnings of $2,750.[78] McGilvray's victory was certainly not the spirit or intent of the all-around title. The GRA board called a special meeting during the Corpus Christi rodeo to discuss the fact that it could be easily won by competing in barrel racing at RCA rodeos, with little support for all-girl rodeos.[79] They amended the rules so that women could count only money won in GRA-sanctioned all-girl rodeos toward the all-around cowgirl title.[80] The rules, which took effect in 1950, also required all-around champions to compete in two or more events. At the same meeting, the GRA elected Binford president, and McGilvray joined the board as one of two directors of sponsor contests (barrel races).[81]

As the election results indicate, the rules change did not reflect any disapproval or dislike for McGilvray. Yet it did indicate a flaw in the system: despite their desire to compete in a variety of rodeo events, financially most cowgirls could not afford to limit themselves to all-girl rodeos. Moreover, the all-girl contests clashed with one of the oldest traditions in rodeo: cowgirls marrying cowboys and following the circuit with their husbands. Single women who competed exclusively in all-girl rodeos obviously had limited opportunities to meet cowboys, while married ones had to leave their husbands to compete in all-girl rodeos. The rules change did protect the integrity of the all-around competition and help promote the all-girl rodeos, but it did not change the financial disparity. In 1953, Jackie Worthington narrowly defeated Wanda Harper (Bush) for the all-around cowgirl title, $1,976 to $1,937. Harper also won $3,462 in barrel racing, making her champion of that event. Wanda's barrel racing winnings alone exceeded the winnings of RCA steer roping champion Ike Rude, and her combined winnings were only $459 less than those of RCA team roping champion Ben Johnson. More to the point, Harper's barrel racing winnings totaled more than the combined earnings of all other GRA event champions that year![82]

While their earnings were low, cowgirls still enjoyed a supportive environment for their efforts. Girls' high school basketball teams had an almost fanatical following in rural west Texas and Oklahoma. Their stars enjoyed the kind of local celebrity that most communities reserved for male athletes. This was most unusual. In many places parents and teachers encouraged girls to become cheerleaders and pep squad members rather than athletes. Betty Hartman, who wrote about women's participation in sport in the late fifties, described the situation this way:

> What does the average American man expect of women? He expects the woman to be a "lady." Being ladylike does not, by any stretch of the imagination, mean a muscled Amazon who can literally hold her own with men. It means a woman who is well-groomed, a good mother, a competent homemaker; a woman who takes an interest in her husband's affairs . . . a woman who, above all, displays more feminine than masculine qualities. Nowhere in analyses of the American woman is there a desire to have a woman be an Olympic champion, a professional golfer, or a great and outstanding athlete.[83]

Hartman found that when girls insisted upon sports participation, mothers frequently steered them away from "masculine" activities like softball, volleyball, and basketball toward the more acceptable, feminine activities of swimming, tennis, and golf.[84]

Of course, a few women overcame the problems and prejudices to achieve success in a variety of sports. Babe Didrikson, track star of the 1932 Olympic Games, earned new fame as an amateur golfer. In 1947, she became the first American to win the British Women's Amateur Championship.[85] When the Olympic Games were restored in 1948, Fannie Blankers-Koen of the Netherlands scored a major breakthrough. Thirty years old and the mother of two, Fannie won four of the nine gold medals available to women in track and field, delivering a serious blow to the myth that strenuous sport destroyed women's reproductive systems.[86]

Even fans who cheered female Olympic heroines often found women's professional sports unacceptable. In 1934, Wilson Sporting Goods hired Helen Hicks to give golf clinics and help design women's equipment. Believing the name "woman golfing professional" was undesirable, Wilson executives gave her the title "Business Woman Golfer." Things were no better ten years later when a small but determined group founded the Women's Professional Golf Association (WPGA). They expected that the all-male Professional Golf Association (PGA) would help them organize and allow some form of affiliation. The PGA was at first quite benevolent and encouraging, but ultimately withdrew their support. That left the women completely on their own, with no hope for a formal alliance with the men's group. The WPGA struggled for four years, but finally succumbed to the financial problems that had plagued them from the start.[87]

In 1950, the Ladies Professional Golf Association (LPGA) received their charter. They were no more successful than the WPGA in obtaining support from the men, and endured many years of financial difficulty. Yet they managed to survive, partly because they had one thing the WPGA lacked, a name star. Thanks largely to the celebrity of cofounder Babe Didrikson Zaharias, the LPGA attracted enough corporate funding to stay in business.[88]

In many ways, the cowgirls were more fortunate than the golfers. From the outset they had worked not only with rodeo committees but with the RCA itself. Their work became easier in 1950 when the GRA headquarters moved to the Livestock Exchange Building in Fort Worth, Texas, close to RCA headquarters.[89] Thereafter cowgirl representatives often appeared at RCA board meetings. On January 30, 1955, GRA president Jackie Worthington and RCA president Bill Linderman signed the following historic agreement still in effect today:

> Only Rodeo Cowboys' Association, Inc. cards will be honored by the Girls' Rodeo Association and the Rodeo Cowboys' Association, Inc. will strongly urge and recommend the use of G.R.A. girls in barrel racing in related events. In the case of straight rodeos, the Rodeo Cowboys' Association, Inc. will insist that such events conform to Rodeo Cowboys' Association, Inc. and G.R.A. rules and regulations.
>
> This agreement shall be in effect until such time as it is terminated by action of either of the parties hereto.[90]

Although there were some early efforts to change the agreement, the RCA board stood by it and referred appropriate requests, protests, and rules interpretations to the GRA for resolution.[91]

RCA support resulted in part from the fact that rodeo remained a family business, with many GRA members having fathers, brothers, and/or husbands who were RCA members. While cowboy organizations consistently resisted actions that would threaten their incomes or status, by that time they certainly recognized that some kind of women's event was going to remain a part of most rodeos. For married cowboys in particular, the GRA barrel racing circuit represented a marked improvement over the invitation-only, amateur sponsor contests. The barrel races paid actual cash purses, and growth of their circuit meant that rodeo couples could again travel and compete together, as they had in the prewar era.

The GRA also made progress on other fronts. Sanctioned roping contests spread across the West, sometimes offering sizable purses to the winners. In 1948 a jackpot calf roping at Claude, Texas, attracted a top field including Sawyer, Binford, Barton, Worthington, and Montgomery.[92] From that time through the mid-fifties, communities in Texas, New Mexico, Oklahoma, Colorado, Wyoming, and Nebraska scheduled events such as matched calf roping, jackpot calf roping, and team roping.[93] Nineteen-year-old Ruby Gobble launched her professional career at the 1950 Pikes Peak or Bust Rodeo at Colorado Springs, where she won the cowgirl calf roping. Gobble also took the title at a highly publicized Northwest all-girl calf roping at Laramie, Wyoming, on July 11, 1952. Other top finishers included Dixie Reger (Mosley), Judy Hays, Wanda Harper, Blanche Altizer, and Margaret Montgomery.[94]

All-Girl Rodeos

All-girl rodeos also grew, with twenty-four held in 1950 alone.[95] Binford and Farr produced contests in Amarillo, San Angelo, and Seymour, Texas, as well as Colorado Springs, Colorado, awarding a trailer to the all-around champion at each one. Publicity for their contests continued to be extraordinary. Of the second Amarillo Tri-State All Girl Rodeo, the *Amarillo Times* noted: "All Girl Rodeo is no joke, son." The article went on to explain that the rodeo featured thirty girls from eight states in a "grueling two-hour show of horsemanship, trick roping, bronc taming and general feminine hell-raising."[96]

Some of their best write-ups, as well as the worst, came in conjunction with a Colorado Springs all-girl rodeo held in July 1951. Bill Totten was arguably the most sexist reporter ever to cover women's rodeo. He gave the following description of Binford and Farr: "Anyone expecting to see a pair of raw-boned, weather beaten scare crows would be shocked to see this pair. Both are neat, well groomed, attractive young ladies who look like they know the difference between a powder puff and a piggin string . . . they don't look like rodeo contestants, but like a couple of nice girls in their twenties . . . who might be more at home on the GAS range."[97]

Totten seemed interested to learn that rodeo did not interfere with women's child bearing. Other locals reported that most of the cowgirls were married, and that losing members to marriage was the biggest problem facing the all-girl rodeo business.[98] Photos showed Judy Hays and her son, and Rae Beach riding a bull. The caption on the latter read "Rae Beach . . . cute looker from Bell Gardens, California."[99] A photo of Blanche Altizer roping had this caption: "The Champ herself demonstrates how a member of the 'weaker sex' goes about a man's job on the range."[100]

Sexist write-ups notwithstanding, Colorado Springs gave the GRA and the producers a rousing welcome. Community support was excellent, with local civic groups contributing in several ways.[101] On one occasion the producers met with the Colorado governor as part of a publicity stunt. Their outfits, much like the ones described earlier, so impressed the governor that he called in staff members to take notes. Binford's and Farr's outfits, he exclaimed, represented exactly the look that he wanted for the capital guides.[102] The papers also covered the actual competition quite fairly, giving the names of both day money and final winners along with several action photos.[103] Their last photo of Rae Beach also had a different caption from the earlier one; it read: "She rides them rough as they come."[104]

The women did not maintain a monopoly on the business for very long. Attracted by their success, several men including Rubin Porter, Delbert Lyons, Dub Spence, and Jerry Rippeteau began producing all-girl rodeos. Lyons's May 1950 contest at Coleman, Texas, overcame the bad weather to draw the largest crowd yet for the sport.[105] That same year, Rippeteau introduced all-girl rodeo to Corpus Christi, Texas, where he produced the championship event. Subsequently, the finals moved to larger cities such as Dallas and Tulsa, where Rippeteau's 1954 contest drew sizable crowds and extensive press.[106] Still, their publicity rarely came close to the quality and quantity Nancy and Thena Mae elicited. Promotion for some of the championships men produced was nonexistent. For example, when the GRA finals took place in Dallas on April 2–4, 1953, only one article appeared in the *Dallas Morning News*. Frank X. Tolbert, who wrote "local color" columns for years, did a piece on cowgirl Aria Kesis, a "displaced person" from Latvia. Although he did note that contestants hailed from throughout the United States, Tolbert gave no other insights into the rodeo. The *News*, which reported women's sports quite well for the fifties, was surely not to blame. It carried both local and national stories on women's sports ranging from the traditionally feminine golf and swimming to the often controversial AAU women's basketball.

**First Annual
CowHand—CowBelle
All-Girl Championship Rodeo**

Rodeo Officials

Rodeo Producers
   Then Mae Farr
   Nancy Binford
Rodeo Clown
   Dixie Lee Reger

Timers
   Mrs Tom Coleman
   Mrs. Tad Lucas

Grand Entry and Introductions
Bareback Bronc Riding
Calf Roping Contest
Wilma Standard—Roman riding
Barrel Racing
Virginia Hadley—Car Jump
Cutting Horse Contest
Trick Riding
Ribbon Roping Contest
Trick Roping—Virginia Hadley
Brahama Bull Riding

Contests in boldface type. Program for June 25, 1951. From the National Cowgirl Hall of Fame and Western Heritage Center, Hereford, Texas.

Official Program
All Girls
World's Championship Rodeo
Fair Park Grandstand

Grand Entry
Introduction of Officials
Bareback Bronc Riding
Trick Roping Exhibition
Championship Calf Roping
Roman Riding Exhibition
Cutting Horse Contest Finals
Trick Riding Exhibition
Presentation of Awards
Bucking Ford Act
Barrel Race
Bull Riding
The Eyes of Texas Ride

Contests in boldface type. Program for April 4, 1952. From the National Cowgirl Hall of Fame and Western Heritage Center, Hereford, Texas.

Therefore the fault must belong to the promoters, who did a poor job of promoting, and purchased no ads.[107]

The situation was better for the 1954 championships. Lengthy articles, several accompanied by action photos, appeared in the *Morning News,* beginning a week before the rodeo. The coverage was fair, and gave good insights into the similarities and differences between men's and women's rodeo. Although the published articles were excellent, coverage stopped when the rodeo started. Results never appeared. The sponsoring Eastern Star Temple of Dallas may have publicized the event with posters, but neither they nor they producers ever purchased ads.[108]

An excellent public relations campaign surrounded the first all-girl rodeo in Natchez, Mississippi, in 1951. The community went all out to support the efforts. Publicity began fully a month before the rodeo opened. There were few ads, but those published were as large as half a page, and were paid for by local merchants. The *Natchez Times* provided superior coverage throughout the contest. In what was then essentially a country town, the biggest news of the rodeo was that Margaret Montgomery had flown all the way from Australia just to participate.[109] This fact appeared in almost every article about Margaret, and made her the star of the show before she ever rode into the arena. Although the paper had only a single page devoted to sports, it reported the names of all contestants, day money winners, and final winners.[110] In the end, reporters concluded that the rodeo was "one of the finest western programs seen here in years."[111]

Two years later, things were quite different, and coverage did not even approach the 1951 event. During the intervening time, the paper had changed owners, editors, and staff. In place of local news and human interest stories, they devoted much space to canned articles from wire services. They filled the sports section with major and minor league baseball, leaving room for only half as many rodeo articles as before. Lack of publicity and support from the press produced lack of community involvement. The enthusiasm was clearly missing, and the contest lost $500 in one night.[112]

Although it is uncertain whether they could have overcome the problems associated with the Natchez paper, Binford and Farr usually had an advantage over male producers. The very fact that they were rodeo producers was newsworthy. Female rodeo producers seemed almost an oxymoron, and reporters and the public came to see what they were like. The two were inevitably impressive, with their knowledge, winning personalities, and natty attire. They were masters of public relations, photographed with mayors and governors and interviewed at length by the local media. Like such renowned producers as Guy Weadick and W. T. Johnson, they became famous in their own right and their very presence enhanced the popularity of their rodeos.

Tri-State All Girl Rodeos also attracted more publicity than those produced by males because they were really "all-girl," down to the judges, clowns, and support staff. At most other all-girl rodeos, only the contestants were female. Consequently, Tri-State productions were far more interesting than other all-girl rodeos, and provided journalists with many unique stories. Articles often stressed the fact that women fulfilled all the roles except announcing. Because of their unique position, even the male announcers were subjects of feature stories.[113]

Reporters at one Natchez all-girl rodeo questioned the absence of female officials. The producer explained that most rodeo officials were former contestants who had been injured or had retired, and that women's rodeo was so new that none of the cowgirls was too old to compete.[114] This was of course ridiculous. The real explanation was probably that the producer, who also staged RCA rodeos, wished to employ his male colleagues. Binford and Farr never had that experience.

The male producers certainly spent very little on public relations, but their actual financial results are unknown. Despite their excellent publicity and support, Nancy and Thena Mae had managed to break even but had never showed a profit. Predictions that their all-girl rodeos would play Madison Square Garden were never realized, and Tri-State All Girl Rodeos ceased operations at the end of the 1951 season.[115] Despite the men's poor publicity efforts, there were quite a few of them producing GRA contests, and Nancy and Thena Mae felt that all-girl rodeos were sufficiently established to succeed without their corporation.

Binford had by that time completed her term as GRA president, and soon turned her attentions to other pursuits. By 1955 she had left behind the women's rodeo business that she had profoundly influenced. Farr succeeded Binford as GRA president and continued to compete through 1954.[116] Still, the departure of these pioneer producers was a major loss to the profession. They alone produced contests for women organized by women with women's special interests and needs in mind. Such events have been extremely rare in the history of women's athletics, and have never again been a part of rodeo.

Between 1947 and 1955, GRA members threw themselves wholeheartedly into their sport, attending meetings and competing in rodeos with great enthusiasm. Many learned new events to help fill the rosters and make the contests a success. The women also went out of their way to be helpful to newcomers. They were anxious to enforce their dress code, yet did not want to exclude anyone. Therefore, when an individual appeared at one of their all-girl rodeos improperly attired, someone near her size would try to talk with her and offer to lend her the needed garments. Looking back on those years, the women felt that these gestures were well received, and helped them increase participation as well as to achieve their other goals.[117]

In order to help more women participate, several of the Texas members opened their homes in summer to cowgirls from out of state, enabling them to live close to most of the GRA events. Ruby Gobble spent several summers at the Binford ranch, while Rae Beach hired on as a full-time ranch hand with Thena Mae Farr's father. During the six months each year she lived at the Farr ranch, she did all kinds of work including branding and dehorning cattle and digging post holes.[118] Throughout this period the camaraderie and friendship within the group were much stronger than the competition between individuals, since all the women wanted their sport to succeed. Wanda Bush, a GRA founder still active in the nineties, has fond memories of the old circuit where "everyone rooted for one another, we helped one another out with problems, we were an inspiration to one another. . . . Today it's a lot more professional. . . . There's a lot more money but a lot of the fun is gone."[119] Women like Barton, Mosley, and Binford also stress that the most important aspect of their careers was the enduring friendships forged during years of working together in the GRA and competing together in the rodeos. They also agreed that they would follow the same rodeo careers again.[120]

The most outstanding athlete of the early years was Jackie Worthington. On more than one occasion, she entered every contest in the rodeo, and during her thirteen years on the circuit won eighteen titles in four different events, as well as six all-around championships.[121] Another star was Dixie Mosley, who was the official GRA clown from 1948 until 1953. Once the organization was formed, Dixie devoted her entire career to women's rodeos, serving as clown and contract performer. She also competed in many of the contests, enjoying her greatest success in calf roping. Her dedication helped the fledgling organization survive, and she was GRA vice president from 1950 to 1952.[122]

The GRA also attracted Madison Square Garden veterans Vivian White, Tad Lucas, Claire Thompson, and Lucyle Roberts. These seasoned competitors gave the organization the benefits of their experience and professionalism. White, Roberts, and Thompson all competed in saddle bronc riding, with Roberts active in the GRA for more than a decade. Lucyle frequently appeared in full Indian costume, adding much color and variety to the contests and publicity photos.[123] She won her last championship at age forty-two, when she took the GRA saddle bronc title in 1951. Thereafter, she did contract work in the United States and performed at several rodeos in Cuba and Puerto Rico before retiring in 1960. In 1962 she became a policewoman in Yokum, Texas, where she worked for the next four years.[124]

The most renowned convert to the GRA was Tad Lucas, whose very presence added credibility and publicity to the rodeos. She competed in saddle bronc riding and showed another side of her talents by sharing clowning chores with Dixie in 1949 and 1950. She also gave bronc and trick riding exhibitions at many all-girl rodeos, and sometimes served as an official. Lucas spent several terms on the GRA board as a director, first for contract acts and later for saddle bronc riding.[125]

After a display of initial enthusiasm, many women began to drift away in the mid-fifties. All of them had been ardent supporters of the GRA, especially the all-girl rodeos, and had hoped to develop women's rodeo into a full-time career. Most of them traveled the circuit each summer, and some used vehicles designed especially for that purpose. Once involved, some discovered they did not really like the constant travel or the distances involved. For several, a memorably arduous and unpleasant trip had been from Amarillo, Texas, to Burwell, Nebraska, less than nine hundred miles.[126] These particular women were certainly different from their predecessors, who were on the road most of the year, covering hundreds of thousands of miles and loving the gypsy life-style. These GRA cowgirls also differed from the earlier professionals in other significant ways. Whereas most of the pioneer cowgirls had come from the lower levels of the socioeconomic scale, many of the GRA members were quite wealthy, and several were millionaires.[127] While they did aspire to professional careers, rodeo for them was not a matter of economic survival as it had been to women like Randolph, Mulhall, and Blancett. That was just as well, for although Mosley was able to show a profit from her winnings and contract work combined, most of the others were lucky to break even. Several like Barton and Gobble left professional rodeo for economic reasons, and to those who remained it was an expensive hobby rather than a source of income.

The bride wore boots: wedding of rodeo star Dixie Lee Reger and William C. Mosley,
August 30, 1953. Photo courtesy of Dixie Reger Mosley, Amarillo, Texas.

One other important difference between the two groups of cowgirls was that many in the forties and fifties were single at the time of their major participation, and several remained so. Rather than marrying cowboys and joining their husbands on the RCA circuit, some women developed diverse interests and left rodeo to concentrate on cutting horse contests, ranching, and the like. Others like Mosley married nonprofessionals and quit the circuit to be with their families.[128]

During this period of transition and change, several cowgirls of the pre–World War I era made news. Florence LaDue and Guy Weadick retired from the entertainment world to their ranch at High River, Alberta, following the collapse of vaudeville. Guy continued to produce Canadian rodeos and occasionally had some role with the Calgary Stampede. In 1949, Calgary pioneers Guy and Florence Weadick, Ed Echols, and Fannie Sperry Steele made a guest appearance at the Stampede. Instead of the skirts of their rodeo days, Fannie and Florence both wore trousers into the arena on that occasion.[129] Fannie, by that time widowed, still operated the ranch she and Bill had run for so long. She continued to hunt and fish, to break and shoe her own horses, and to trail them across the Continental Divide to pasture once a year.[130]

In 1950 the Weadicks decided to retire to a warmer climate, and purchased a new home in Phoenix, Arizona. The citizens of High River gave them a farewell party, honoring both for their contributions to rodeo in western Canada. Parting gifts included a check for $10,000.[131] A year to the day later Florence died suddenly of heart failure, leaving a grieving Guy to make the move alone.[132]

He was not alone for long. Soon after his arrival in Arizona, he looked up Dolly Mullins, a longtime family friend who had won the trick riding at the first Calgary Stampede. The couple married at Nogales, Mexico, in April of 1952.[133] Three months later, they traveled to Calgary, Dolly's first return visit since 1912. Guy was the guest of honor on the fortieth anniversary of his founding the stampede, and as part of the ceremonies, they donated the medals she and Florence had won in 1912 to the Stampede.[134]

The next year, Guy and Dolly sold their home in Phoenix and moved to Los Angeles, where their life was far from serene. He had a long-standing reputation as a heavy drinker, and she was by that time apparently an alcoholic. By November of 1953 the two apparently separated, and Dolly wrote Guy that she wanted to dissolve their marriage. She added that she was working eight hours a day and did not want him "making a nuisance of himself."[135] A month later, Guy Weadick died, still legally married to Dolly. His obituary in the *Albertan* listed his "wife Dolly" as a survivor, and she attended the funeral in the widow's role. There she informed the family that she intended to take all of Guy's estate, although a will made four months before their marriage had left it all to his siblings. The family did manage to obtain his most personal belongings, and then apparently lost contact with Mullins. The end of her sad story remains a mystery.[136]

More information is available concerning some of her contemporaries. Tillie Baldwin died in 1950 at age seventy, having spent many years as a riding instructor.[137] Sixty-four-year-old Prairie Lillie Allen died at New York City in 1951, following a two-year illness that had kept her away from the Madison Square Garden rodeo where she had been a popular guest. News varied concerning later Garden veterans. Iva Jacobs, bedridden with tuberculosis in California, sent word she would like to talk rodeo with someone.[138] Mildred Mix Horner Morris, 1939 Madison Square Garden bronc riding champ, had remarried and moved to Arizona where she had a new baby. Florence Randolph taught trick riding in Oklahoma.[139] Bill and Mary Parks continued to perform with Eskew's J. E. Ranch rodeo, the last to abandon cowgirl bronc riders and the first to include a women's barrel racing exhibition.[140] Parks sometimes competed on the Florida barrel racing circuit, as did former all-girl rodeo producer Fay Kirkwood.[141] Velda Tindall Smith, a trick, bronc, and relay rider since the twenties, had struggled through the war giving contract performances with her two daughters. She later remarried, and returned to competition as a GRA barrel racer until she was injured in a 1953 race.[142]

During the fifties and early sixties several female athletes achieved major successes but only minor fame. One was American diver Patricia McCormick, who accomplished something no woman has done before or since. She won both the springboard and platform diving gold medals in two successive Olympic Games, those of 1952 and 1956.[143] Althea Gibson won the prestigious Wimbledon tennis tournament in 1957, the first black athlete to do so, but she missed the glory that today's Wimbledon champions enjoy. Two years after Gibson's victory, an American woman also achieved international acclaim in Olympic track. Wilma Rudolph, a black from rural Tennessee who had overcome crippling polio and an assortment of childhood diseases to become a world-class athlete, won three gold medals at the 1960 Rome Olympics and became a household word.[144] While none of these three realized the publicity or incomes they would enjoy today, they gained more recognition than women competing in basketball, volleyball, and softball, who usually toiled in total obscurity.

The GRA too lacked national recognition, but several of the pioneer members stayed with their organization long enough to have their daughters join them as fellow members. Jackie Worthington competed through 1961. Rae Beach, another veteran of the 1947 Tri-State All Girl Rodeo, served as GRA bronc riding director from 1951 to 1954. She competed through 1963, winning eight GRA bronc riding crowns, and died in 1991. Betty Baron Dusek, the first GRA calf roping director, won fourteen titles, including one all-around and nine in roping during a career that extended from 1948 to 1970. She is still a WPRA member.[145]

Wanda Bush, who first collected GRA calf and ribbon roping prizes in 1950, began roping with her father as a youngster. She won several Junior Rodeo Association championships before joining the GRA as a charter member. During the fifties, she battled Worthington for the all-around championship, winning it eight times between 1952 and 1969. She took eight titles in calf roping, seven in ribbon roping, two in cutting, two in barrel racing, and one in flag racing, for a total of twenty-eight.[146] Bush's daughter Shana, who now competes in barrel racing on the PRCA Circuit, was born in 1959. By that date women's barrel racing had become an integral part of the rodeo scene, and successful cowgirls spent five months or more following the tour. They competed in as many as forty-five rodeos annually and could earn up to $5,600 at their sport.[147] Also in 1959 changes in rodeo itself presented the women with a new challenge. That year, the venerable Madison Square Garden rodeo ended its historic run as America's number one rodeo, while the RCA established its own national championship, the National Finals Rodeo. The NFR, first held at Dallas, involved the top fifteen money winners in each of the RCA's standard events. (Team roping and steer roping were not included). Money won at the finals is added to the year's total to determine the world champion in each event. Since that time, the cowboys themselves have assumed almost total control over their sport, and have turned the NFR into America's premier rodeo, the place where the world champions really earn their crowns, no singers perform, and the contestants are undisputed stars. The GRA had been ten years ahead of the cowboys in determining annual champions at a final rodeo, yet they rightly perceived that having their barrel racing finals at the NFR would be a public relations bonanza. They made a concerted effort to be included.

The World's Richest Rodeo

The woman who initiated the effort was Billie McBride, GRA president from 1957 to 1959. She was the barrel racing champion from 1955 to

Billie McBride, former GRA president, competing in a barrel race. She was the GRA barrel racing champion from 1955 through 1958. Photo courtesy of the National Cowgirl Hall of Fame and Western Heritage Center, Hereford, Texas.

1958, barrel racing director from 1953 to 1956, and GRA secretary from 1962 to 1964. Billie could hardly have avoided some kind of career involving horses, since her father first lifted her into a saddle when she was only two weeks old. During the fifties, she and her husband, rancher and RCA calf roper Wilson McBride, followed the rodeo circuit with their daughter Alva Gene, who began competing in barrel races at age ten.[148]

In January of 1959, Billie made a formal presentation to the RCA board requesting the barrel racing finals be included at the NFR. She told the board that the GRA usually took 10 percent of the purse at regular rodeos, but they were willing to defer to the RCA National Finals Rodeo Committee (NFRC) on that subject. She also stated that the women could be used for pivots and in the grand entry. The board refused the request, noting that the NFR was for RCA members only. McBride protested, suggesting that some GRA members also belonged to the RCA. The board tabled the matter, stating they would take it up again at the next meeting. They never did.[149]

Though the women were unsuccessful in their first attempt to join the NFR, they were able to hold their barrel racing championships in conjunction with the RCA National Steer Roping Championship at Clayton, New Mexico, in 1959. This was because the NFRC recognized a need for some relief between six rounds of steer roping, and itself suggested that a barrel race would be the perfect solution. Supporters asserted that the event was very popular in the Clayton area, and that the women could provide the grand entry, pivots, hostesses, and color. Their rationale for allowing the women at the steer roping finals but not the NFR was that the NFR was a rodeo, sponsored by the RCA, while the steer roping finals was not a rodeo and was not sponsored by the RCA but by the local committee. Nonetheless, they warned Clayton promoters to watch the publicity and not let the women diminish the significance of the steer roping competition.[150]

The following year Chandler, Arizona, bid to sponsor the RCA steer roping and team roping finals along with the GRA barrel racing contest. The NFRC wanted to split their two events, allowing the barrel race to be held in conjunction with either of them so long as it was billed as an "added attraction."[151] In 1960 and 1961, the GRA held the barrel racing finals with the RCA team roping finals at Scottsdale, Arizona, and Santa Maria, California.[152]

Clearly the men speaking about the GRA proposals at these meetings had mixed feelings. Board and commission members agreed to allow women's contests in their events only to add relief or color, and demanded that the women act as pivots, hostesses, and so forth, in order to participate. They also exhibited a persistent fear that cowgirl contests might in some way overshadow the RCA events, and took great pains to ensure that the women's publicity was not too abundant.

GRA representatives continued their efforts to have the barrel racing finals added to the NFR, while the NFRC persisted in refusing their request. The women also decided they no longer wished to be a part of the RCA team or steer roping finals. Beginning in 1962, they held the barrel racing finals at Dallas, Texas, independent of any RCA contests. During those years the RCA did make several concessions regarding holders of GRA and RCA cards, enabling women to compete in events sponsored by both organizations and allowing women holding either GRA or RCA cards to compete in RCA-sanctioned team roping contests.[153]

By that time, many changes were taking place in American life. Westerns like "Bonanza" and "Rawhide" were among the top television programs of the decade, but the sixties are better known for other things. The tragedies of assassination, triumphs in outer space, and protests over the

Vietnam war characterized the times. It was also a period of activism, particularly for the causes of civil rights and world peace. In this environment women finally overcome the antifeminist sentiments of the postwar era in favor of militancy. The catalyst for the new movement was Betty Friedan's 1963 polemic *The Feminine Mystique,* which captured a huge and receptive audience.[154] With more than 40 percent of women in the work force that year, Congress passed the Equal Pay Act. In 1964, Title VII of the 1964 Civil Rights Act prohibited discrimination on the basis of sex as well as race. Despite this progress, leaders like Friedan soon realized that the new laws were not being enforced, and in 1966 they formed the National Organization of Women (NOW) to pressure governments on their behalf in the same way civil rights organizations were working for blacks.[155]

The women's sports revolution, an outgrowth of the women's movement, did not really begin until the mid-seventies. One of its leaders, Billie Jean King, was the top female tennis player in the world in 1967. She was also an amateur with no official earnings to report, since neither open tennis nor the Virginia Slims Tour existed. Nineteen sixty-seven was also the year physical educators finally reversed their long-standing opposition to women's varsity sports. They established the mechanisms to sanction and promote intercollegiate sports for women, which became widespread by the late seventies. While these changes were still in the future, 1967 marked the beginning of a new era for cowgirls who finally achieved their long-sought goal of inclusion in the NFR. Their careful attention to public relations and working with committees and promoters finally turned the tide.

Change began when the 1967 RCA board responded to a request for inclusion of barrel racing finals in the NFR by stating that it was up to the GRA, as long as they were willing to accept RCA cards as entries.[156] The real breakthrough came later that year when NFR promoters from Oklahoma City met with the RCA board. The promoters wanted the NFR to include the GRA barrel racing finals because the popular event would increase ticket sales. They were so eager to hold the barrel race that they offered to put up the prize money themselves to obtain approval. By a vote of eight to three, the board approved the inclusion of the event, with a $2,500 purse coming from the sponsor's half of the budget and not the profit.[157]

Loretta Manuel was the first cowgirl to win her barrel racing title at the NFR. Oddly, she had only $6,050 in winnings, the lowest total since 1959. Of course, this was a much smaller amount than the male champions collected at the NFR, much less the $51,995 total earnings of all-around cowboy Larry Mahan, though Manuel did win more than RCA steer roping champion Bob Altizer, who collected only $5,696.[158] Her situation was fairly typical of the times. That year, Jack Nicholas, the leading male golfer, won $188,998. The top female golfer, Kathy Whitworth, earned only $32,937.[159]

The results of the NFR and the women's role in it definitely pleased the Oklahoma City sponsors. In March of 1968, Stanley Draper of Oklahoma City proposed to the NFRC that GRA barrel racing finals be held at the NFR for as long as the rodeo was held in Oklahoma City. He also advocated a minimum prize of $2,500, to be included in the regular budget. "Discussion was held and these matters were agreed upon by the commission."[160] This was a major victory for the cowgirls, and barrel racing became an integral and popular part of the NFR during its twenty-five years in Oklahoma City.

The inclusion of the GRA barrel race at the NFR meant cowgirls had at last come full circle and had returned to the spotlight as featured contestants at America's premier rodeo. The scene had shifted from Madison Square Garden to Oklahoma City, yet the result was the same. Popularity and publicity for cowgirls increased dramatically, as did their share of the prize money. Since 1967, the champion barrel racer has earned more than the RCA steer roping champion, and sometimes surpassed the team roping winner as well. By the mid-eighties, women's earnings matched and sometimes exceeded those of other RCA event champions.[161]

Naturally, its inclusion in the NFR made barrel racing more popular than ever, and exacerbated the financial disparity between it and the all-girl rodeos. Even with the many advantages of the barrel racing circuit, all-girl rodeos might also have thrived under the right leadership. The enthusiastic participants, community support, overwhelmingly favorable press, and record crowds all suggested a bright future, and quickly brought several male producers into the business. Still, women could not earn a living from the limited number of contests available, and the only answer to that dilemma would have been growth. That would have required selling all-girl rodeos on a national basis, a major challenge at a time when women's sports were themselves in recession. It would also have taken years of skill, dedication, and financing such as Weadick, Austin, and Johnson had used to establish rodeo itself throughout the United States. Certainly the abilities and leadership of Binford and Farr would have been critical, and they would have needed much help over a long period of time.

It is impossible to know whether all-girl rodeos could have succeeded even under the best of circumstances. One thing is certain: without Nancy and Thena Mae, the contests ceased growing in the mid-fifties, never exceeding thirty per year. The departure of the two founders was a major blow to the future of the contests, and one from which they have never recovered. Binford and Farr brought much more to their jobs than just skills. To them, the all-girl rodeos were special and personal in a way they could never be for their male counterparts. Unlike the men, the two women had no financial involvement with other aspects of the rodeo business but did have a strong personal stake in the all-girl rodeos.

Even though those very special contests did not thrive, the legacy of Binford and Farr, along with Mosley, Barton, Harper, Montgomery, Altizer, and the other GRA pioneers, endures today. The organization they created has benefited thousands of women. Today, as the WPRA, it is the oldest organization of female professional athletes in America, and the only one controlled and managed entirely by women.

Chapter Six

Cowgirls Hit the Jackpot, 1967–1990s

Cowgirls have experienced tremendous progress since 1967. WPRA membership and prize money have grown, while commercial sponsorships and television coverage undreamed of only a few years ago have become a reality. The biggest changes transpired in the last ten years. In the 1990s the world champion barrel racers earned an average of $111,170. Along with the WPRA's accomplishments, however, have come some problems. These include the continuing financial disparity between the barrel racing circuit and the all-girl rodeos, and between men's and women's purses at the NFR, along with the lack of consistent media exposure that plagues the sport as a whole.

WPRA membership reached its zenith of 3,000 in 1975, dropped to 2,000 in 1979, and stands at approximately 1,300 today. The total prize money available to WPRA winners rose dramatically. It was $29,000 in 1949, $500,000 in 1975, and more than two million dollars by 1990.[1] Barrel racing champions earned an average of $7,500 in the sixties; $22,000 in the seventies; and $82,000 in the eighties. Since 1980, the champion has earned at least $40,000 annually. The all-time high was $152,000 earned by Charmayne James in 1986, one of two seasons in which she earned more than the second and third place finishers combined.[2]

One reason for the tremendous surge was the WPRA's decision in 1980 to demand that rodeos pay women prizes equal to those paid men. They sent an ultimatum to 650 rodeo committees across the country that if the purses were not equal by 1985, the WPRA would not participate.[3] The results were phenomenal, as the average annual winnings for the barrel racing champion jumped from $47,000 before 1985 to $118,000 during the last half of the decade. Most of the other really significant changes have also taken place since 1980, and those developments are the focus of the remainder of this chapter.

All of these events occurred amidst a rapidly changing society, and during a period some characterize as a "women's sports revolution." It is almost impossible from such a short perspective to summarize the past twenty-five years. Certainly the Vietnam war, America's longest and most acrimonious, is a key factor in the sixties and seventies. Memorable for a different reason is the Watergate break-in and its aftermath. During the same time, science and technology finally put a man on the moon and an artificial heart into a man. Financial matters got top billing in the "go-go eighties," as Americans tried to have it all. Before the decade ended, many of the financial wizards and golden boys were behind bars, and many formerly prosperous economies were in deep trouble. The end of the booming eighties and the beginning of the nineties paralleled unforgettable change abroad. The fall of the Berlin wall and the collapse of Soviet communism signaled the end of the cold war, a change whose global impact is only beginning to be felt.

The introduction of personal computers was a major technological triumph of the eighties, and helped hasten computerization of all aspects of life from education to banking to cooking. Today, few Americans can avoid interacting with computers on some level, even though the machines have yet to penetrate more than 28 percent of American homes. Another technological breakthrough, cable television, grew phenomenally during the same period, reaching almost 60 percent of American homes by 1991.[4] Cable had many benefits, not the least of which was presenting sports previously absent from the screen, thereby providing promoters, governing agencies, and athletes with new revenue. Rodeo was one of the beneficiaries. The Entertainment and Sports Network (ESPN) shows the men's NFR, while the Nashville Network (TNN) telecasts PWRA finals. Both networks have more than fifty million subscribers.[5]

During these decades, American women enjoyed considerable progress in business, industry, government, and education, while continually reaching the so-called glass ceiling that kept most from the top administrative positions. Women's salaries remained no better than 70 percent of men's nationwide, and females remained disproportionately represented at the lowest socioeconomic levels and pay ranks. One visible area of significant progress for females was sport. While the best-known athlete of the sixties and seventies was unquestionably heavyweight boxer Muhammad Ali, tennis player Billie Jean King was close behind. Both earned their place in history as sports champions, but their other activities raised them above the level of mere sports heros.

The federal government indicted Ali for draft evasion when he refused induction into the army as a conscientious objector. He lost his titles and his licence to fight, but eventually won both back. In the process he became "a focal point of the massive social and cultural unrest of the 1960s."[6] King led the battle for "open" tennis: allowing professional players to compete in important events like Wimbledon and the U.S. Open. Soon after winning that battle in 1968, she began the struggle to obtain equal prizes for females. Her efforts led to the formation of the Virginia Slims Professional Tour for women, but most importantly to her landmark "Battle of the Sexes" match against Bobby Riggs at the Houston Astrodome. Before a record crowd on September 20, 1973, King defeated Riggs. She collected $100,000 and became a major figure in the fight for sports equity for American women, and a key figure in the revived feminist movement.[7] She created the Women's Sports Foundation and started a women's sports magazine while maintaining her position as the premier woman tennis player in the world.[8] That same year, Robyn Smith became the first female jockey to win a stakes race; Little League baseball opened its doors to women the following year.[9]

King's triumph came at a time when women's equality attracted considerable government attention. In 1972 the Senate passed the Equal Rights Amendment (ERA) and sent it to the states for ratification.[10] Congress also passed Title IX of the Educational Amendments of 1972, which read in part: "No person in the United States shall on the basis of sex be excluded from participation in, be denied the benefits of, or be subjected to discrimination under any education program or activity receiving Federal financial assistance."[11]

The law, which took effect in 1975, affected sixteen thousand public school systems and twenty-seven hundred colleges and universities. Although it covered every aspect of the educational process, the greatest publicity focused on athletics, which quickly became a battleground. The NCAA fought Title IX with all of its resources, but failed to stem the tide. The results were nothing short of a revolution.

For once, physical educators were ready for the sweeping changes. The DGWS, one of the physical education groups that had opposed women's varsity competition for decades, began sanctioning a few national cham-

pionships for college women in 1967, and in 1971 established a new organization, the Association for Intercollegiate Athletics for Women (AIAW).
Thus as Title IX took effect, a governing agency already existed, and wom-
en first received athletic scholarships in 1973. The AIAW grew rapidly in
the ensuing years, as member schools increased from 280 to 790 in just
eight years. Threatened by this entity, the NCAA in 1981 began offering
its own national championships for women, along with financial incentives
the AIAW could not afford to provide. By 1982, the AIAW ceased to exist,
and women's intercollegiate sports came under the jurisdiction of the
male-dominated NCAA and its smaller counterpart, the National Association of Intercollegiate Athletics (NAIA).[12]

The WPRA's rise began later, but cowgirls too have paid a price for being part of a traditionally male activity. One of the few rodeos that refuses
to comply with their equal funding ultimatum is the NFR, which still pays
women only half as much as men.[13] One reason that the NFR refuses to
award equal prizes to women is that it is run directly by the PRCA, which
in turn maintains that women are merely guests and not full participants.
The cowboys assert that without the women, they would have more money to split among themselves and hope the women "don't make too much
trouble and get our membership upset about this."[14] The women contend
that they deserve equal money, since their travel expenses are equal to if
not greater than those of cowboys, they must wear more expensive costumes than the men, and barrel racing is the second most popular event
in rodeo, behind only bull riding.[15] Though they took a hard line, women
were not shut out of the NFR. Since 1985 Purina Mills has underwritten
the barrel racing purse at the NFR, thereby bringing it into compliance.
Thanks to their sponsorship, cowgirls have been able to abide by their
ultimatum and still compete in the world's richest rodeo. This solution was
a result of the WPRA's popularity, as well as their constant efforts toward
public relations and good rapport with their sponsors.[16]

The Purina contribution brings the WPRA barely into compliance.
While enabling the cowgirls to compete in the NFR and have access to
the many prizes and benefits, it still exacerbates the inequity between
cowboys and cowgirls. At the end of the regular 1991 season, two women
were among the top ten money winners in all of rodeo. After the NFR,
only one woman, Charmayne James Rodman, was even in the top fifteen,
and she was last on that list.[17]

Still, rodeo and tennis are the only professional sports where women
have come close to equity, where female champions have reached the top

of the money lists and remained in close contention. In 1990, tennis player Steffi Graf won $1,921,853, to $1,995,901 for Stefan Edberg.[18] The
reason for women's success in rodeo and tennis is in part the fact that in
both sports they have demanded equity. However, equally helpful is the
fact that in those two sports, unlike almost all others, men and women
compete together at the same tournaments, before the same audiences
and under the auspices of the same producers. Due to their totally different circumstances, female golfers have made minimal progress toward
equity. In 1990, the top woman golfer won only 70 percent as much as the
top male.[19] Title IX has yet to erase the differences at the intercollegiate
level. A 1991 NCAA survey found that even though women now make up
almost half of the student body at most universities, athletic departments
spend twice as much on men's scholarships and three times as much on
men's operating expenses as they do on women's programs. Moreover, the
average coaching salary was $71,511 for males and $39,177 for females.[20]

Women's progress in the Olympics has been quite significant in recent
years. In the 1968 Summer Games, only 14 percent of the competitors
were female. In 1988, that percentage rose to 26.[21] The number of events
for women increased from 22 percent in 1968 to 34 percent in 1992.
American women improved greatly in their Olympic efforts as a result of
Title IX and the opportunities for coaching and scholarships that it provided. Women contributed only 9 percent of America's gold medals in
1976, while they won 33 percent of the gold at the 1988 Olympics. Wom-
en won all five of the U.S.'s gold medals at the 1992 Olympic Winter
Games, as well as nine of the eleven total medals collected by the United
States. Cowgirls got into the Olympics in 1988 when the sponsors of the
Winter Games at Calgary scheduled a rodeo as a demonstration event.
Two teams, representing the United States and Canada, competed in the
popular event and won Olympic medals for their efforts. The series was
such a hit that it has continued as the annual Wrangler Showdown, sponsored by Wrangler Jeans.

The Showdown is only one of the opportunities open to WPRA members. They have many more options than their predecessors, thanks to the
innovative leadership of recent years. In addition to competing nationally, barrel racers have the alternative of participating in the circuit system
or the divisional tour championship. The circuit system, which parallels a
similar PRCA program, divides the country into twelve regional competitive circuits. "Contestants can compete within their circuit not only for
prize money, sport and prestige, but also for a circuit championship."[22]

Cowgirls earn points toward the circuit championship only when competing within their home circuit. Each self-governing circuit then holds its own finals rodeo, with winners advancing to the Dodge National Circuit Finals Rodeo (DNCFR), along with the regular season champs from each circuit. The 1991 DNCFR had a total purse of $200,000.[23]

The primary goal of the circuit system is to provide competitive and championship opportunities for WPRA members "whose vocational or family commitments rule out the possibility of a world title. . . . They limit their travel to their circuit or region." Even though they do not travel from coast to coast, these individuals have the opportunity to compete in the same rodeos with world champions.[24] This happens because competing for the circuit title does not preclude a qualifying athlete's participation in the NFR. Many men and women participate in as many home circuit events as possible and also tour the nation in an effort to reach the National Finals. Since 1983, approximately one-third of circuit barrel racing champions were full time professionals who won enough to qualify for the NFR as well as the DNCFR. The most successful were Marlene Eddleman, a nine-time NFR participant and 1983 world champion who also won the Mountain States circuit championship from 1986 to 1989; Rose Webb, who won the Sierra circuit title in 1985, 1987, 1988, and 1990, qualifying for the NFR in all of those years; and Charmayne James Rodman who won four championships on two different circuits during years she took the world's championship. Kelly Fletcher, 1990 DNCFR barrel racing champion, collected approximately $5,000 in prizes and bonuses. She also qualified for the NFR, bringing her total earnings to more than $32,000.[25]

The newest WPRA program is the divisional tour championship, introduced in 1989 so that the WPRA could approve barrel races held at events other than PRCA rodeos. Participants accumulate points in the same manner as in the circuit system, and this "enables WPRA members who compete at the pro level, but do not haul to rodeos to strive toward a championship."[26] Divisional tour championships are available in circuits offering ten or more approved events annually. Currently, the Wrangler divisional tour finals take place during the women's NFR.[27]

An example of the monetary awards available in nonrodeo competition became quite evident in June of 1990. Three WPRA members took home $160,000, or 47 percent of the total purse at the thirteenth annual Old Fort Days Futurity and Derby at Fort Smith, Arkansas. Betty Roper's check for $54,282 was the largest ever paid a barrel racer on a single run, and still only part of the $61,064 she collected at Fort Smith.[28] It was also more than she ever earned on the PRCA barrel racing circuit. In 1987, her best year on that tour, Roper finished fifth with $39,451.[29]

Yet another championship opportunity awaits WPRA members forty years old and older: Senior Pro Rodeo and the National Senior Pro Rodeo Finals, sponsored by the National Old Timers Rodeo Association (NOTRA) of Roundup, Montana. In 1991, WPRA member Wanda Cagliari made rodeo history. Her combined winnings in team roping, ribbon roping, and barrel racing made her the top money winner in Senior Pro Rodeo. She thereby became the first woman to take their all-around championship. Wanda competed in thirty rodeos in 1991. She won $10,000, as well as the championship saddle and buckle. Her achievement appeared in several national publications.[30] No stranger to championship competition or big-time rodeo, Wanda was the WPRA 1980 rookie of the year, 1981 NFR qualifier, as well as a contract trick rider.[31] Wanda was one of three women competing in both roping and riding at the senior finals rodeo. Approximately one-third of the barrel racers competing at the senior finals were WPRA members, while none of the women who competed exclusively in roping belonged.

Of course, the big money still goes to the top barrel racers on the PRCA tour. During the past five years, the average combined winnings for the top five women was $359,355. In a classic case of the rich getting richer, women like Rodman and Eddleman who finish atop the money lists, both overall and at selected rodeos that comprise circuits underwritten by corporate sponsors, earn additional bonuses at year's end. Sponsors include Sharp Electronics, Wrangler Jeans, Coors Beer, Dodge Trucks, Purina Mills, and Copenhagen/Skoal. Most are part of series that also include all of the sanctioned PRCA events. However, Wrangler recently introduced a special Wrangler Jeans Pro Barrel Racing Tour with no PRCA equivalent. Women accumulate points at PRCA rodeos selected for that purpose by WPRA directors, and successful athletes' bonuses can exceed $60,000.[32]

Another benefit women have attained through their close relationship with the PRCA is participation in the computerized entry system known as PROCOM. This enables any member of PRCA or WPRA to enter by phone any sanctioned rodeo. In addition, two participants may elect to "buddy" their entries, so both will be assigned to the same day or go-round. Normally buddies must compete in the same events, but husbands

Jimmie Gibbs Munroe, WPRA president since 1978, competing in a barrel race. Photo by Bern Gregory, Black Jack, Missouri.

and wives are also allowed to buddy, which is of course a great advantage to their schedules and expenses.[33]

Even though their earnings have increased dramatically, today's cowgirls still have much in common with their predecessors. Eighty-four percent live in the western states where rodeo originated, more than half of them on ranches. A random sample of 1992 WPRA members found that more than half had at least one relative in rodeo. Almost half are also married, and 90 percent of their husbands are rodeo cowboys. Seventeen percent are divorced.[34] Unlike their predecessors, almost all present-day WPRA members are either high school students or high school graduates. Over one-third attended college.[35] Still, the lives and achievements of current WPRA leaders and champions show many parallels to those of their predecessors from the nineteenth century to the present.

Much of the credit for the tremendous progress in prize money, sponsorship, and publicity must go to Jimmie Gibbs Munroe, WPRA president since 1978. Wife of PRCA champion saddle bronc rider Bud Munroe, she is the granddaughter of Colonel Zack Miller, cofounder of the legendary

101 Ranch Wild West. She grew up around cattle and horses, and competed in Junior Rodeo while in high school. She was active in Intercollegiate Rodeo while earning a degree in education from Sam Houston State University, and served two years on the board of directors of the National Intercollegiate Rodeo Association (NIRA).[36]

She joined the WPRA in 1973, competing in barrel racing, calf roping, and steer undecorating. She qualified for eleven NFRs, and won three national titles between 1974 and 1986. In 1975 Jimmie was the last cowgirl to win the all-around and barrel racing titles in the same year, as she also took the GRA tie-down title. She served the WPRA as all-girl rodeo director for two years before assuming the presidency. Her background in both barrel racing and all-girl rodeos, as well as her NIRA experience, made her uniquely qualified to accept that challenge.[37]

According to Munroe, the major achievements of the WPRA under her leadership have been electric timers, additional sponsors, and equal money. The sponsors "give a large number of contestants an opportunity to reap their benefits throughout the year, . . . [and] . . . bonus money awarded to the year-end winners by the sponsors has been terrific."[38]

Also important to the WPRA have been Lydia Moore, executive secretary since 1973, and Pam Minick, a rodeo sports commentator, team roper, and former Miss Rodeo America, who has been first vice president since 1983. Her contributions in the area of public relations are invaluable. Minick began competing in 4-H activities as a youngster, and won the Nevada barrel racing title while still in high school. The versatile Minick also won the PWRA breakaway calf roping title in 1982, and now concentrates on team roping, both in PWRA and charity events.[39]

The first woman to earn a PRCA announcer's card, Minick has done both films and commercials, and is a hostess/commentator on weekly rodeo series on ESPN and TNN. Her addition as commentator for the women's events at the NFR was a welcome change, as female announcers for women's sports events remain a rarity. She does an excellent job of promoting and explaining the various WPRA and PWRA programs. She and her husband, a former PRCA bull rider and stock contractor, live near Fort Worth, Texas, where she handles the advertising for his business establishment.[40]

WPRA executive secretary Lydia Moore came to her position with a strong rodeo background. Her father was a saddle bronc rider and member of the CTA while her mother was a Hall of Fame circus equestrienne. As a child, Lydia performed at rodeos with the family's trick roping and riding contract act. Once they settled down in St. Louis, she began competing in flag and barrel racing, and helped form the Missouri chapter of the GRA. She finished among the top fifteen in 1972, collecting more than $25,000 in awards and bonuses, while working full time. For her, the WPRA position was a dream come true.[41] Munroe summed up Moore's contributions to the organization on the occasion of her receiving the 1991 WPRA/Coca-Cola Woman of the Year Award: "When Lydia took over as secretary-treasurer she received the records of the association in a box— a cardboard box. So when we say we've grown from a shoe box operation to a strong association of organized women we mean it literally and Lydia has been a vital part of that growth. There were 400 members and 100 approvals at the time she assumed the duties. . . . Now we have 2,000 members and over 700 approvals."[42]

While these three women have provided the leadership, Charmayne James Rodman has been the premier athlete and superstar. She burst on the scene as a fourteen-year-old rookie in 1984, winning the Rookie of the Year title and both WPRA and NFR barrel racing championships. Raised on a small feedlot and farming operation near Clayton, New Mexico, Charmayne showed her equestrian skills by age four. She could defeat women twice her age at barrel racing by the time she was eleven. Charmayne showed unique abilities with horses at an early age as well. She has won all of her titles on Scamper, a horse she bought at a feedlot for $1,200, and trained herself.[43] She also mastered breakaway roping, but decided to focus on barrel racing and became a full-time professional at age thirteen. Loving the competition and the tour, she finished high school through correspondence courses.[44]

Charmayne has earned nine consecutive world titles, and more than twenty-five sponsor's championships. In 1987, she was the leading money winner in all of rodeo, thus becoming the first woman to wear the prestigious #1 in the NFR. In 1988 she finished the NFR with $130,540 in official prize money. Her winnings surpassed even those of the all-around cowboy, who won $121,546 competing in two events.[45] In 1990, she was the first athlete in the sport to reach the $100,000 mark, finally winning her crown with $130,328, including $44,251 in NFR money.[46]

On November 6, 1988, Charmayne married PRCA team roper Walt Rodman, and now lives in Galt, California. Since her marriage she has added team roping to her repertoire, first competing in that event at the Hereford, Texas, All Women's Rodeo in 1989.[47] An extraordinarily popular athlete, Rodman has played a key role in increasing the WPRA's visibility in the national media. She is by far the most successful and best-

Charmayne James Rodman, the first "million dollar cowgirl," team roping with WPRA vice president Pam Minick at the Hereford, Texas, All-Girl Rodeo. Photo by Trela Miller, Tuttle, Oklahoma.

known cowgirl of the modern era, and perhaps of all time. Her achievements have not gone unnoticed. On June 19, 1992, the National Cowgirl Hall of Fame inducted Charmayne James Rodman and Jimmie Gibbs Munroe.[48]

The lack of visibility and superstars like Charmayne has created a big problem for the struggling all-girl rodeos. Only fifteen contests occurred annually through the seventies, reaching their nadir in 1987, when only three took place.[49] That year the WPRA established the Professional Women's Rodeo Association (PWRA), a separate division for all-women's events, and elected Betty Gayle Cooper the first director. Cooper, the holder of eight PWRA championships and member of a distinguished rodeo family, began to make some progress.[50] In 1988 the PWRA sanctioned fifty-three events, including five all-women rodeos, and awarded $128,605 in prizes, $3,000 at the finals rodeo.[51] In 1989, forty-two women collected prizes in PWRA contests. Individual earnings ranged from $14 to $5,145. By 1990, the number of all-girl rodeos had risen to ten.[52] Since 1985, Coors Light Women's National Finals Rodeo has been held at the Lazy E Arena in Guthrie, Oklahoma, and televised (delayed tape) on TNN.[53]

Sanctioned PWRA contests include bareback bronc riding, bull riding, team roping, tie down calf roping, and breakaway calf roping. There are many more ropers than riders, and they also have the advantage of more contests in which to compete.[54] Some of the women who participate in PWRA contests also compete in barrel racing, although no one has won both the all-around and the barrel racing titles in the same year since 1975.[55] Today, PWRA members make up less than 10 percent of the total WPRA membership and collect less than 1 percent of the prizes. The rest goes to barrel racers, who had more than six hundred sanctioned rodeos open to them.[56]

The barrel racers have done an excellent job of public relations, and their popular champions have been a welcome sight at the PRCA rodeos. On the other hand, the women in the PWRA contests could do a much better job of selling themselves. While sponsorship and television coverage have improved, they have a long way to go. The PWRA members have apparently chosen to ignore the importance of appearance and grooming as a public relations tool. Even on their televised finals rodeo, few wear the "dashing outfits" promised in their publicity. In fact many do not even bother to wear the western attire required by the PWRA rules, but instead compete in rugby sweaters and the like.[57] While much of the fault lies with the contestants, the PWRA leadership must share the blame for failing to

Kathy Morales, competing in the bronc riding at a PWRA all-woman rodeo in the nineties. Photo by Trela Miller, Tuttle, Oklahoma.

Betty Gayle Cooper Ratliff, former PWRA president, on her barrel racing horse. Photo courtesy of the National Cowgirl Hall of Fame and Western Heritage Center, Hereford, Texas.

enforce its own rules. They could learn a lot from the GRA founders, or even the PRCA, when it comes to the importance of image in selling your sport. Of course, feminists insist that clothing should be irrelevant in athletic performance, and that the cowgirls should be judged solely on their skills. Unfortunately, as long as athletes must depend on sponsors and television to provide their prize money, they will have to take appearances into account. There are few professional sports today, male or female, that don't maintain and enforce some kind of dress code.

Another move that would greatly help the PWRA would be including barrel races at more all-women rodeos. While a barrel race is now held at the all-women's finals rodeo, the regular presence of nationally known stars like Charmayne James Rodman, Marlene Eddleman, and Martha Josey would be extremely beneficial. These women would bring additional publicity and credibility to the contests, both of which would be a big help to the sport and the other contestants. Of course that would not solve all the problems facing all-women rodeos. While women still have ample opportunities to compete in a variety of roping events in high school, college, and senior rodeo, as well as PWRA-sanctioned jackpots and the like, the PWRA is about the only organization sanctioning bronc and bull riding for women. Opportunities for women to learn and perfect their skills in these rough stock events continue to diminish. Today, with the low prize money, there is little incentive for newcomers to take up the activities, while the limited number of participants makes it difficult to find sponsors and increase prizes. It remains to be seen if a solution exists for this dilemma, or the contests will die for lack of interest. Perhaps Paula Sage, newly elected (1992) PWRA director, will be able to build on Cooper's achievements and move the division into a more lucrative era.

On the barrel racing circuit the issues remain whether women will continue to be welcome in the NFR and whether their official prize money will eventually catch up to the men's. For despite the success of the WPRA, the cowgirls are, in the end, totally dependent on the PRCA for their presence in the big time and at the NFR. Should the cowboys decide to add team roping to their premier event, the women would probably be out. Although that seems unlikely given the popularity of barrel racing, anything can happen. On the other hand, PWRA's attempt to have more women's contests added to standard rodeos is constantly thwarted by the widespread belief that rodeos are too long already. Consequently, the growing number of PWRA team roping events at PRCA rodeos is an achievement in itself.

The women faced a new challenge in 1990, when a cowboy sued for the

right to compete in WPRA barrel races because no similar contests existed for males on the PRCA circuit. Perhaps the most important date in the
WPRA's recent history was June 29, 1990, when Judge Pasco M. Bowman
of the United States Court of Appeals for the Eighth Circuit ruled that the
"WPRA may remain an all female organization." In his ruling the judge
stated that the WPRA was exempt from the law under question (Title VII
of the Civil Rights Act of 1964) because they had fewer than fifteen employees. He also ruled that being female was a bona fide occupational
qualification for competing in women's professional rodeo, just as it would
be for competing in women's golf or tennis.[58] The *Women's Pro Rodeo
News* concluded their article on the lawsuit by stating: "This has always
been the position of the WPRA. It is hoped that this decision will terminate this expensive and lengthy litigation and deter other men from attempting to compete against women in the WPRA."[59]

The WPRA appears to be free from this threat, and financially secure
thanks to fees paid annually by sanctioned rodeos. Consequently, it is in a
stronger position than any of the previous agencies that attempted to organize and conduct sports competition by and for women. The Women's
World Games (formerly women's Olympics) ceased to operate soon after
International Olympic Games added women's track and field, and it took
women nearly forty years to achieve the same number of contests in the
latter that they had in the former. As mentioned above, the all-woman
AIAW lasted only ten years before the NCAA forced it out of business by
luring away most of the membership with financial incentives it could not
match. So far, the WPRA has managed to maintain its independence.
Because of that, cowgirls have choices that women in many other sports
have lost. Whether cowgirls want to compete for hundreds of dollars in
bronc and bull riding, thousands of dollars in roping, or hundreds of thousands of dollars in barrel racing, the WPRA is there for them! Certainly, it
would not be available to the PWRA women if not for the income and
publicity generated by the barrel racing circuit. That is hardly different
from the situation in intercollegiate athletics, where a few so-called revenue sports support the many nonrevenue activities of member schools.

This may explain the members' loyalty. The 1992 WPRA still includes
fourteen women who joined before 1960. Among them are two GRA
charter members, Billie McBride and Wanda Harper Bush. Substantial
publicity went recently to Sherry Johnson, who joined the GRA in 1957,
and won the world championship in barrel racing in 1962. Thirty years
later, fifty-three-year-old Johnson finished in the top fifteen to earn her
eleventh trip to the NFR, her first since 1972. She was the oldest female

contestant, with fifteen-year-old Angie Meadors the youngest.[60] Meadors had a better NFR, but Johnson reaped plenty of publicity, sharing the spotlight with steer wrestler Roy Duvall, competing in his twenty-third NFR.[61]

Several superstars from past generations lived to see the progress and triumphs of recent decades as they were inducted into the National Cowgirl Hall of Fame and the National Rodeo Hall of Fame. Fannie Sperry Steele, who died in 1983 at age ninety-five, rode horseback until she was eighty-seven years old.[62] Bertha Blancett and Vera McGinnis also lived into their nineties. Although she was unable to attend her induction ceremonies, Vera donated many trophies to both halls of fame before she died. Tad Lucas died February 23, 1990, at age eighty-seven, having spent many years on the board of directors of the Rodeo Historical Society and attended many Hall of Fame functions.[63] Margie and Alice Greenough are active in their eighties, still performing in western films and television programs, and attending Hall of Fame inductions and National Finals Rodeos.[64] Jackie Worthington and Thena Mae Farr lived to enjoy their inductions into the National Cowgirl Hall of Fame, but died soon thereafter, Farr in 1985 and Worthington two years later. Nancy Binford, Dude Barton, and Dixie Mosley still live in west Texas, where Binford and Barton are ranchers. All three are active in the affairs of the National Cowgirl Hall of Fame, and maintain the close ties developed during their years in the GRA.[65]

One of their colleagues is still in the WPRA, still winning barrel races and headlines. Wanda Harper Bush, a GRA charter member, maintains an active interest in competing long after most of her peers have retired. After earning early recognition as a roper, Wanda gradually began focusing her attention exclusively on barrel racing, and qualified for the NFR eight times. She also became a teacher and horse trainer, while holding a variety of GRA offices.[66] Her most recent triumph came in 1992. Following back surgery and a year's layoff, Wanda climbed back in the saddle to collect the biggest purse in a career that has spanned five decades. On March 23, she won $28,577.88 at the Old Fort Futurity Days at Fort Smith, Arkansas.[67] Had she been competing in a sanctioned rodeo, that single day's winnings would have put her second on the 1992 money list behind Charmayne James Rodman.[68]

Cowgirls have faced a variety of challenges through the years and have overcome many obstacles in their efforts to succeed as professional athletes. Today, they earn more money than ever before in the history of the sport, and are featured at the top rodeos in North America. Yet they have lost the one thing that made them exceptional among all female athletes in American history, the ability to compete as equals with men in otherwise all-male contests. Whether that is even the goal of 1990s cowgirls is open to question, for women have never agreed on what would be the best of both worlds in sport. Some want gender-appropriate contests for men and for women in the same big events, some aspire for separate but equal events, others aim for total equality: one set of contests open to all regardless of gender. Cowgirls are the only female athletes to have experienced all three, making their story a singular chapter in the history of women's sports. Most important to that chapter is the WPRA, which has maintained its unique status among sports governing agencies. It remains as it has always been, an organization of women, governed entirely by women, and designed to meet the distinctive needs, interests, and abilities of women. Surely that is the secret to its success, and its hope for the future. One admiring reporter summed up the organization's achievements this way: "the ladies have 'sold' their contest, their professionalism, their association, and themselves."[69]

Appendix

Table A.1

Women's Participation in Professional Rodeo, 1882–1955

Event	Total Group		Careers-3 years or more		Career-less than 3 years	
	number of women	percent	number of women	percent	number of women	percent
	607	100	218	36	389	64
Bronc Riding	183	30	112	51	71	18
Trick Riding	92	15	85	39	7	<1
Racing Relay	268	44	80	37	188	48
Roping	121	20	72	33	49	13
Barrel Racing	100	16	42	19	58	15
Bull Riding	33	5	16	7	17	4
Cutting	30	5	16	7	14	4
Steer Riding	47	8	37	17	10	3
Flag Racing	55	9	26	12	29	7
Average Career	5.0 years	—	12.0 years	—	1.1 years	—
Average Number of Events	1.53	—	2.25	—	1.1	—
Performer as well as Contestant	152	25	133	61	19	5

Table A.2

Women's Participation in Professional Rodeo through 1912

Event	Total Group		Careers-3 years or more		Career-less than 3 years	
	number of women	percent	number of women	percent	number of women	percent
	39	100	27	69	12	31
Bronc Riding	21	54	18	67	3	25
Trick Riding	13	33	12	44	1	8
Racing Relay	22	56	14	52	8	66
Roping	18	46	14	52	4	33
Barrel Racing	0	0	0	0	0	0
Bull Riding	0	0	0	0	0	0
Cutting	0	0	0	0	0	0
Steer Riding	3	8	3	11	0	0
Flag Racing	0	0	0	0	0	0
Average Career	14 years	—	19 years	—	1.2 years	—
Average Number of Events	2	—	2.3	—	1.3	—
Performer as well as Contestant	23	59	23	85	0	0
Wild West	19	49	19	70	0	0

Table A.3

Women's Participation in Professional Rodeo through 1919

Event	Total Group		Careers-3 years or more		Career-less than 3 years	
	number of women	percent	number of women	percent	number of women	percent
	145	100	62	43	83	57
Bronc Riding	66	46	43	69	23	28
Trick Riding	43	23	40	65	3	4
Racing Relay	91	63	36	58	55	66
Roping	32	22	19	31	13	16
Barrel Racing	0	0	0	0	0	0
Bull Riding	0	0	0	0	0	0
Cutting	0	0	0	0	0	0
Steer Riding	12	8	11	18	1	1
Flag Racing	0	0	0	0	0	0
Average Career	7 years	—	15 years	—	1.2 years	—
Average Number of Events	1.6	—	2.2	—	1.1	—
Performer as well as Contestant	56	39	47	76	9	11
Wild West	40	28	35	56	5	6

Table A.4

Women's Participation in Professional Rodeo, 1920–36

Event	Total Group		Careers-3 years or more		Career-less than 3 years	
	number of women	percent	number of women	percent	number of women	percent
	265	100	136	51	129	49
Bronc Riding	108	41	89	65	19	15
Trick Riding	77	29	74	54	3	2
Racing Relay	168	63	66	49	102	79
Roping	52	20	43	32	9	7
Barrel Racing	6	2	6	4	0	0
Bull Riding	6	2	6	4	0	0
Cutting	2	<1	2	1	0	0
Steer Riding	38	14	32	24	6	5
Flag Racing	5	2	5	4	0	0
Average Career	7.7 years	—	14 years	—	1.1 years	—
Average Number of Events	1.7	—	2.4	—	1.1	—
Performer as well as Contestant	108	41	104	76	4	3

Table A.5

Women's Participation in Professional Rodeo, 1931–47

Event	Total Group		Careers-3 years or more		Career-less than 3 years	
	number of women	percent	number of women	percent	number of women	percent
	262	100	137	52	125	48
Bronc Riding	96	37	76	55	20	16
Trick Riding	67	26	66	49	1	<1
Racing Relay	113	43	51	37	62	50
Roping	70	27	54	39	16	13
Barrel Racing	39	15	28	20	11	9
Bull Riding	12	5	9	7	3	2
Cutting	17	6	13	9	4	3
Steer Riding	37	14	30	22	7	6
Flag Racing	41	16	23	17	18	14
Average Career	8.2 years	—	15 years	—	1.1 years	—
Average Number of Events	1.9	—	2.6	—	1.1	—
Performer as well as Contestant	104	40	97	70	7	6

Table A.6

Women's Participation in Professional Rodeo, 1947–55

	Total Group		Careers-3 years or more		Career-less than 3 years	
Event	number of women	percent	number of women	percent	number of women	percent
	166	100	63	37	103	62
Bronc Riding	40	24	21	33	19	16
Trick Riding	12	7	11	17	1	0
Racing Relay	5	3	5	8	0	0
Roping	47	29	30	48	17	16
Barrel Racing	86	52	39	62	47	46
Bull Riding	29	17	14	22	15	14
Cutting	27	16	16	25	11	11
Steer Riding	7	4	7	11	0	0
Flag Racing	37	22	22	35	15	14
Average Career	6.1 years	—	14 years	—	1.1 years	—
Average Number of Events	1.8	—	2.6	—	1.2	—
Performer as well as Contestant	23	14	21	33	2	2

Table A.7

Cowgirl Champions at Madison Square Garden

Year	Bronc Riding			Trick Riding		
	Winner	Prize	Purse	Winner	Prize	Purse
1922	Bonnie McCarroll	$400		Bonnie Gray and Mabel Strickland tie	$350 ea	$1000
1923	Rose Smith	$875	$3175	Mabel Strickland	$800	$2200
1924	Reine Shelton	$125+		Mabel Strickland		
1925	No Madison Square Garden Rodeo					
1926	Grace Runyon	$700+	$2800	Tad Lucas	$600	$3000
1927	Marie Gibson	$600	$2000	Florence Randolph	$900+	
1928	Brida Miller	$600+		Tad Lucas	$900	$1700
1929	Bea Kirnan	mount money only		Tad Lucas	$700	$2000
1930	not available			Tad Lucas	$650	$1700
1931	Marie Gibson	$200+	$2300	Tad Lucas	$1100	$3000
1932	Ruth Roach	$526	$2300	not held		
1933	Rose Davis	$570	$2775	Florence Randolph	saddle/ trophy	
1934	Vaughn Krieg	$615	$2775	Betty Myres	$750	$2500
1935	Rose Davis	$557	$2775			
1936	Ruth Wood	$450+	$2775			
1937	Brida Gafford	$449	$2775			
1938	Vivian White	$595	$3475			
1939	Mildred Mix Horner	$715	$3650			
1940	Alice Greenough	not available				
1941	Vivian White	not available				
Average		$560	$2763		$750	$2300

+incomplete data

Table A.8

Rodeo Cowgirl Honorees in the National Cowgirl Hall of Fame and
Western Heritage Center, Hereford, Texas

Honoree	Induction	Honoree	Induction
Alice **Adams** Holden	1983	Mary Williams **Parks**	1979
Ann Lee Aldred	1983	Ruth Parton	1988
Blanche **Altizer** Smith	1976	Sue Pirtle	1981
Mary Ellen "Dude" Barton	1984	Jerry Ann **Portwood** Taylor	1986
Nancy Binford	1979	Dixie Lee **Reger** Mosley	1982
Faye Hudson **Blackstone**	1982	Lucyle Garmes	
Shelly **Burmeister**	1990	(Roberts) Richards	1987
Wanda Harper Bush	1978	Ruth **Roach** Salmon	1989
Betty Gayle **Cooper** Ratliff	1987	Margie **Roberts** Hart	1987
Gene Krieg Creed	1982	Charmayne James Rodman	1992
Bernice Hoppe **Dean**	1986	Fern Sawyer	1976
Mildred **Douglas** Chrisman	1988	Rhonda Coy Sedgwick	1977
Jewel Frost **Duncan**	1976	Mike Reid Settle	1977
Thena Mae **Farr**	1985	Reine Hafley **Shelton**	1983
Flaxie Fletcher	1983	Nancy Kelly Sheppard	1991
Mamie **Francis** Hafley	1981	Lorraine Graham Shoultz	1981
Ruby Gobble	1982	Betty Sims Solt	1990
Bonnie Jean **Gray** Harris	1981	Fannie **Sperry Steele**	1978
Alice **Greenough** Orr	1975	Mabel **Stickland** Woodward	1992
Margie **Greenough** Henson	1978	Sissy Thurman	1975
Juanita **Hackett** Howell	1986	Karen Womack Vold	1978
Faye **Johnson** Blesing	1978	Dora Rhoads Waldrop	1979
Lynn Jonckowski	1991	Joan Wells	1989
Martha Arthur **Josey**	1985	Vivian **White** Dillard	1985
Kathy Kennedy	1984	Jackie Worthington	1975
Vaughn **Krieg** Husky	1989	Sydna **Yokley** Woodyard	1977
Ann Lewis	1981	Isora DeRacy **Young**	1979
Tad Barnes **Lucas**	1978		
Billie Hinson **McBride**	1981		
Vera **McGinnis** Farra	1979		
Goldia Fields **Malone**	1981		
Margaret Elizabeth			
Owens Montgomery	1976		
Lucille Mulhall	1977		
Jimmie Gibbs Munroe	1992		
Ollie Osborn	1982		

Most prominent professional name in bold
type when more than one last name is listed.
Where women used several different names,
none is emphasized.

Information provided by the National
Cowgirl Hall of Fame and Western Heritage
Center, Hereford, Texas.

Table A.9

Rodeo Cowgirl Honorees in the National Rodeo Hall of Fame at the National Cowboy Hall of Fame, Oklahoma City, Oklahoma

Honoree	Induction Year
Bertha Kapernick **Blancett**	1975
Ava Colburn	1987
Bernice **Dossey** Bolen	1991
Alice **Greenough** Orr	1983
Margie **Greenough** Henson	1983
Eloise "Fox" **Hastings** Wilson	1987
Tad Barnes **Lucas**	1968
Vera **McGinnis** Farra	1985
Lucille **Mulhall**	1975
Florence Hughes **Randolph**	1968
Ruth **Roach** Salmon	1990
Maggie Rowell	1985
Fern Sawyer	1991
Reine Hafley **Shelton**	1991
Fannie **Sperry Steele**	1975
Mabel **Strickland** Woodward	1981
Vivian **White** Dillard	1991

Most prominent professional name in bold type when more than one last name is listed. Where women used several different names, none is emphasized.

Information provided by the Rodeo Historical Society, National Cowboy Hall of Fame, Oklahoma City, Oklahoma.

Tad Barnes Lucas is the only cowgirl honored by the ProRodeo Hall of Fame and Museum of the American Cowboy at Colorado Springs, Colorado.

Notes

Abbreviations

NRHOF   National Rodeo Hall of Fame at the National Cowboy Hall of Fame, Oklahoma City, Oklahoma.

PRHOF   ProRodeo Hall of Fame and Museum of the American Cowboy, Colorado Springs, Colorado.

CGHOF   National Cowgirl Hall of Fame and Western Heritage Center, Hereford, Texas.

Glenbow   Glenbow Museum and Archives, Calgary, Alberta, Canada.

BBD   *The Billboard*

CBBD   "The Corral," *The Billboard*

H&H   *Hoofs and Horns*

NYT   *New York Times*

LAT   *Los Angeles Times*

MFP   *Manitoba Free Press*

WT   *Winnipeg Tribune*

Introduction

1. Kenneth Springer, "Rodman Sets New World Record at Houston Wins $18,546!" *Women's Pro Rodeo News*, 1 Apr. 1992, 1.

2. Based on all of the data collected for this book, including but not limited to rodeo programs, prize lists, and day sheets, as well as scrapbooks and memorabilia, photographs, and files on individual cowgirls housed in the archives of the National Rodeo Hall of Fame at the National Cowboy Hall of Fame, Oklahoma City, Okla. (NRHOF); ProRodeo Hall of Fame and Museum of the American Cowboy, Colorado Springs, Colo. (PRHOF); National Cowgirl Hall of Fame and Western Heritage Center, Hereford, Tex. (CGHOF); and the Glenbow Museum and Archives, Calgary, Alberta, Canada (Glenbow); interviews with Mary Ellen

Barton, Hereford, Tex., 15 Mar. 1988; Nancy Binford, Hereford, Tex., 15 Mar. 1988; Alice Greenough and Marjorie Greenough, Tucson, Ariz., 19 May 1988; Tad Lucas, Fort Worth, Tex., 26 Feb. 1988; Dixie Reger Mosley, Hereford, Tex., 15 Mar. 1988 and 17 June 1989; and Isora DeRacy Young, Stephenville, Tex., 27 Feb. 1988; BBD, 1897–1944; *The Wild Bunch*, 1915–17; H&H, 1929–48; *Fort Worth Star Telegram*, Feb.–Mar. 1917–48; NYT, Oct.–Nov. 1922–48; *Chicago Tribune*, May–Nov. 1922–47.

3. Interview with Ollie Osborn, "Cowgirls of Eastern Oregon," Audio Tape HO 820630, National Public Radio, 1982.

4. Based on sources given in n. 2 above. Although the history extends through 1992, the statistics include women who were active in professional rodeo through 1955.

5. Shelly Armitage, "Rawhide Heroines," in *The American Self*, ed. Sam B. Girgus (Albuquerque: University of New Mexico Press, 1981), 169.

6. Ibid., 171.

7. See n. 2 above.

8. Publicity for the 1912 Calgary Stampede stated that Dolly Mullins was from Mexico. However, Mullins, whose maiden name was Dorothy Roberts, was born in Brooklyn, New York, in 1893. Guy Weadick Papers, M1278, B1 F34, Glenbow.

9. "1991 Top 15 Barrel Racers," *Women's Pro Rodeo News*, 1 Dec. 1991, 13.

10. Even her obituary in *The Billboard* gives only this name. ("Mrs. Ed Wright Killed," BBD, 15 Aug. 1917, n.p.)

11. For an excellent discussion of the current status of western women's history, see *Montana Magazine of Western History* 41 (Spring 1991), especially Sara Deutsch, "Coming Together, Coming Apart—Women's History in the West," 58–61, and Glenda Riley, "Western Women's History—A Look at Some of the Issues," 66–70.

12. The most recent and comprehensive book on women's sport history is Allen Guttmann's *Women's Sports: A History* (New York: Columbia University Press, 1991).

13. Other books about cowgirls include Joyce Gibson Roach, *The Cowgirls* (Denton: University of North Texas Press, 1990), and Teresa Jordon, *Cowgirls: Women of the American West* (Garden City: Anchor Books, 1984).

14. "In Praise of Cowgirls," *Texas Monthly*, Nov. 1987, 110.

Chapter One: Overview

1. William H. Goetzmann and William N. Goetzmann, *The West of the Imagination* (New York: W. W. Norton Co., 1986).

2. Mary Lou LeCompte, "The Hispanic Influence on the History of Rodeo, 1823–1932," *Journal of Sport History* 12 (Spring 1985): 21–38.

3. Ibid.; Richard W. Slatta, *Cowboys of the Americas* (New Haven: Yale University Press, 1990), chap. 8; Kristine Fredriksson, *American Rodeo* (College Station: Texas A&M University Press, 1985), 139–40.

4. Don Russell, *The Wild West* (Fort Worth: Amon Carter Museum of Western Art, 1970), 1–5.

5. Lonn Taylor and Ingrid Maar, *The American Cowboy* (Washington, D.C.: Library of Congress, 1983), 67–69.

6. Vincente Oropeza, who was Cody's "Chief of Vaqueros," billed himself as the "premier charro Mexicano" of the world. Given the opportunity, he attempted to explain the term *charro* to Anglo reporters. See for example, *San Antonio Daily Express,* 29 July 1891, 1; see also LeCompte, "Hispanic Influence on the History of Rodeo."

7. Sarah J. Blackstone, *Buckskins, Bullets, and Business: A History of Buffalo Bill's Wild West* (New York: Greenwood Press, 1986), 62.

8. Col. Bailey C. Haynes, *Bill Pickett, Bulldogger: The Biography of a Black Cowboy* (Norman: University of Oklahoma Press, 1989), 155–56.

9. Russell, *Wild West,* 31–42; Taylor and Maar, *American Cowboy,* 67–69; LeCompte, "Hispanic Influence on the History of Rodeo," 35–36.

10. James F. Hoy, "From Folk Game to Professional Sport: Early Rodeo in Kansas," *International Folklore Review,* Summer 1983, 143–51; and James F. Hoy, "Early-Day Rodeo Events," paper presented to the Western History Association, Sacramento, Calif., Oct. 1985.

11. See Intro. n. 2.

12. Milt Riske, *Those Magnificent Cowgirls* (Cheyenne: Wyoming Publishing, 1983); Willard Porter, *Who's Who in Rodeo* (Oklahoma City: Powder River, 1982), 28–29, 90–91, 126–27; Beth Day, *America's First Cowgirl* (New York: Julian Messner, 1955), 28–29, 57–58; Dee Marvine, "Fannie Sperry Wowed 'em at the First Calgary Stampede," *American West,* Aug. 1987, 30–37; Katherine Harris, "Homesteading in Northeastern Colorado, 1873–1920: Sex Roles and Women's Experience," in *The Women's West,* ed. Susan Armitage and Elizabeth Jameson (Norman: University of Oklahoma Press, 1987), 165–78; Jameson, "Women as Workers, Women as Civilizers: True Womanhood in the American West," in *Women's West,* 145–64; Virginia Rowe Terrett, "(Mrs.) Ridin', Ropin', Wranglin', Rodman," *Western Horseman,* Nov. 1949, 22, 46–48; Vera McGinnis, *Rodeo Road: My Life as a Pioneer Cowgirl* (New York: Hastings House, 1974); Fannie Sperry Steele and Helen Clark, "A Horse beneath Me Sometimes," *True West,* Feb. 1956, 8 13, 36 37, 45 46; and Jordon, *Cowgirls,* 200 235.

13. *Wyoming Tribune,* 1 Sept. 1904, 1; Robert D. Hanesworth, *Daddy of 'em All: The Story of Cheyenne Frontier Days* (Cheyenne: Flintlock, 1967), 44–48; Mary Lou LeCompte, "Wild West Frontier Days, Roundups and Stampedes: Rodeo before There Was Rodeo," *Canadian Journal of History of Sport* 12 (Dec. 1985): 54–67. From 1906 to 1946 the Denver Post Trophy went to the winner of the cowgirls relay race.

14. LeCompte, "Wild West Frontier Days," 54–67.

15. See Intro. n. 2.

16. "Rain and Cold Fail to Keep Eleven Thousand away from the Second Performance," *Calgary Daily Herald,* 4 Sept. 1912, 6.

17. LeCompte, "Wild West Frontier Days," 63–67.

18. John E. Hartwig, "Has the RAA Been a Success?" BBD, 29 Mar. 1930, 13; Tex Sherman, "Keep the Rodeo Game Clean," BBD, 19 Oct. 1929, 61.

19. "Out of the Wild West, Scorn B'way Heat," *New York World,* 1 Aug. 1916, 4; Sperry to Weadick, 8 July 1912, Weadick to Sperry, 11 July 1912, letters in the Guy Weadick Papers, M12 87, File #1, Glenbow; Liz Stiffler and Tona Blake, "Fannie Sperry-Steele: Montana's Champion Bronc Rider," *Montana Magazine*

of Western History 32 (Spring 1982): 51; Mary Lou LeCompte, "Cowgirls at the Crossroads: Women in Professional Rodeo, 1885–1922," *Canadian Journal of History of Sport* 20 (Dec. 1989): 27–48.

20. NYT, *New York Post, New York World, New York Herald,* Aug. 1916.

21. Bill King, *Rodeo Trails* (Laramie: Jelm Mountain Press, 1982), 166–79; "Cheyenne Frontier Data," *Ketch Pen,* Fall 1988, 7; Yakima Canutt, "Hinkle and Hoolihaning," *The Wild Bunch,* Nov. 1982, 11; "Early Day Record," *Ketch Pen,* Fall 1988, 9.

22. For further discussion of this situation, see Foghorn Clancy, *My Fifty Years in Rodeo* (San Antonio: Naylor Company, 1952), 185–203ff.

23. Marie Gibson to Freda Ashby, 1 May 1927, letter in the Vera McGinnis Correspondence, NRHOF.

24. Ibid.

25. CBBD, 1914–45; see, for example, 11 June 1927, 83; 30 May 1936, 39.

26. CBBD, 1914–45.

27. H&H, 1934–36, see esp. "Chuck Wagon Chatter" by Tex Sherman, and "Eastern Rodeo Chat" by Herbert S. Maddy.

28. *The Wild Bunch,* 1916, 1917; Kathryn B. Stansbury, *Lucille Mulhall* (privately published, 1985), 109–14.

29. Tom B. Saunders, "How the Word Rodeo Originated as Applied to Western Events," *Quarter Horse Journal,* June 1968, 31–32.

30. Mosley interview, 1989; H&H, 1929–48.

31. Roach, *Cowgirls,* sect. 2.

32. Ibid., 197–99. A former cowgirl who demanded anonymity, and is called Pearl Mason in the book, is the most outspoken and bitter. Since her name and identity are concealed, it is impossible to even attempt to ascertain the true nature of her anger and the validity of her claims.

33. Edna L. Shaw, "Rodeo Managers Form Association," BBD, 16 Feb. 1929, 65.

34. Mosley interview, 1989.

35. Shaw, "Managers Form Association," 65; "Rules Governing Contests Approved by the Rodeo Association of America," BBD, 13 Apr. 1929, 57–58; "Rodeo Association of America Issues Certificates of Award under New Rules," BBD, 6 Apr. 1929, 65; Fredriksson, *American Rodeo,* 22.

36. Fredriksson, *American Rodeo,* 36–52ff.

37. Ibid., 79–88.

38. Minutes of the PRCA and National Finals Rodeo Committee, PRHOF.

39. H&H and BBD, 1939–45.

40. Interviews with Binford, Barton, and Mosley, 1988; *WPRA/PWRA Official Reference Guide,* vols. 7 and 8 (Blanchard: Women's Professional Rodeo Association, 1990, 1991).

41. *The Wilson Report: Moms, Dads, Daughters and Sports* (River Grove, Ill.: Wilson Sporting Goods, 1988).

42. Uriel Simri, *Women at the Olympic Games* (Netanya, Israel: Wingate Institute, 1979), 12.

43. Mary A. Boutilier and Lucinda SanGiovanni, *The Sporting Woman* (Champaign: Human Kinetics, 1983), 23–47; Donald J. Mrozek, "Sexual Fears of Wom-

en as Athletes," in J. A. Mangan and Roberta J. Park, *From Fair Sex to Feminism* (London: Frank Cass, 1987), 282–98; Ellen W. Gerber et al., *The American Woman in Sport* (Reading: Addison Wesley, 1974), 3–273; Timothy J. Curry and Robert M. Jiobu, *Sports: A Social Perspective* (Englewood Cliffs: Prentice Hall, 1984), 161–68; Helen Lenskyj, *Out of Bounds* (Toronto: Women's Press, 1986), 17–53.

44. Stanley Eitzen and George H. Sage, *Sociology of North American Sport*, 4th ed. (Dubuque: Wm. C. Brown, 1989), 292.

45. Frontier here refers to recently settled areas with a low ratio of people to inhabitable space. Some of the women who made the move west did attempt with varying degrees of success to maintain or regain their former genteel life-styles, but few could have survived the trip or the homesteading experience and also remained pale, frail, and incapable of exertion.

46. Jameson, "Women as Workers, Women as Civilizers," 150ff.

47. Harold Seymour, *Baseball: The People's Game* (New York: Oxford University Press, 1990), 475.

48. Frances B. Cogan, *All American Girl* (Athens: University of Georgia Press, 1989), 257–62; Carroll Smith–Rosenberg, *Disorderly Conduct: Visions of Gender in Victorian America* (New York. Oxford University Press, 1985), 245–95.

49. Lenskyj, *Out of Bounds*, 95.

50. Boutilier and SanGiovanni, *Sporting Woman*, 23–47; Mrozek, "Sexual Fears of Women as Athletes," 292–93; Gerber, *American Woman in Sport*, 3–273; Curry and Jiobu, *Sports*, 161–68.

51. Mrozek, "Sexual Fears of Women as Athletes," 294.

52. Lenskyj, *Out of Bounds*, 83–86; June Sochen, *Enduring Values: Women in Popular Culture* (New York: Praeger, 1987), 116–18; Eitzen and Sage, *Sociology of North American Sport*, 299–300; Betty G. Hartman, "On Intercollegiate Competition for Women," *Journal of Health and Physical Education* 29 (Mar. 1958): 24.

53. Lenskyj, *Out of Bounds*, 83–86; Boutilier and SanGiovanni, *Sporting Woman*, 34ff.; Lois W. Banner, *American Beauty* (New York: Alfred A. Knopf, 1982), 285; William Henry Chafe, *The American Woman: Her Changing Social, Economic, and Political Roles, 1920–1970* (New York: Oxford University Press, 1972), 199–225; Hartman, "Intercollegiate Competition for Women," 24.

54. Gerber, *American Woman in Sport*, 75, 163.

55. Eitzen and Sage, *Sociology of North American Sport*, 299–300. Ohio State University had sponsored a women's intercollegiate golf tournament since 1941, and the USLTA also sponsored intercollegiate tennis competition.

56. See Gerber, *American Woman in Sport*, 3–167; Joan S. Hult, "The Governance of Athletics for Girls and Women: Leadership by Women Physical Educators," *Research Quarterly for Exercise and Sport* 57 (1986): 64–76; Peggy Burke, "The Effect of Current Sports Legislation on Women in Canada and the U.S.A.—Title IX," in *Her Story in Sport*, ed. Reet Howell (West Point: Leisure Press, 1982), 330–42.

57. Nancy L. Struna, "Beyond Mapping Experience: The Need for Understanding in the History of American Sporting Women," *Journal of Sport History* 11 (Spring 1984): 130–31.

58. Janice A. Beran, "Daughters of the Middle Border, Iowa Women in Sport

and Physical Activity, 1850–1910," *Iowa State Journal of Research* 62 (Nov. 1987): 168–81; Kevin Cook, "The Iowa Girl Stands Tall," *Sports Illustrated,* 13 Feb. 1989, 67–86; Lenskyj, *Out of Bounds,* 100.

59. Armitage and Jameson, Introduction to *Women's West,* 5; Lillian Schlissel, "Frontier Families: Crisis in Ideology," in *American Self,* 161–65; Sandra L. Myres, *Westering Women and the Frontier Experience: 1800–1915* (Albuquerque: University of New Mexico Press, 1982), 261, 270; Harris, "Homesteading in Northeastern Colorado," 165–78; Susan Armitage, "Women and Men in Western History: A Stereoptical Vision," *Western Historical Quarterly* 16 (Oct. 1985): 392; Jameson, "Women as Workers, Women as Civilizers," 159.

60. Harris, "Homesteading in Northeastern Colorado," 175.

61. Ibid., 170–76; Myres, *Westering Women,* 160–64; Terrett, "(Mrs.) Ridin', Ropin', Wranglin', Rodman," 24, 46–48; Steele and Clark, "Horse beneath Me Sometimes," 8–13.

62. Interviews with Lucas, A. Greenough, and M. Greenough.

63. A. Greenough interview; Jordon, *Cowgirls,* 218.

64. Greenough and Lucas interviews; McGinnis, *Rodeo Road.*

65. See Intro. n. 2.

66. Young, Binford, Barton interviews; archives, CGHOF.

67. *WPRA/PWRA Official Reference Guide,* vols. 7 and 8; *Women's Professional Rodeo Association Reference Guide* (Fort Worth: Western Media Services, 1985).

68. Slatta, *Cowboys of the Americas,* 210ff.

69. Elizabeth Atwood Lawrence, *American Rodeo: An Anthropologist Looks at the Wild and the Tame* (Knoxville: University of Tennessee Press, 1982), 80, 92.

70. Ibid., 92.

71. *Prorodeo Sports News,* 15 Jan. 1992, 2.

72. Ibid.

73. Joan S. Hult, "Women to the Mainstream of Sport History," paper delivered to the History Academy of the National Association for Sport and Physical Education, Las Vegas, Nev., 13 Apr. 1987, 8.

74. Young interview; Jackie Worthington files, CGHOF; WPRA 1985 *Reference Guide.*

75. Hult, "Women to the Mainstream," 18.

76. See Intro. n. 2.

77. Boutilier and SanGiovanni, *Sporting Woman,* 185.

78. Ibid., 198.

79. Ibid., 183–218; John Hargreaves, *Sport, Power, and Culture* (Cambridge: Polity Press, 1986), 152–54; Gerber, *American Woman in Sport,* 263–66; Felicia E. Halpert, "You Call This Adorable?" *MS,* Oct. 1988, 36–39.

80. See Intro. n. 2. On the desirability of athletic women see Lenskyj, *Out of Bounds,* chap. 4; Boutilier and SanGiovanni, *Sporting Woman,* 23–47; Mrozek, "Sexual Fears of Women as Athletes."

81. LAT, 10 Aug. 1935.

82. *Amarillo Daily News,* 24 Sept. 1947, 1.

83. WT, 12 Aug. 1913, 3.

84. *San Antonio Express,* 9 Mar. 1928, 4.

85. *New York Sun,* 16 Oct. 1933, in Alice Greenough scrapbook, Tucson, Ariz.

86. *Wyoming Tribune,* 31 Aug. 1904, 5.

87. Dorothy M. Brown, *Setting a Course: American Women in the 1920s* (Boston: Twayne Publishers, 1987), 43.

88. MFP, 14 Aug. 1913, 10; WT, 14 Aug. 1913, 5.

89. *San Antonio Express,* 9 Mar. 1928, 4.

90. Ibid.

91. David Wallechinsky, *The Complete Book of the Olympic Games* (New York: Penguin Books, 1988), 141.

92. Greenoughs, Lucas interviews; Gene Creed files CGHOF; Lynn Haney, *Ride 'em Cowgirl* (New York: G. P. Putnam's Sons, 1975), 112–14; McGinnis, *Rodeo Road.*

93. See Intro. n. 2.

94. CBBD, 19 Nov. 1942, 52; CBBD, 5 Sept. 1936, 41; H&H, Jan. 1939, 14; Sarah Wood-Clark, *Beautiful Daring Western Girls* (Cody: Buffalo Bill Historical Center, n.d.), 22; "The Rodeo Cowgirls," *Official Program, Boston Garden Rodeo,* 1934, n.p.; Faye Blackstone files, CGHOF; and many more.

95. Deutsch, "Coming Together, Coming Apart," 60.

96. Lucas interview.

97. Jordon, *Cowgirls,* 201–14; Lucas files, CGHOF, NRHOF; H&H, 1949–54.

98. Slatta, *Cowboys of the Americas,* 210.

99. "Cowgirls of Eastern Oregon."

100. See Intro. n. 2.

101. CBBD, 10 Aug. 1929, 54; CBBD, 19 Oct. 1929, 61; CBBD, 1 Sept. 1934, 32; CBBD, 8 Sept. 1934, 36; CBBD, 9 Mar. 1940, 32; CBBD, 7 Oct. 1933, 31; H&H, Apr. 1940, 15; *Ketch Pen,* Spring 1988, 21. The actual death rate is quite low, but the fear of death or injury was very real nonetheless.

102. See Intro. n. 2.

103. Ibid.

104. "In Praise of Cowgirls," *Texas Monthly,* Nov. 1987, 110.

105. Lucas, Young interviews; Kenneth Springer, "James Heads Entire Delegation," *Womens Pro Rodeo News,* 1 Dec. 1987, 1–2; Bruce Anderson, "Having a Barrel of Fun," *Sports Illustrated,* 15 Dec. 1986, 85.

106. Lucas, Young, Greenough, Binford, Barton, Mosley interviews.

107. Tana Mac, "Half-Century Queen of the Rodeo," *Quarter Horse Journal,* Jan. 1962, 174.

108. McGinnis, *Rodeo Road,* 25.

Chapter 2. Wild West Frontier Days, 1880s–World War I

1. Don Russell, *The Lives and Legends of Buffalo Bill* (Norman: University of Oklahoma Press, 1960), 313; Russell, *Wild West,* 21; Wood-Clark, *Beautiful Daring Western Girls.*

2. Early Wild West show cowgirls included Adele Von Ohl Parker, Bessie Farrell, Nellie Braden, Emma Galindo, Annie Shaffer, Lillian Smith, Claraleo McFadden Rodman, Amy Jacobs, Emma Hicock, Pancha Aguria, Edna Willoughby,

and Della Farrell. Milt Hinkle, "Cowgirls—Rodeo's Sugar and Spice," *Frontier Times,* Oct./Nov. 1971, 38–43; Russell, *Lives and Legends of Buffalo Bill,* 339; Wood-Clark, *Beautiful Daring Western Girls;* BBD, 1 May 1918, 29; 18 Sept. 1915, 23; 10 Dec. 1921, 101; Terrett, "(Mrs.) Ridin', Ropin', Wranglin', Rodman," 24, 46–48.

3. BBD, 1897–1920; Glenn Shirley, *Pawnee Bill* (Lincoln: University of Nebraska Press, 1958), 170.

4. See Intro. n. 2.

5. *Cheyenne State Leader,* 20 Aug. 1909, 4.

6. Jan Todd, "The Strong Lady in America: Professional Athletes and the *Police Gazette,*" paper presented at the North American Society for Sport History, 27 May 1989, Clemson, S.C.

7. Sara M. Evans, *Born for Liberty: A History of Women in America* (New York: The Free Press, 1989), 157.

8. Deutsch, "Coming Together, Coming Apart," 60.

9. Todd, "Strong Lady in America."

10. McGinnis, *Rodeo Road,* 123.

11. Glenn R. Vernam, *Man on Horseback* (Lincoln: University of Nebraska Press, 1964), 385–89.

12. Donna M. Lucey, *Photographing Montana, 1894–1928: The Life and Work of Evelyn Cameron* (New York: Alfred A. Knopf, 1990), 204.

13. Ibid., 203–5, 175.

14. See esp. the vintage photographs in Hallie Crawford Stillwell, *I'll Gather My Geese* (College Station: Texas A&M University Press, 1991), and Ada Moorehead Holland, *Brush Country Woman* (College Station: Texas A&M University Press, 1988).

15. Stillwell, *I'll Gather My Geese,* 22.

16. See Intro. n. 2.

17. Paula Welch, "The Debut of Margaret Abbott," paper presented to the North American Society for Sport History, May 1982, Manhattan, Kans.; Paula Welch, "America's First Women Olympians: A Reflection of Sport," paper presented to the North American Society for Sport History, May 1985, LaCrosse, Wisc.; David Chester, *The Olympic Games Handbook* (New York: Charles Scribner's Sons, 1975), 13–36.

18. *Biographical Dictionary of American Sports: Outdoor Sports,* s.v. Eleonora Sears.

19. NYT, 14 Aug. 1910.

20. "A Genuine and Fascinating Cowgirl," *Police Gazette,* 16 Sept. 1893, 7.

21. See, for example, Day, *America's First Cowgirl.*

22. Stansbury, *Lucille Mulhall,* i–10ff.

23. Ibid., 15.

24. Stansbury, letter to the author, 12 Dec. 1990.

25. Stansbury, *Lucille Mulhall,* 69–91.

26. "Wants Divorce from Lucile [*sic*] Mulhall," BBD, 28 Mar. 1914, 22.

27. Stansbury, *Lucille Mulhall,* ii.

28. "Cowboys Ball Novel Feature," *San Antonio Express,* 5 May 1917, 7.

29. McGinnis, *Rodeo Road*, 125ff.; Lajuana Newman, "Ruth Roach Salmon, A Pioneer Cowgirl" (printed by the author, Lewisville, Tex., 1989), 2; Ruth Roach induction, National Cowgirl Hall of Fame, 17 June 1989.

30. Jake Page, "New Mexico's Gray Ranch: The Natural Preserve as Big as All Outdoors," *Smithsonian*, Feb. 1992, 31.

31. Laurence Urdang, ed., *The Timetables of American History* (New York: Touchstone, 1981), 244–49.

32. Evans, *Born for Liberty*, 148, 180.

33. Ibid., 145–73.

34. David F. Burg, *Chicago's White City of 1893* (Louisville: University of Kentucky Press, 1976), xii.

35. Ibid., xiv.

36. Russell, *Lives and Legends,* 374; Jan Todd, "Bernarr Macfadden Reformer of Feminine Form," *Journal of Sport History* 14 (Spring 1987): 64.

37. Burg, *Chicago's White City of 1893,* 256–57.

38. Russell, *Wild West,* 43; William Cronon, "Revisiting the Vanishing Frontier: The Legacy of Fredrick Jackson Turner," *Western Historical Quarterly* 18 (Apr. 1987): 160.

39. Blackstone, *Buckskins, Bullets, and Business: A History of Buffalo Bill's Wild West,* 62.

40. Russell, *Lives and Legends,* 374–75.

41. Ibid., 374–78.

42. Ibid., 376.

43. Shirley, *Pawnee Bill,* 117–20ff.

44. Writers contributing to the confusion include Mary Lou LeCompte, "Champion Cowgirls of Rodeo's Golden Age," *Journal of the West* 28 (Apr. 1989): 88, and "Cowgirls at the Crossroads: Women in Professional Rodeo: 1885–1922," 29; Roach, *Cowgirls,* 83–84; Clifford P. Westermeir, *Man, Beast, Dust—The Story of Rodeo* (Denver: World Press, 1947), 83; and Mary Lou Remley, "From Sidesaddle to Rodeo," *Journal of the West* (July 1978): 46.

45. Blancett to Kipling, 9 Dec. 1971. Letter in Kipling, C. Collector, Notes, Clippings, etc. of Early Riders: File M4300, Glenbow.

46. *Wyoming Tribune,* 1 Sept. 1904, 5; Hanesworth, *Daddy of 'em All,* 47–48; Warren Richardson "History of the First Frontier Days Celebration," *Annals of Wyoming* 19 (Jan. 1947): 43.

47. *Wyoming Tribune,* 31 Aug. 1904, 5.

48. Ibid., 1 Sept. 1904, 5; Hanesworth, *Daddy of 'em All,* 47–48; Ann Nelson, Historian, Wyoming State Archives, letter to the author, 10 Apr. 1990.

49. *Wyoming Tribune,* 31 Aug. 1904, 5; and 1 Sept. 1904, 5.

50. Nelson, letter to the author.

51. *Cheyenne Daily Sun Leader,* 3 July and 24 Aug. 1899; *Cheyenne Leader,* 28 Aug. 1901, 4.

52. Milt Riske, *Cheyenne Frontier Days* (Cheyenne: Frontier Printing, 1984), 215–16; Hanesworth, *Daddy of 'em All,* 164–65.

53. In bulldogging, the hazer rides along the steer's "off" side to keep the animal running in a straight line until the contestant has jumped onto its back.

54. Virgil Rupp, *Let 'er Buck* (Pendleton: Pendleton Roundup Committee, 1987), 6, 19. Different sources give conflicting dates for Blancett's achievement, but Rupp's is the only one based on the Pendleton Roundup committee records.

55. Glenn Shirley, *Hello Sucker* (Austin: Eakin Press, 1989), 17.

56. Armitage, "Rawhide Heroines," 176–77; Dee Brown, *The Gentle Tamers: Women of the Old Wild West* (Lincoln: University of Nebraska Press, 1958), 188–89.

57. *Porterville Recorder* (California), 5 Sept. 1973; Jerry Armstrong, "Picked Up in the Rodeo Arena," *Western Horseman,* May 1955, 38–39; Porter, *Who's Who,* 28–29.

58. Although sanctioned by the PRCA, steer roping is contested in only four of the twelve PRCA circuits, and is not included at the National Finals Rodeo. The top winners do not earn even half as much as the champion team ropers. See Omar S. Barker, "Rodeo Then and Now," Official Program: Rodeo de Santa Fe (1960), 6–7; Hanesworth, *Daddy of 'em All,* 36–37, 59–63; Clancy, *Fifty Years,* 9; *Fort Worth Gazette,* 5 Dec. 1890.

59. *Calgary Daily Herald,* 26 Aug. 1912, 16.

60. "Woman Champion: She Is a Wonder with the Lariat at Steer Roping," *Police Gazette,* 24 June 1905, 6.

61. "Rain and Cold Fail to Keep Eleven Thousand away from the Second Performance."

62. "Dorothy Morrell Makes Hit," BBD, 12 June 1915, 23.

63. BBD, 8 May 1915, 57; 5 June 1915, 42.

64. Evans, *Born for Liberty,* 167.

65. Ibid., 168.

66. Simri, *Women at the Olympic Games,* 23.

67. James H. Gray, *A Brand of Its Own* (Saskatoon: Western Producer Prairie Books, 1985), 30–41.

68. LAT, 4 Feb.–25 Mar. 1912.

69. Ibid., 14, 15, and 17 Mar. 1912. A potato race was a team event. A large box of potatoes was placed at one end of the arena, with an empty box for each team placed at the opposite end. Riders were required to spear the potatoes with long pointed sticks, and carry them back to their box, with the team collecting the most potatoes the winners. Contestants also tried to knock opponents' potatoes off their sticks.

70. LAT, 12, 15, and 17 Mar. 1912.

71. H&H, Jan. 1944, 3; Cleo Mackey, *The Cowboy and Rodeo Evolution* (Dallas: Cleo Mackey Publishing, 1979), 39.

72. LAT, 4 Feb.–25 Mar. 1912.

73. "The Champion Rough Rider Who Never Saw a Ranch," *New York World Magazine,* 3 Sept. 1916, 5; *New York Journal American,* 24 Oct. 1958; BBD, 25 May 1927, 73; BBD, 25 June 1927, 72; Tillie Baldwin files, NRHOF.

74. Maryanne Dolan, *Vintage Clothing: 1880–1960* (Florence, Ala.: Books America, n.d.), 100.

75. MFP, 12 Aug. 1913, 11; "Champion Rough Rider," 5; photo #NA–1029–18: Roman Races at the Winnipeg Stampede, 1913, Glenbow; Rupp, *Let 'er Buck,* 10.

76. "Cowgirls of Eastern Oregon."

77. "Rain and Cold Fail to Keep Eleven Thousand away from the Second Performance"; Stansbury, *Lucille Mulhall.*

78. *Porterville Recorder,* 5 Sept. 1953, 73; Tillie Baldwin files, NRHOF.

79. Jon Tuska, *The Filming of the West* (Garden City: Doubleday, 1976), 71–77; Rupp, *Let 'er Buck,* 9–12.

80. Goetzmann and Goetzmann, *West of the Imagination,* 305–6.

81. "Weadick Travelled a Rocky Road before Hitting Pay Dirt In 1912," *Calgary Herald,* 9 July 1949, 24; Jerry Armstrong, "The Man Who Started the Stampede," *Western Horseman,* Aug. 1959, 6, 7, 62–65; Gray, *Brand of Its Own,* 30–41.

82. Fred Kennedy, *The Calgary Stampede Story* (Calgary: T. Edwards Thonger, 1952), 19–21.

83. "Weadick Travelled a Rocky Road," 24; Armstrong, "Man Who Started the Stampede," 6, 7, 62–65; Gray, *Brand of Its Own,* 30–41.

84. "Weadick Travelled a Rocky Road," 24. LaDue used several stage names, including Flora LaDue and Flores LaDue.

85. *Calgary Herald,* 7 Sept. 1949 and 15 Dec. 1953; Guy Weadick, "Here and There," BBD, 13 Jan. 1912, 23; BBD, 5 Oct. 1907, n.p.; Guy Weadick Papers, M1287, File #35, Glenbow.

86. "Florence Weadick Passes On," H&H, Nov. 1951, 16; "Weadick Travelled a Rocky Road," 24; CBBD, 29 Mar. 1924, 75.

87. Chester Byers, *Cowboy Roping and Rope Tricks* (New York: Dover Publications, 1966), 82–83; *Argonne Association of America, World's Championship Cowboy Contests, Official Program* (New York: R. R. Doubleday, 1922), 15–16; Porter, *Who's Who,* 94–95; Vincente Oropeza files, NRHOF; Richard M. Ketchum, *Will Rogers: His Life and Times* (New York: American Heritage, 1973), 20; LeCompte, "Hispanic Influence on the History of Rodeo," 21–38.

88. *Calgary Herald,* 12 Sept. 1912, 2.

89. Ibid.

90. Hargreaves, *Sport, Power, and Culture,* 151–54; Gerber, *American Woman in Sport,* 249–72; Boutilier and SanGiovanni, *Sporting Woman,* 183–218; Mangan and Park, *From Fair Sex to Feminism,* 7, 216–18.

91. James F. Taylor, "How Six Years' Practice and a Sixth Sense Made Flores La Due a Champion," *New York World Magazine,* 17 Sept. 1916, 16; "Champion Rough Rider," 5.

92. Porter, *Who's Who,* 126–27; "Fannie Sperry Steele," H&H, May 1945, 5; Stiffler and Blake, "Fannie Sperry-Steele," 48–52.

93. Stiffler and Blake, "Fannie Sperry-Steele," 46–48; "Fannie Sperry Steele," H&H, May 1945, 5; Mac, "Half-Century Queen of the Rodeo," 27; Steele and Clark, "Horse beneath Me Sometimes," 8.

94. Stiffler and Blake, "Fannie Sperry-Steele," 49–51; Lucas, Young interviews 1988.

95. Stiffler and Blake, "Fannie Sperry-Steele," 50; Fannie Sperry files, CGHOF, NRHOF.

96. Sperry to Weadick, 8 July 1912.

97. Weadick to Sperry, 11 July 1912.

98. Riske, *Cheyenne Frontier Days,* 180–83.

99. CBBD, 1 Mar. 1930, 59; "Stampede Closes with Naming of Champions," WT, 18 Aug. 1913, 5; Stiffler and Blake, "Fannie Sperry-Steele," 51; "Stampede Ended Saturday with Awarding of World's Championships," MFP, 18 Aug. 1913, 4–5.

100. Weadick to Sperry, 11 June 1912.

101. George J. Rempel, "Goldie St. Clair Was a World Champion Saddle Bronc Rider," *Calgary Herald Magazine,* 3 July 1970, 12. Although she moved to Alberta in 1913 and spent much of the remainder of her life there, St. Clair was not a Canadian, and not a "home town heroine" at the Stampede.

102. Stiffler and Blake, "Fannie Sperry-Steele," 51–52; "Fannie Sperry Steele," H&H, May 1945, 5; *Calgary Herald,* 9 Sept. 1912, 16.

103. Marvine, "Fannie Sperry Wowed 'em at First Calgary Stampede," 30–36; Stiffler and Blake, "Fannie Sperry-Steele," 48–53.

104. *Porterville Recorder,* 5 Sept. 1973; "The Stampede Program, Sept. 2, 1912," Calgary Exhibition and Stampede Papers, M1287, Glenbow; *Calgary Herald,* 6 Sept. 1912, 2, and 7 Sept. 1912, 16.

105. BBD, 16 Oct. 1915, 23; Marvine, "Fannie Sperry Wowed 'em at First Calgary Stampede," 30–36; Stiffler and Blake, "Fannie Sperry-Steele," 53–54.

106. LAT, 12–18 Feb. 1913.

107. Blancett apparently did not compete in any rodeos in 1913.

108. McGinnis, *Rodeo Road,* 13–14. The account of McGinnis's life that follows is taken from this work, which is cited by page number in this section.

109. John Goodwin, Tom Brosnahan, and Marilyn Wood, *Arthur Frommer's Dollarwi$e Guide to Canada* (New York: Frommer/Paasmantier Publishing Corp., 1980), 458–59.

110. WT, 31 July–18 Aug. 1913; MFP, 31 July–19 Aug. 1913.

111. Ibid.

112. "Large Crowd Attends Stampede on Opening Saturday Afternoon," WT, 11 Aug. 1913, 5.

113. "Woman to the Fore as Steer Roper," MFP, 11 Aug. 1913, 10; "Civic Holiday at the Stampede," MFP, 12 Aug. 1913, 10; WT, 12 Aug. 1913, 3; "Stampede Ended Saturday with Awarding of World's Championships."

114. "Stampede Closes with Naming of Champions."

115. WT 14 Aug. 1913, 5; MFP, 14 Aug. 1913, 10.

116. McGinnis, *Rodeo Road,* 46.

117. Ibid., 22–167.

118. WT, 13 Aug. 1913, 5.

119. MFP, 14 Aug. 1913, 10; WT, 14 Aug. 1913, 5; "Stampede Closes with Naming of Champions."

120. "Blanche McGaughey's Sensation," WT, 12 Aug. 1913, 3.

121. "Much Dissatisfaction over Women's Bronc Riding Title Won by Fannie Sperry Steele," MFP, 18 Aug. 1913, 4.

122. "Stampede Closes with Naming of Champions."

123. MFP and WT, Aug. 1913.

124. Rupp, *Let 'er Buck,* 19; Photo, "Tillie Baldwin: Only Woman Bulldogger in the World," copyright 1913 by E. H. Paige, Tillie Baldwin files, NRHOF; Photo #NA–446–107, Glenbow. Eloise Fox Hastings is usually called "The First Woman Bulldogger," but she never performed the feat until 1924, and was at best fourth behind Baldwin (1913), Blanche McGaughey (1914), and Anita Ingles (1922). See Reba Perry Blakely, "Three Good Hands," *The Wild Bunch,* Aug. 1984, 11; Guy Weadick, "Here and There," BBD, 16 May 1914, 59.

125. Counted from sources listed in Intro. n. 2.

126. See Intro. n. 2.

127. See, for example, Remley, "From Sidesaddle to Rodeo," 48.

128. Photo from the collection of Gilbert Pittman, Wichita, Kans.

129. Guy Weadick, "Here and There," BBD, 20 July 1912, 23; Rhonda Sedgwick, "Women's Western Fashions, More Practical than Vain," *Side Saddle,* 1985, 41.

130. Stiffler and Blake, "Fannie Sperry-Steele," 54–56; "Fannie Sperry Steele," H&H, 5.

131. Stiffler and Blake, "Fannie Sperry-Steele," 54–56; "Fannie Sperry Steele," H&H, 5.

132. *The Wild Bunch,* May 1915, 4; Jan. 1916, 16.

133. Stansbury, *Lucille Mulhall,* 99.

134. Tona Blake and Liz Stiffler, "Top Cowboys and Cowgirls Performed in Montana's 1916 Wild West Presentation," *The Wild Bunch,* Feb. 1983, 15; McGinnis, *Rodeo Road,* 121–27.

135. Blake and Stiffler, "Top Cowboys and Cowgirls," 15; McGinnis, *Rodeo Road,* 121–27.

136. NYT, 6–13 Aug. 1916; *New York World,* 1–15 Aug. 1916; *New York Tribune,* 5–14 Aug. 1915.

137. *The Wild Bunch,* Sept. 1916, 14; Guy Weadick and Calgary Stampede Papers, Glenbow.

138. Unidentified clipping, Fox Hastings files, NRHOF; "Cowgirls of the Rodeo, Interesting," BBD, 25 Jan. 1922, 108.

139. Foghorn Clancy, "Memory Trail," H&H, July 1937, 17; Westermeir, *Man, Beast, Dust,* 48–49.

140. NYT, 14–17 Aug. 1916; *New York World,* 15–20 Aug. 1916; *New York Tribune,* 14–20 Aug. 1916; *New York Evening Post,* 26 July–10 Aug. 1916; *New York Herald,* 3–20 Aug. 1916.

141. *Chicago Tribune,* 17–28 Aug. 1916; *The Wild Bunch,* Sept. 1916, 3.

142. BBD, 2 Sept. 1916, 26; *The Wild Bunch,* Sept. 1916, 3, 14.

143. Mac, "Half-Century Queen of the Rodeo," 174.

144. *The Wild Bunch,* Sept. 1916, 4, 5, 9; Stansbury, *Lucille Mulhall,* 109.

145. McGinnis, *Rodeo Road,* 47.

146. Ibid., 123–26.

147. Ibid., 128–33; BBD, 19 Aug. 1916, 24.

148. McGinnis, *Rodeo Road,* 133–34.

149. *The Wild Bunch,* Sept. 1916, 11.

150. LeCompte, "Champion Cowgirls."

151. See Intro. n. 2.

152. McGinnis, *Rodeo Road*, 150–53; BBD, 3 Feb. 1917, 23; "Wimmin's Writes," BBD, 20 Jan. 1917, 23.

153. *The Wild Bunch*, Apr. 1917, 3, 9.

154. Newman, "Ruth Roach Salmon," 1–7; Roach files, CGHOF.

155. Clancy, *Fifty Years*, 16; *San Antonio Express*, 2, May 1917, 3.

156. *San Antonio Express*, 2 May 1917, 3, and 6 May 1917, 5; Riske, *Cheyenne Frontier Days*, 49; Gray, *Brand of Its Own*, 53.

157. *San Antonio Express*, 8 May 1917, 6. Clyde Lindsey took third.

158. *The Wild Bunch*, 1915–17.

159. Shirley, *Hello Sucker*, 3. Cited by page number in the paragraph that follows.

Chapter 3. Champion Cowgirls in the Golden Age of Sport, 1919–29

1. Dorothy Brown, *Setting a Course*, chap. 1.

2. Benjamin Rader, *American Sports: From the Age of Folk Games to the Age of the Spectator* (Englewood Cliffs: Prentice Hall, 1983), 177.

3. Dorothy Brown, *Setting a Course*, 42–43.

4. Ibid., chap. 3.

5. Ibid., 85.

6. Ibid., 50, 73–74; Evans, *Born for Liberty*, 174.

7. Evans, *Born for Liberty*, 175.

8. Dorothy Brown, *Setting a Course*, 43.

9. Shirley, *Hello Sucker*, v, 43–44ff.

10. Ibid., chaps. 6–12.

11. A few old timers such as Dorothy Morrell always wore divided skirts in rodeo, and some women wore them in Wild West shows through 1930, whereas bloomers totally vanished. See BBD, 1920–30.

12. See Intro. n. 2.

13. BBD, 1896–1940; Program, 1936 Calgary Stampede, Calgary Stampede and Exhibition Papers, A7 W361 A, Glenbow; Mac, "Half-Century Queen of the Rodeo," 27.

14. See Intro. n. 2.

15. Vernam, *Man on Horseback*, 409–10.

16. Ibid.

17. Ibid.

18. BBD, 1912–29; "Star of Buffalo Bill's Circus Dies in Poverty," unidentified clipping from Dayton, Ohio, in the archives of the Buffalo Bill Historical Center, Cody, Wyo.; Ohio Department of Health, Division of Vital Statistics, Certificate of Death: Lulu Bell Parr, 17 Jan. 1955.

19. BBD, 2 Aug. 1913, 25; BBD, 27 Sept. 1913, 26; BBD, 29 Oct. 1913, 122; BBD, 6 Feb. 1915, 23; BBD, 27 Feb. 1915, 23; "Princess Mohawk's Wild West," BBD, 28 Aug. 1915, 23; BBD, 11 Sept. 1915, 56; *The Wild Bunch*, July 1916, 7; BBD, 3 Mar. 1917, 53; BBD, 24 Aug. 1919, 26; Sally Gray, "Florence Hughes Randolph, Part I," *Quarter Horse Journal*, Mar. 1971, 42–50.

20. *The Stampede Detailed Programme,* 25–30 Aug. 1919, Calgary Stampede and Exhibition Papers, M2160, fib 29a, Glenbow; Gray, "Florence Hughes Randolph, Part I," 50.

21. Porter, *Who's Who,* 102–3; Sally Gray, "Florence Hughes Randolph, Part II," *Quarter Horse Journal,* Apr. 1971, 144.

22. Gray, "Florence Hughes Randolph, Part I," 50.

23. BBD, 1919–25; Florence Randolph files, NRHOF; Porter, *Who's Who,* 103.

24. *Fort Worth Star Telegram,* 13 Mar. 1919, 12.

25. Stansbury, *Lucille Mulhall,* 115–17; Porter, *Who's Who,* 90–91; Stansbury, letters to the author, 1989–91.

26. *Porterville Recorder,* 5 Sept. 1973 and 5 July 1979, NRHOF; CBBD, 10 Dec. 1932, 33; CBBD, 9 Dec. 1933, 31; CBBD, 24 Oct. 1934, 39; CBBD, 15 Dec. 1934, 37; CBBD, 2 July 1938, 34; LAT, 10 Sept. 1933. A pickup is a mounted arena official whose job it is to assist bronc riders from their horses and then lead the broncs out of the arena.

27. Stiffler and Blake, "Fannie Sperry-Steele," 45–51; "Fannie Sperry Steele," H&H, 5; Steele and Clark, "Horse beneath Me Sometimes," 9–16ff.

28. Gray, *Brand of Its Own,* 53; Calgary Stampede and Exhibition Papers, Glenbow.

29. "The Stampede at Calgary," BBD, 20 Sept. 1919, 53 and 89.

30. *The Stampede Detailed Programme,* 25–30 Aug. 1919, Calgary Exhibition and Stampede papers, Glenbow.

31. CBBD, 20 Jan. 1933, 76; CBBD, 22 Aug. 1925, 63; CBBD, 25 May 1927, 73; "101 Ranch," BBD, 25 June 1927, 72; Clancy, "Memory Trail," H&H, Jan. 1944, 3.

32. CBBD, 22 Mar. 1924, 89; CBBD, 25 July 1925, 61; CBBD, 3 Dec. 1932, 49; CBBD, 22 July 1933, 29; CBBD, 16 May 1936, 37.

33. CBBD, 29 Oct. 1927, 67.

34. Ibid.

35. MGM Trophy, NRHOF.

36. "Rodeo Champions Chosen," NYT, 31 Oct. 1932, 32; "Garden Rodeo," NYT, 5 Nov. 1932, 5.

37. "MGM Trophy Reaches Fred Beebe's Rodeo," BBD, 10 Sept. 1932, 35; CBBD, 8 Oct. 1932, 35. Beebe produced the Madison Square Garden rodeo in 1927, but not thereafter. Randolph won the trophies at Beebe's 1931 and 1932 rodeos at St. Louis. Many of Randolph's trophies and memorabilia were destroyed by fire, and Randolph is deceased, so the mystery may never be solved.

38. Gerber, *American Woman in Sport,* 206.

39. Gray, "Florence Hughes Randolph, Part II," 126.

40. McGinnis, *Rodeo Road,* 172–73.

41. Ibid., 182–208.

42. Gray, "Florence Hughes Randolph, Part 1," 54.

43. Riske, *Cheyenne Frontier Days,* 215–16; Hanesworth, *Daddy of 'em All,* 164–65; CBBD,19 Aug. 1922, 63.

44. Remley, "Sidesaddle to Rodeo," 49.

45. Lorena Trickey trophies and files, NRHOF; CBBD, 4 Dec. 1920, 62; CBBD, 12 Aug. 1924, 115; BBD, 1920–25.

46. Tad Lucas files, CGHOF and NRHOF; "World Champion Cowgirl Tad Lucas Dies at 87," *Prorodeo Sports News,* 7 Mar. 1990, 26.

47. Capt. Dan Fox, "Tad Lucas," H&H, Oct. 1937, 9; Lucas files, CHGOF, NRHOF.

48. Fox, "Tad Lucas," 9; Lucas files, CHGOF, NRHOF; Porter, *Who's Who,* 78–79; Lucas interview; CBBD, 1922.

49. Willard Porter, "Tad," *True West,* Sept. 1988, 32; Fox, "Tad Lucas," 9; "Dick Ringling's Rodeo Closes Successfully," BBD, 24 Nov. 1923, 128.

50. Telephone interview with Mitzi Lucas Riley, 30 Nov. 1990; Certificate of Marriage Registration, City of New York, 13543–1924.

51. Lucas files, CGHOF, NRHOF; Lucas interview; "90,000 See Start of British Rodeo," BBD, 21 June 1924, 5; Porter, *Who's Who,* 78–79; Fox, "Tad Lucas," 9.

52. Dorothy Brown, *Setting a Course,* 42–43; Wallechinsky, *Complete Book of the Olympic Games,* 497–98; Frank G. Menke, *The Encyclopedia of Sports,* 5th ed. (New York: A. S. Barnes, 1975), 967–68.

53. Lewis H. Carlson and John J. Fogarty, *Tales of Gold* (Chicago: Contemporary Books, 1987), 78.

54. Tex Austin files, NRHOF.

55. The big news in New York in Nov. 1922 pertained to elections. Much of the publicity the rodeo did receive concerned Austin's successful court battle with the ASPA over the bulldogging events.

56. NYT, 5–14 Nov. 1922; *New York Tribune,* 5–13 Nov. 1922; *New York Herald,* 3–11 Nov. 1922.

57. BBD, Jan.–Oct. 1922.

58. CBBD, 21 Oct. 1922, 74; CBBD, 12 Aug. 1922, 63; "Best Show Ever," BBD, 7 Oct. 1922, 74. Strickland repeated as champion in 1923. CBBD, 8 June 1923, 75.

59. Porter, *Who's Who,* 128–31; "Cowgirls of the Rodeo," 108; *The Wild Bunch,* 1915–19; BBD, 1914–22.

60. NYT, 6 Nov. 1922, 3; *New York Tribune,* 3 Nov. 1922.

61. *New York Herald,* 3 Nov. 1922, 12.

62. BBD, 18 Nov. 1922, 5.

63. NYT, 5 Nov. 1922, 20.

64. "Cowgirls of the Rodeo," 108.

65. Ibid.

66. BBD, 18 Nov. 1922, 6.

67. BBD, 25 Nov. 1922, 5, 110.

68. "Cowgirls of the Rodeo," 108.

69. Ibid.; BBD, 6 Nov. 1915, 23; *The Wild Bunch,* Aug. 1983, 13; Reine Shelton files, CGHOF.

70. *The Wild Bunch,* Aug. 1983, 13; BBD, 1922–25.

71. BBD, 18 Nov. 1922, 6.

72. Clancy, *Fifty Years*, 51–55.

73. BBD, 18 Nov. 1922, 6. Except for 1925, when the Garden was closed, annual rodeos took place from 1922 though 1959.

74. See for example, Section 4 of the *New York Herald*, 12 Nov. 1922.

75. BBD, 4 Aug. 1923, 77.

76. Porter, *Who's Who*, 104; BBD, 17 Nov. 1923, 85.

77. "Dick Ringling's Rodeo Closes Successfully," 128; BBD, 28 Apr. 1923, 78; CBBD, 1924–35.

78. Porter, *Who's Who*, 104; CBBD, 1919–30; McGinnis, *Rodeo Road*, 180–82. Lucas later claimed to have created the first "Mexican Suit" (press release, National Cowboy Hall of Fame and Western Heritage Center, 3 Nov. 1977; Jane Pattie, "The Clothes Horse," *Quarter Horse Journal*, Mar. 1970, 59–66; Roach, *Cowgirls*, 124), but photos support McGinnis as the originator.

79. Vaughn Krieg scrapbook, Gene Creed files, CGHOF.

80. Ibid.; BBD, 1925–40; H&H 1929–40. Gene married bulldogger Shorty Creed in 1931. Vaughn Krieg followed her onto the rodeo circuit in 1927, and was also well known for the costumes that she made.

81. BBD, 28 July 1923, 75.

82. CBBD, 24 Oct. 1923, 83; CBBD, 17 Nov. 1923, 85; CBBD, 8 Dec. 1923, 83; "Dick Ringling's Rodeo Goes over Big," BBD, 17 Nov. 1923, 5, 123; "Dick Ringling's Rodeo Closes Successfully," 128.

83. BBD, 1 Nov. 1924, 77 and 100; BBD, 8 Nov. 1924, 5 and 103; NYT, 20 Oct. 1924.

84. Porter, *Who's Who*, 20–21; Russell, *Wild West*, 106; BBD, 28 July 1923, 75; BBD, 1920–30; LAT, Aug. 1935; *Chicago Tribune*, 1921–29.

85. Vera McGinnis files, CGHOF. Tad Lucas was still using her maiden name, and is listed on the program as Tad Barnes; Randolph is listed as Fenton, the name of her husband at the time.

86. McGinnis, *Rodeo Road*, 182–208; Vera McGinnis files, trophies, and memorabilia, CGHOF.

87. McGinnis, *Rodeo Road*, 182–208; Vera McGinnis files, trophies, and memorabilia, CGHOF.

88. McGinnis, *Rodeo Road*, 204–5.

89. Ibid., 208.

90. Ibid., 182–208ff.; CBBD, 1922–34.

91. CBBD, 3 May 1924, 78; CBBD, 14 June 1924, 73; CBBD, 5 July 1924, 71.

92. "90,000 See Start of British Rodeo," 5; "Injuries at Rodeo," BBD, 28 June 1924, 6.

93. *Detroit News*, 2 Nov. 1924, 2; Rupp, *Let 'er Buck*, 35, 40, 167.

94. Gray, "Florence Hughes Randolph, Part II," 142.

95. See Intro. n. 2.

96. Ibid.

97. "Burnette's Houston Rodeo," BBD, 5 Apr. 1924, 75; "Houston Rodeo Has Very Auspicious Start," BBD, 22 Mar. 1924, 255.

98. BBD, Jan.–Dec. 1924.

99. Clancy, *Fifty Years*, 35; Fox Hastings files, NRHOF.

100. Rupp, *Let 'er Buck*, 35.

101. Ibid.; photos, BBD, 7 June 1924, 7; Fox Hastings files, NRHOF.

102. Unidentified clipping, Fox Hastings files, NRHOF.

103. CBBD, 29 Oct. 1927, 67. Claire Belcher is referred to as Claire Thompson hereafter.

104. CBBD, 19 Nov. 1927, 65. Although the two women never competed in the bulldogging contest, the *New York Times* did report that their husbands, bulldoggers Mike Hastings and Bob Belcher, were arrested following an altercation that stemmed from comments about their wives' bulldogging abilities (NYT, 27 Oct.–4 Nov. 1927).

105. CBBD, 17 Dec. 1927, 65; CBBD, 23 May 1929, 97.

106. *Boston Post*, 1 Nov. 1936; "101 Ranch Show," BBD, 30 Apr. 1927, 10; *Houston Post*, 29 June 1928; CBBD, 1926–29.

107. CBBD, 28 Dec. 1929.

108. Fox Hastings files, NRHOF; *New York Evening Journal*, 3 Nov. 1926; "Second Annual World Series Rodeo Opens," BBD, 5 Nov. 1927, 63; *Houston Post*, 19 June 1928; CBBD, 16 Nov. 1929, 59.

109. BBD, 10 Nov. 1913, 26; BBD, 15 Sept. 1917, 40; BBD, 20 July 1918, 54; CBBD, 8 Sept. 1917, 28; "Wimmin's Writes," BBD, 4 Aug. 1917, 28.

110. "William Smith Killed," BBD, 12 May 1923, 16.

111. CBBD, 2 June 1923, 75.

112. CBBD, 12 Nov. 1927, 65.

113. CBBD, 26 Nov. 1927, 63.

114. Lorena Trickey trophies, NRHOF.

115. Edith S. Armstrong, "Tip Your Hat to the Greenoughs," *Tucson Daily Star*, 26 Feb. 1976.

116. Jordon, *Cowgirls*, 214–21; Mary Cates, "Marjorie Greenough—Bronc Rider," H&H, May 1939, 19; Greenoughs interviews.

117. Also known as the IXL Wild West among other names, it was the same outfit with which Florence Randolph toured from 1913 to 1915.

118. Jordon, *Cowgirls*, 214–21; Cates, "Marjorie Greenough," 19; Greenoughs interviews; Armstrong, "Tip Your Hat to the Greenoughs"; BBD, 23 Mar. 1929, 96–97.

119. CBBD, 5 Oct. 1929, 61, CBBD, 19 Oct. 1929, 61; Milt Hinkle, "The Pale-Horsed Rider," *Frontier Times*, Sept. 1967, 26–7.

120. CBBD, 19 Oct. 1929, 61.

121. Ibid.

122. Cover, *The Wild Bunch*, Nov. 1915; "Best Show Ever," 74; CBBD, 5 Oct. 1929, 61; CBBD, 19 Oct. 1929, 61; Roach, *Cowgirls*, 118; and Hinkle, "Cowgirls—Rodeo's Sugar and Spice," 40.

123. Rupp, *Let 'er Buck*, 44.

124. See for example CBBD, 7 Dec. 1929, 115; CBBD, 4 Jan. 1930, 59; CBBD, 18 Jan. 1930, 59; CBBD, 25 Jan. 1930, 61; CBBD, 1 Mar. 1930, 59; CBBD, 29 Mar. 1930, 97; H&H, May 1938, 18.

125. Simri, *Women at the Olympic Games*, 23; Shaw, "Rodeo Managers Form Association," 65; BBD and H&H, 1929–30.

126. Fredriksson, *American Rodeo*, 22; CBBD, 15 Feb. 1930, 59.

127. CBBD, 8 Feb. 1930, 57; Hartwig, "Has the RAA Been a Success?" 13.

128. McGinnis, *Rodeo Road*, 211–16.

129. Ibid.; Haney, *Ride 'em Cowgirl*, 114; Gray, "Florence Hughes Randolph, Part I," 50.

130. CBBD, 29 July 1922, 83; CBBD, 2 Sept. 1922, 65; CBBD, 17 Nov. 1923, 85; CBBD, 24 Nov. 1923, 83; CBBD, 8 Dec. 1923, 83; "Dick Ringling's Rodeo Closes Successfully," 128.

131. Tad Lucas Trophies, NRHOF; CBBD, 1925–36.

132. Tad Lucas Trophies, NRHOF; CBBD, 1925–36; "Rodeo Champions Chosen," 32; "Garden Rodeo," 5.

133. CBBD, 17 Aug. 1940, 46–47.

134. Fox, "Tad Lucas," 9.

Chapter 4. Home on the Range, 1930–47

1. Allan M. Winkler, "Pearl Harbor Was Relatively Insignificant," *Chronicle of Higher Education*, 4 Dec. 1991, A64.

2. Susan Ware, *Holding Their Own: American Women in the 1930s* (Boston: Twayne Publishers, 1982), xi–xxi, 199.

3. Ibid., xvi.

4. Clancy, *Fifty Years*, 184–210.

5. Susan M. Hartmann, *The Home Front and Beyond: American Women in the 1940s* (Boston: Twayne Publishers, 1982), 18 and 92.

6. June Sochen, *Herstory: A Woman's View of American History* (New York: Alfred Publishers, 1974), 313.

7. BBD, 12 Oct. 1929, 57.

8. Fredriksson, *American Rodeo*, 37.

9. H&H, Jan. 1936 through Mar. 1937.

10. Fredriksson, *American Rodeo*, 46.

11. See Intro. n. 2.

12. Fredriksson, *American Rodeo*, 37–39.

13. Tad Lucas files, CGHOF, NRHOF.

14. Greenough interviews and scrapbooks; CBBD, 7 Apr. 1934, 7; CBBD, 4 Aug. 1934, 37; CBBD, 31 Dec. 1938, 101; H&H, Dec. 1940, 12. Buck jumping was the Australian term for bronc riding.

15. Ware, *Holding Their Own*, 27; Sochen, *Herstory*, 313.

16. *Information Please Almanac* (Boston: Houghton Mifflin, 1989), 54.

17. CBBD, 24 Nov. 1934, 39.

18. Ibid., 25 Apr. 1936, 39.

19. Wallechinsky, *Complete Book of the Olympic Games*.

20. Ware, *Holding Their Own*, xviii.

21. See Intro. n. 2.

22. Gray, "Florence Hughes Randolph, Part II," 126; Lucas and Greenough interviews; Roach, *Cowgirls*, 121–227.

23. Greenough interviews.

24. Ware, *Holding Their Own*, xvii.

25. Greenough interviews.

26. BBD, 1922–36; Madison Square Garden programs and prize lists, PRHOF; Lucas interview. See, for example, CBBD, 28 Apr. 1934, 40; CBBD, 19 May 1934, 37.

27. CBBD, Jan.–Dec. 1932.

28. CBBD, 26 July 1930, 65.

29. BBD, 29 Oct. 1934, 75; H&H Sept. 1937, 20–21.

30. *San Antonio Express*, 4–13 Oct. 1928.

31. BBD, 28 Sept. 1929, 65; BBD, 19 Oct. 1929, 61; BBD, 26 Oct. 1929, 63; BBD, 29 Oct. 1934, 1 and 75.

32. CBBD, 7 Nov. 1931, 33.

33. Ibid.; "Boston Rodeo Sets Record," BBD, 21 Nov. 1931; "The Story of *The Billboard* and Col. W. T. Johnson's Rodeos," BBD, 29 Oct. 1934, 75; "Gate of 17-Day Garden Rodeo $236,412; Attendance 235,000," BBD, 5 Nov. 1932, 3; CBBD, 1931–34.

34. Patricia A. Florence, "The Little Turtle That Grew," *Pro Rodeo Sports News,* 29 Oct. 1986, 3.

35. "Gate of 17-Day Garden Rodeo $236,412; Attendance 235,000," BBD, 5 Nov. 1932, 3; CBBD, 1922–32.

36. Greenough and Young interviews; Lucyle Richards (Roberts) files, CGHOF; *Boston Sunday Post,* Nov. 1936, n.p.; "Insurance Starts 1946," *Ketch Pen,* Spring 1988, 28.

37. "Col. Johnson Signs Band for Five Years' Rodeos," BBD, 26 Nov. 1932, 34.

38. "The Story of *The Billboard,* and Col. W. T. Johnson's Rodeos," 75.

39. CBBD, 1929–33.

40. CBBD, 1 Apr. 1930, 39; CBBD, 9 July 1930, 55; CBBD, 27 Sept. 1930, 57.

41. Sam Cohen, "Lucyle Roberts, 'Queen of the Saddle,' Rides Here," unidentified 1934 clipping, Lucyle Richards files, CGHOF.

42. CBBD, 4 Aug. 1934, 37; CBBD, 12 May 1934, 40; Lucyle Richards files, CGHOF.

43. CBBD, 1932–39; Newman, "Ruth Roach Salmon," 15–16.

44. CBBD, 7 Oct. 1933, 31; Marie Gibson files, NRHOF.

45. CBBD, 25 Apr. 1936, 39; "Maynard Offering Outstanding Wild West Circus Performance," BBD, 16 May 1936, 34 and 37.

46. Clancy, "Memory Trail," H&H, July 1937, 17.

47. Clancy, "Prairie Lillie Allen," H&H, July 1951, 11.

48. CBBD, 22 Sept. 1934, 37; CBBD, 4 May 1935, 63.

49. Stansbury, *Lucille Mulhall,* 115–17; Porter, *Who's Who,* 90–91; Stansbury, letters to the author, 1989–91.

50. Jordon, *Cowgirls,* 209; Tad Lucas files, CGHOF and NRHOF; Lucas interview; Jane Pattie, "Rodeo's First Lady, Tad Lucas," *Quarter Horse Journal,* June 1961, 36.

51. H&H, Sept. 1938, 18.

52. "Cowboy Championships Start This Afternoon," LAT, 3 Aug. 1935, 7.

53. Kristine Fredriksson, "Growing Up on the Road, Children of Wild West Shows and Rodeos," paper presented to the North American Society for Sport

History, 19 May 1984, Louisville, Ky.; H&H, June 1938, 5. It should be noted that while this article stated that the Sheltons were at "the height of their careers," Reine was then thirty-six years old, and a twenty-two-year veteran of competitive rodeo.

54. Jordon, *Cowgirls*, 214; M. Greenough interview.

55. A. Greenough interview.

56. Fredriksson, *American Rodeo*, 39–40; Florence, "Little Turtle That Grew," 3; "Johnson's Rodeo," BBD, 14 Nov. 1936, 3 and 87.

57. Dr. Ivan E. Johnson, letter to the author, 4 June 1991.

58. Ibid., Porter, *Who's Who*, 110–11.

59. CBBD, 14 Nov. 1936, 3, 87, 89; CBBD, 5 Dec. 1926, 67; *Boston Post*, 3 Nov. 1936, 7; Florence, "Little Turtle That Grew," 3, 43; "Col. W. T. Johnson, Rodeo Producer, Ranchman, Dies," *San Antonio Express News*, 26 Sept. 1943, n.p.

60. Fredriksson, *American Rodeo*, 36–51.

61. Hooper Shelton, *Fifty Years a Living Legend* (Stamford: Shelton Press, 1979), 94.

62. Rodeo programs, prize lists, and day sheets, PRHOF; Binford, Barton, Mosley interviews; Jane Mayo, *Championship Barrel Racing* (Houston: Cordovan, 1961), 6–7; H&H, Nov. 1935, 22; Jan. 1946, 14.

63. Lenskyj, *Out of Bounds*, 83–86; Boutilier and SanGiovanni, *Sporting Woman*, 34ff.; Banner, *American Beauty*, 285; Chafe, *American Woman*, 199–225.

64. Binford, Barton, Mosley interviews.

65. Young interview.

66. Young, Binford, Barton interviews; clipping, "Cowgirls Organize Group Here," n.p., n.d., in Nancy Binford scrapbook, CGHOF.

67. Ibid.

68. Lawrence, *Rodeo*, 36.

69. Due in part to pressure from humane societies, most states outlawed steer roping around the turn of the century, and it remains illegal in many states today. Although sanctioned by the Professional Rodeo Cowboys Association (PRCA), steer roping is not included at their National Finals Rodeo.

70. H&H, CBBD, *Western Horseman*, 1935–42; Jewel Duncan scrapbook and files, CGHOF.

71. Young interview.

72. Clipping from *Pecos Enterprise and Gusher*, 19 July 1935, Duncan files, CGHOF.

73. Clipping of Tex Sherman article from *Ranch Romances*, n.p. n.d., Duncan files, CGHOF.

74. CBBD, n.p., n.d., Duncan files, CGHOF.

75. CBBD, 29 Aug. 1936, 54; H&H, Feb. 1937, 30; Oct. 1938, 13; Isora Young files, CGHOF.

76. H&H, Apr. 1937, 23.

77. *Pecos Enterprise Gusher*, 23 Apr. 1937, n.p., Duncan files, CGHOF.

78. Young interview; Duncan and Young files, CGHOF.

79. CBBD, 1 Apr. 1939, 32.

80. Young interview; Duncan and Young files, CGHOF.

81. CBBD and H&H, 1930–41.

82. CBBD, 18 Mar. 1939, 38 and 57.

83. CBBD, 10 Aug. 1940, 33.

84. CBBD, 7 Dec. 1940, 42; *Fort Worth Star Telegram,* Dec. 1940.

85. CBBD, 7 Dec. 1940, 42; *Fort Worth Star Telegram,* Dec. 1940.

86. "Official Program, Daily Insert. T. E. Robertson All American Championship Rodeo and Bull Fight," St. Louis, Mo., 25 Mar.–1 Apr. 1942, from Dixie Reger Mosley scrapbook, Amarillo, Tex.; CBBD, 16 May 1942, 50; CBBD, 6 June 1942, 38.

87. Fredriksson, *American Rodeo,* 36–51; CBBD, 6 June 1942, 38.

88. Clancy, *Fifty Years,* 221–22.

89. H&H, May 1938, 12; CBBD, 30 Apr. 1938, 37.

90. Lucas, Greenough interviews.

91. Jordon, *Cowgirls,* 230.

92. *Madison Square Garden Magazine,* 1939, 35, PRHOF.

93. Clancy, *Fifty Years,* 225.

94. "Madison Square Garden Rodeo," H&H, Dec. 1939, 13.

95. NYT, 20 Oct. 1939; 1939 Madison Square Garden World's Championship Rodeo program, 44, PRHOF; "World's Championship Rodeo, Aided by World Series Joust, Opens Long Run to 11,000 House," BBD, 14 Oct. 1939, 3, 45.

96. "World's Championship Rodeo Aided by World Series Joust," 3, 45.

97. Madison Square Garden Rodeo programs and memorabilia, PRHOF; NYT, 29 Sept., 6, 7, and 10 Oct. 1940.

98. "13000 at Garden Rodeo Opening Night," BBD, 19 Oct. 1940, 3, 33.

99. Madison Square Garden and Boston Garden programs, PRHOF; NYT, Oct. 1939–45; CBBD, 1939–42.

100. CBBD, 13 Apr. 1940, 47; Binford scrapbook, CGHOF.

101. CBBD, 13 Apr. 1940, 47; Binford scrapbook, CGHOF; Madison Square Garden program, PRHOF.

102. Barton files, CGHOF; "Mary Ellen 'Dude' Barton," *Matador Tribune,* 17 Mar. 1988, 1.

103. Barton files, CGHOF; "Mary Ellen 'Dude' Barton," 1.

104. *Fort Worth Star Telegram,* 10–23 Mar. 1942; Barton interview.

105. *Fort Worth Star Telegram,* 10–23 Mar. 1942; 1942 Madison Square Garden program, PRHOF. Boyd won only one go-round of the 1942 musical chairs.

106. "Career Cowboys," *Time,* 16 Oct. 1939, 59; H&H, July 1939, 15; copy of a contract, State of New York, County of New York, Sept. 1939, whereby Madison Square Garden Corporation agrees to pay J. L. Yokley $450 for the services of his daughter Sydna to rope calves, exhibition, during thirty-six rodeo performances from 4 to 29 Oct. She is to work in the exhibition put on by the other seven Texas ranch girls and "be ready at all times to work on publicity and promotional activities," Sydna Yokley files, CGHOF.

107. Foghorn Clancy, "Madison Square Garden Rodeo," H&H, Dec. 1939, 10.

108. Alva Johnston, "Tenor on Horseback," *Saturday Evening Post,* 2 Sept. 1939, 18.

109. Herbert S. Maddy, "Eastern Rodeo," H&H, June 1940, 9.

110. Rodeo programs and memorabilia, PRHOF.

111. Maddy, "Eastern Rodeo," H&H, June 1940, 9; ibid., Sept. 1940; ibid., 6 and Dec. 1940, 8; "Garden Rodeo Keeps Pace for First Week," BBD, 26 Oct. 1940, 41 and 58; "New Attendance Mark Is Set at Hub City Rodeo," BBD, 23 Oct. 1940, 39.

112. BBD, 1896–1940; 1936 Calgary Stampede program, Calgary Stampede and Exhibition Papers, A7 W361 A, Glenbow; Mac, "Half-Century Queen of the Rodeo," 27.

113. Clancy, Fifty Years, 196.

114. CBBD, 1 Mar. 1941, 42, CBBD, 26 Apr. 1941, 45; "Autry, Eskew Draw 'em at Washington," BBD, 19 Apr. 1941, 46; "Pittsburgh Rodeo with Autry," BBD, 24 May 1941, 3; Maddy, "Eastern Rodeo," July 1941, 9; ibid., Aug. 1941, 8; ibid., Jan. 1942, 9; ibid., Feb. 1942, 6; Boston Garden and Madison Square Garden Rodeo programs, PRHOF; Alex Gordon and Ruth Gordon, The Gene Autry Story (Los Angeles: Champion Records, 1989), audiocassette.

115. CBBD, 3 May 1941, 45; CBBD, 10 May 1941, 47; CBBD, 17 May 1941, 44; CBBD, 10 Oct. 1941, 40; CBBD, 11 Nov. 1941, 41; Maddy, "Eastern Rodeo," Nov. 1941, 7; ibid., July 1941, 9; ibid., Aug. 1941, 8; ibid., June 1942, 3.

116. Douglas B. Green, "Gene Autry," in Stars of Country Music: Uncle Dave Macon to Johnny Rodriguez, ed. Bill C. Malone and Judith McCulloh (Urbana: University of Illinois Press, 1975), 145–47.

117. Roy Merlock, "Gene Autry and the Coming of Civilization," in Shooting Stars: Heroes and Heroines of Western Film, ed. Archie P. McDonald (Bloomington: Indiana University Press, 1987), 89.

118. Ibid., 92–96.

119. Johnston, "Tenor on Horseback," 18.

120. Green, "Gene Autry," 149.

121. Gene Autry with Mickey Herskowitz, Back in the Saddle Again (Garden City: Doubleday, 1978), 39–40.

122. Ibid., 52.

123. Armitage, "Rawhide Heroines," 177; William W. Savage, Jr., The Cowboy Hero (Norman: University of Oklahoma Press, 1979), 84, 98–100.

124. Savage, Cowboy Hero, 84 and 98.

125. Ibid., 98–99.

126. A. Greenough interview.

127. Ware, Holding Their Own, 14ff.

128. Lois W. Banner, Women in Modern America: A Brief History (New York: Harcourt Brace Jovanovich, 1974), 171–86.

129. CBBD, 24 May 1941, 46; "Autry to Launch Streamlined Rodeo," BBD, 21 June 1941, 47.

130. Fredriksson, American Rodeo, 65–78.

131. Eddie O'Brien, "Rodeo Chat," H&H, Apr. 1943, 3.

132. Clancy, Fifty Years, 238–43.

133. Fredriksson, American Rodeo, 65–78.

134. Menke, Encyclopedia of Sports, 967–68.

135. Merrie A. Fidler, "The All American Girls' Professional Baseball League, 1943–1954," in *Her Story in Sport*, 590–607.

136. Tex Sherman, "Out of the Chutes," *Ranch Romances*, 16 Jan. 1942.

137. H&H, Oct. 1942, 2.

138. Jane Pattie, "Fay Kirkwood," *Sidesaddle*, 1988, 61.

139. Ibid., 63.

140. *Bonham Daily Favorite*, 6 June 1942, 4. The Indian attire is virtually identical to swimsuits being modeled by film stars on the preceding page, except that the Indian's outfit is strapless.

141. Ibid., daily through 11 June 1942.

142. Ibid., 6–28 June 1942.

143. Ibid.

144. Ibid., 7–29 June 1942.

145. Ibid., 26 June 1942, 1.

146. Musical chairs was conducted much as the traditional game, except that participants were on horseback. When the music stopped, they had to dismount and run for the nearest chair. Flag races required contestants to start behind a line at least twenty yards from a post to which was attached a container holding a flag. The rider had to carry a flag to the post, exchange it for the one already there, make a sharp right turn to another post, switch flags again, and then ride back across the starting line. Reining contests of the forties were similar to contemporary cloverleaf barrel races, except that they used much smaller obstacles. Straightaway rather than cloverleaf barrel races were standard. In cutting, contestants "cut" steers or calves out of a group and drove them into an enclosure or pen. See Mayo, *Championship Barrel Racing*.

147. Barton files, CGHOF.

148. Ibid.

149. Farr files, CGHOF.

150. *Wichita Falls Record News*, clipping, n.p., n.d., from Mosley scrapbook.

151. Jim Scarboro, "Tip Your Hat . . . Monte Reger . . . Tip Your Hat," pt. 1, *Quarter Horse Journal*, July 1970, 30–33, 44–46, 98–99; pt. 2, Aug. 1970, 38–42; pt. 3, Sept. 1970, 40–43, 50–52, 74; Mosley interviews, scrapbook.

152. Mosley scrapbook.

153. Pattie, "Fay Kirkwood," 63.

154. Vaughn Krieg files, CGHOF.

155. Ibid.

156. Ibid.

157. Ibid.; CBBD, 1 July 1939, 35.

158. Krieg files, CGHOF.

159. Ibid.; Vaughn Krieg's Flying V All Cow-Girl Rodeo program, Krieg files, NRHOF.

160. *Paris Morning News*, 24 Aug.–6 Sept. 1942.

161. Earl Armstrong, "Midwest Contract News," H&H, Mar. 1947, 10.

162. CBBD, 4 Dec. 1943, 39 and 55.

163. *Sidesaddle*, 1989, 2; Maddy, "Eastern Rodeo," Mar. 1942, 8; CBBD, 24 Jan. 1942, 39.

164. Lucas and Greenough interviews.

165. "Autry's Houston Rodeo," H&H, Apr. 1942, 11.

166. Clancy, *Fifty Years*, 238.

167. Advertisements for Flying A Rodeos, H&H, 1942; see, for example, Apr. 1942, 11.

168. Ibid.

169. Sherman, "Out of the Chutes," *Ranch Romances*, 15 Jan. 1943, 137; BBD, 12 Sept. 1942, 39.

170. H&H, Sept. 1942, 15.

171. H&H, July–Dec. 1942.

172. Rodeo programs, PRHOF; O'Brien, H&H, Dec. 1942, 6; "Roy Rogers as Star of NY Garden Rodeo Now Official News," BBD, 12 Sept. 1942, 3; "Buffalo Rodeo Draws Below Expectations," BBD, 5 Dec. 1942, 39.

173. Rodeo programs, PRHOF; "Autry's Houston Rodeo," 11; advertisements for Flying A Rodeos, H&H, 1942.

174. Hartmann, *Home Front and Beyond*, 63.

175. Similar things happened in film. See, for example, Sandra Kay Schackel, "Women in Western Films: The Civilizer, the Saloon Keeper, and Their Sisters," in *Shooting Stars*, 197.

176. CBBD, 1941–45; H&H, 1941–46. The women's relay race at Cheyenne did continue until 1946, but this was an anomaly, as relay races were not included on the big-time eastern circuit.

177. BBD and H&H, 1937–42; archives, CGHOF, PRHOF, NRHOF.

178. BBD and H&H, 1937–42; archives, CGHOF, PRHOF, NRHOF; Riske, *Cheyenne Frontier Days*, 215.

179. BBD and H&H, 1943–45; archives, CGHOF, PRHOF, NRHOF.

180. James F. Hoy, "Marge Roberts: Hall of Fame Cowgirl," paper presented to the Western History Association, Oct. 1991, Austin, Tex.; Marge Roberts files, CGHOF.

181. Hoy, "Marge Roberts"; Marge Roberts files, CGHOF.

182. Hoy, "Marge Roberts"; Marge Roberts files, CGHOF.

183. Hoy, "Marge Roberts"; Marge Roberts files, CGHOF.

184. CBBD, 20 Aug. 1938, 31; CBBD, 22 Nov. 1938, 32; Vivian White files, CGHOF.

185. NYT, 27 Dec. 1941, 12; Vivian White files, CGHOF.

186. Clipping from the *Daily Ardmorette*, 13 Sept. 1970, n.p., NRHOF.

187. Tad Lucas interview; A. Greenough interview and scrapbooks; H&H, 1940–50; BBD, 1940–44.

188. Foghorn Clancy, "Eloise Fox Hastings Wilson," H&H, Oct. 1948, 8; CBBD, 15 Dec. 1934, 7.

189. "Grieving Woman Kills Self," *Phoenix Gazette*, 16 Aug. 1948, 12.

190. CBBD, 21 July 1934, 37.

191. *Boston Post*, 1 Nov. 1936.

192. H&H, May 1938, 10–12ff.

193. CBBD, 23 May 1942, 38; CBBD, 26 Sept. 1942, 37.

194. "This and That," H&H, Sept. 1943, 2.

195. CBBD, 9 Dec. 1944, 42.

196. *Tulsa World*, 11 Nov. 1951.

197. *Houston Post,* 3 Dec. 1941, 1.

198. Ibid., 3 May 1941, 2.

199. Ibid., 3 Dec. 1941.

200. Ibid., 28 Apr. 1941, 1.

201. Ibid., 28 Apr. and 4 May 1941; Richards files, CGHOF.

202. *Houston Post,* 28 Apr.–21 May and 1–4 Dec. 1941.

203. Ibid., 28 Apr. 1941, 1.

204. Ibid., 5 Dec. 1941, 1.

205. NRHOF archives.

206. Richards files, CGHOF.

207. Unidentified clipping, Guy Weadick clipping file M1278, File 35, Glenbow.

208. Clancy, *Fifty Years,* 261.

Chapter 5. Back to the Big Time, 1948–67

1. See Intro. n. 2. No effort was made to collect this type of data past 1955, because of missing records, absence of standard publications, and the tremendous proliferation of barrel racing.

2. Kate Weigand, "The Red Menace, the Feminine Mystique, and the Ohio Un-American Activities Commission," *Journal of Women's History* 3 (Winter 1992): 70.

3. Eugenia Kaledin, *Mothers and More: American Women in the 1950s* (Boston: Twayne, 1984), 61–80.

4. Ibid., 36.

5. Gordon Carruth, *What Happened When* (New York: Harper Collins, 1991), 806–12.

6. Dolan, *Vintage Clothing,* 170–80.

7. Banner, *Women in Modern America,* 215–16.

8. Evans, *Born for Liberty,* 245.

9. Carruth, *What Happened When,* 859.

10. Kaledin, *Mothers and More,* preface, 1–17.

11. John W. Wright, ed., *The Universal Almanac, 1992* (Kansas City: Andrews and McMeel, 1991), 251–52.

12. "Republic Studio Rides Again with Western Update," *Austin American Statesman,* 15 Jan. 1992, D9.

13. Carruth, *What Happened When,* 806–12.

14. See Intro. n. 2.

15. Fredriksson, *American Rodeo,* 81–82.

16. "Bigtime Rodeo," *Life Magazine,* 17 Nov. 1947, 126–27.

17. H&H, 1945–48; *Quarter Horse Journal,* 1945–48.

18. Leland Rice, "The Cowboys' Amateur Association of America," H&H, July 1941, 6.

19. H&H, 1945–47.

20. Bean Stew, "Wilma Standard," 7, clipping from *Western Horseman,* July 1959, n.p., in Binford scrapbook and files, CGHOF.

21. *The Buckboard,* Aug. 1947; H&H, Aug. 1946, 5; archives, CGHOF, PRHOF.

22. H&H, Dec. 1944, 8; ibid., 1944–47.

23. H&H, June 1944, 11; Worthington files, CGHOF.

24. Frank Reeves, "Rodeo Cowgirls," *Western Horseman,* July 1949, 52; Worthington files, CGHOF.

25. Binford, Mosley, Barton, Young interviews; Cleo Tom Terry and Osie Wilson, *The Rawhide Tree* (Oxford: Clarendon Press, 1957), 199–203; Margaret Montgomery files, CGHOF.

26. "In Memory, Kathryn Cabot Binford," *Sidesaddle,* 1988, 30.

27. Binford files and scrapbook, CGHOF.

28. Farr files, CGHOF; "In Memory: Thena Mae Farr," *Sidesaddle,* 1986, 8; Shelton, *Fifty Years a Living Legend,* 97.

29. Binford interview.

30. Binford interview and records; "All Girl Rodeo a Knockout," clipping, n.p., n.d., Binford scrapbook, CGHOF.

31. Binford files, CGHOF.

32. "Rodeo Spectators Stetsons off to Feminine Bulldogger," *Amarillo Daily News,* 24 Sept. 1947, 1.

33. Binford files and records, CGHOF; Binford and Mosley interviews.

34. Mosley interviews.

35. Ibid.; Willard Porter, "Dixie Lee Reger," H&H, Sept. 1951, 6.

36. Binford interview and scrapbook, CGHOF.

37. Binford scrapbook and files, CGHOF.

38. *Amarillo Daily News,* 21 Sept. 1947, 20.

39. Photo and article, *Amarillo Daily News,* 21 Sept. 1947, 7.

40. H&H, Sept. 1943, 4.

41. *Amarillo Daily News,* 24 Sept. 1947, 1.

42. "Girls Rodeo Aces Ride Tonight for $3,000 in Prizes," *Amarillo Daily News,* 25 Sept. 1947, 1.

43. Ibid.

44. Unidentified clipping, Binford scrapbook, CGHOF.

45. Ibid.

46. "Girls Rodeo Aces Ride Tonight for $3,000 in Prizes," 1.

47. "Record Crowd Hails Champion Cowgirls," *Amarillo Daily News,* 26 Sept. 1947, 1 and 8.

48. Binford, Barton, Mosley interviews; Binford scrapbook, CGHOF; *Amarillo Daily News,* Sept. 1947.

49. Binford files and records, CGHOF; Binford, Mosley, Young interviews.

50. "Girl's Rodeo Association," H&H, May 1948, 24.

51. "Cowgirls Organize Group Here," n.p., n.d., Binford scrapbook, CGHOF; Binford, Barton, Mosley interviews.

52. "Girl's Rodeo Association," 24.

53. Roach, *Cowgirls,* 119.

54. Ibid., 214.

55. Jordon, *Cowgirls,* 239.

56. Mrs. B. Kalland, "Rodeo Personalities," H&H, Dec. 1951, 17; *WPRA/PWRA Official Reference Guide* (Blanchard: Women's Professional Rodeo Association, 1990), vol. 7, 72; Montgomery files, CGHOF.

57. "Girl's Rodeo Association," 24.

58. Kalland, "Rodeo Personalities," 17; *WPRA/PWRA Official Reference Guide,* vol. 7, 72; Montgomery files, CGHOF.

59. "Cowgirls Organize Group Here"; Binford, Barton, Mosley interviews; "GRA," *Western Horseman,* July 1959, 10–13.

60. GRA rulebooks, Binford scrapbook, CGHOF.

61. Ibid. Sanctioned events were as follows: races—flag races, figure eight and cloverleaf barrel races, line reining; roping events—catch as catch can, team tying, figure eight catch; rough stock events—bareback bronc riding, saddle bronc riding, bull riding.

62. Mayo, *Championship Barrel Racing,* 9; Binford, Barton, Mosley interviews; GRA rulebooks, Binford scrapbook, CGHOF.

63. Binford, Barton, Mosley interviews; GRA rulebooks, Binford scrapbook, CGHOF.

64. RCA minutes, PRHOF.

65. Mary King, "Cowgirls Have the New Look Too," *Quarter Horse Journal,* Nov. 1948, 28–29.

66. Sponsors first participated at Stamford in 1931, but did not compete until 1932. See Shelton, *Fifty Years a Living Legend,* 31–32.

67. Ibid., 94.

68. *Houston Post,* 2–13 Feb. 1950. Cowgirls were in the headlines on 5 Feb., 6, and 6 Feb., 8.

69. BBD, 11 Sept. 1954, 62; BBD, 16 Oct. 1954, 48; NYT, Oct. 1954.

70. See Intro. n. 2.

71. WPRA records, Blanchard, Okla.

72. Binford scrapbook, CGHOF; Binford, Barton, Mosley interviews.

73. *WPRA/PWRA Official Reference Guide,* vol. 7, 4; *Powder Puff and Spurs,* July and Aug. 1950.

74. Foghorn Clancy, *Rodeo Histories and Records* (n.p., 1949–51).

75. Jack Shadoain, "Yuh Got Pecos! Doggone, Belle, Yuh're as Good as Two Men," *Journal of Popular Culture* 12 (Spring 1979): 721.

76. Ibid., 722.

77. Ibid.

78. James Cathey, "Amy McGilvray, World's Champion Cowgirl," *Back in the Saddle,* Dec. 1949, n.p., CGHOF.

79. "GRA to Vote on New Ruling for All Around," clipping in Binford scrapbook, CGHOF.

80. GRA rulebook in Binford scrapbook, CGHOF.

81. Ibid.

82. *Quarter Horse Journal,* May 1954, 22; *PRCA Official Media Guide* (Colorado Springs: Professional Rodeo Cowboys Association, 1987), 184.

83. Hartman, "Intercollegiate Competition for Women," 24.

84. Ibid.

85. Babe Didrikson Zaharias, *This Life I've Led* (New York: Dell Publishing, 1955), 147.

86. Wallechinsky, *Complete Book of the Olympic Games,* 135.

87. Elinor Nickerson, *Golf: A Women's History* (Jefferson: McFarland and Co., 1987), 50–53.

88. Ibid., 53–55; Sally Raque, "You've Come a Long Way Ladies," *Womens Sports and Fitness,* May/June 1990, 61–62.

89. Binford scrapbook, CGHOF.

90. Copy of "AGREEMENT BETWEEN THE Rodeo Cowboys' Association, Inc. and the Girls' Rodeo Association," WPRA files.

91. RCA Board minutes, PRHOF.

92. Binford scrapbook, CGHOF.

93. H&H, 1948–55; *Quarter Horse Journal,* 1948–59; *Western Horseman,* 1949–59.

94. *Quarter Horse Journal,* Aug. 1952, 39–40.

95. Binford scrapbook, CGHOF.

96. *Amarillo Times,* 29 Sept. 1948, n.p., Binford scrapbook, CGHOF.

97. Bill Totten, "Performers Prove Beauty and Rodeo Can Be Mixed," *Colorado Springs Gazette Telegraph,* 21 June 1951, 13.

98. Ibid.; "All Girl Rodeo Wins," *Colorado Springs Sunday News,* n.p., n.d., Binford scrapbook, CGHOF.

99. Ibid.

100. *Colorado Springs Gazette Telegraph,* 17 June 1951, B-1.

101. Ibid., 1–26 June 1951.

102. Ibid., 19 June 1951, 1.

103. Ibid., 22–26 June 1951.

104. Ibid., 20 June 1951, 12.

105. *Powder Puff and Spurs,* July 1950, 7.

106. Rodeo programs and results, NRHOF.

107. *Dallas Morning News,* 1 Mar.–30 Apr. 1951.

108. Ibid., 1 Mar.–30 Apr. 1954.

109. Ibid., 4 Apr. 1951, 4; 8 Apr. 1951, 4.

110. *Natchez Times,* Mar.–Apr. 1951.

111. "All Girl Rodeo to Conclude Stand Today," in ibid., 8 Apr. 1941, 4.

112. Ibid., 9–25 June 1953.

113. See, for example, *Amarillo Times,* Sept. 1947 and Oct. 1948; *Colorado Springs Gazette Telegraph,* June 1951.

114. "Rodeo Arena Manager Here; Girl Performers Arriving and en Route," *Natchez Times,* 3 Apr. 1951, 2.

115. Binford interview.

116. Farr files, CGHOF; H&H 1950–55.

117. Binford, Barton, Mosley interviews.

118. "Empty Saddles," *Ketch Pen,* Winter 1991, 14; "World's Championship Rodeo," *Dallas Morning News,* 1 Apr. 1954, I-11.

119. "Ex Roper Wanda Bush Has 'Try,'" *Fort Worth Star Telegram,* 27 Jan. 1982, 1B, 4B.

120. Binford, Barton, Mosley interviews.

121. *WPRA/PWRA Official Reference Guide,* vol. 7, 72–73; 1961 GRA Championship Rodeo program, n.p., CGHOF. Worthington won seven titles each in cutting and bull riding, three in bronc riding, and one in ribbon roping.

122. Binford, Barton, Mosley interviews; Porter, "Dixie Lee Reger"; Dixie Mosley files, CGHOF.

123. *WPRA/PWRA Official Reference Guide,* vol 7, 72; White and Roberts files, CGHOF.

124. Gloria Shiner, "Texas Cow Tales," H&H, Jan. 1954, 9; ibid., Mar. 1954, 16; ibid., May 1954, 17; Lucyle Roberts files, CGHOF.

125. GRA rulebooks, Binford scrapbook, CGHOF; "Notes from Texas," H&H, Nov. 1949, 9; ibid., Dec. 1949, 9; Jerry Armstrong, "Picked Up in the Rodeo Arena," *Western Horseman,* Aug. 1950, 10–11; H&H, Oct. 1950, 21; H&H, Dec. 1950, 21; *Tulsa Tribune,* 7 Nov. 1951, n.p.; Lucas and Greenough interviews; *WPRA/PWRA Official Reference Guide,* vol. 7, 72; White and Roberts files, CGHOF.

126. GRA rulebooks, Binford scrapbook, CGHOF; "Notes from Texas," 9; ibid., Dec. 1949, 9; Armstrong, "Picked Up in the Rodeo Arena," 10–11; H&H, Oct. 1950, 21; H&H, Dec. 1950, 21; *Tulsa Tribune,* 7 Nov. 1951, n.p.; Lucas and Greenough interviews; *WPRA/PWRA Official Reference Guide,* vol. 7, 72; White and Roberts files, CGHOF.

127. Binford scrapbook, CGHOF; H&H, Aug. 1949, 28; Tony Slaughter, "The Girl with Mink Pants," *Quarter Horse Journal,* July 1954, 6–7.

128. See Intro. n. 2.

129. Guy Weadick clipping files, Glenbow.

130. "Fanny Sperry Steele," H&H, May 1945, 5; Fannie Sperry Steele files, CGHOF, NRHOF.

131. H&H, Nov. 1950, 20; Joe Keller, "Rodeo Highlights of 1950," H&H, Jan. 1951, 9.

132. "Florence Weadick Passes On," 16.

133. Guy Weadick files, M1278 B1 F35, Glenbow. Newspaper clippings state they married at Beverly Hills, Calif., but a copy of the marriage certificate indicates otherwise.

134. "Weadick and New Bride Returning to Stampede," *The Albertan,* 6 July 1952, n.p.

135. Letter in the Guy Weadick Papers, B1F2, Glenbow; Guy Weadick files, NRHOF.

136. Ibid.

137. Clipping from the *New York Journal American,* 24 Oct. 1958, NRHOF.

138. H&H, Oct. 1947, 7; Oct. 1948, 13.

139. Florence Randolph files, NRHOF; H&H, Aug. 1950, 13.

140. H&H, 1947–55.

141. Helen Mills, "News from Florida," H&H, 1953.

142. H&H, 1950–53.

143. Wallechinsky, *Complete Book of the Olympic Games,* 489–93.

144. Ibid., 136–37.

145. *WPRA/PWRA Official Reference Guide,* vol. 7, 72–75; All Girls World Championship Rodeo program, Oct. 28–29, 1961, Duncan Okla., CGHOF.

146. *WPRA/PWRA Official Reference Guide*, vol. 9 (Blanchard: WPRA, 1992), 28–80; Wanda Bush files, CGHOF. Bush may have won more titles than these; the records for 1960–62 are incomplete or missing.

147. *WPRA/PWRA Official Reference Guide*, vol. 7, 72–73; "Ex Roper Wanda Bush Has 'Try'"; McBride files, CGHOF.

148. McBride files, CGHOF.

149. NFRC minutes, 14 Jan. 1959, PRHOF. McBride's suggestion that the women be used as pivots, etc., causes some consternation today. It reflected women's continued willingness to go the extra mile in order to be part of the proceedings, and was ultimately accepted in exactly those words.

150. NFRC minutes, 5 May and 16 Sept. 1959, PRHOF. In order to be called a rodeo, an event must include five standard PRCA contests.

151. RCA Board minutes, 16 Mar. 1960.

152. NFRC minutes, 16–18 Mar. 1960; *WPRA/PWRA Official Reference Guide*, vol. 7, 32; *PRCA Official Media Guide* (1987), 220.

153. RCA Board minutes, 24–27 Nov. 1960, 6 Jan. 1962, 10 Aug. 1965, and 13 May 1967.

154. Banner, *Women in Modern America*, 228–35.

155. Ibid.; Evans, *Born for Liberty*, 274–78.

156. RCA Board minutes, 30 Jan. 1967.

157. Ibid., 13 May 1967. Unfortunately, it is not possible to chronicle this achievement from the women's point of view. Although it is known that many WPRA representatives spent countless hours and traveled thousands of miles pleading their case to the PRCA before finally succeeding with the help of the Oklahoma City promoters, their names will never be known. Alone among all of the organizations and agencies involved with this project, the WPRA refused to allow this writer access to of any of its files, documents, or minutes.

158. *WPRA/PWRA Official Reference Guide*, vol 7, 22–23; *PRCA Official Media Guide* (1987), 195–96. Unlike Manuel, Altizer also competed in calf roping. His combined earnings of $24,302, placed him eighth in the all-around standings, and far above the barrel racing champion. Bob Altizer is the brother of Blanche Altizer Smith, longtime GRA secretary-treasurer.

159. Carruth, *What Happened When*, 997.

160. NFRC minutes, 15 Mar. 1968.

161. *WPRA/PWRA Official Reference Guide*, vol. 7, 22–28; *PRCA Official Media Guide* (1987), 195–217.

Chapter 6. Cowgirls Hit the Jackpot, 1967–1990s

1. WPRA office, Blanchard, Okla.; *WPRA/PWRA Official Reference Guide*, vol. 7, 7.

2. *WPRA/PWRA Official Reference Guide*, vol. 7, 22–28.

3. Rebecca Trounson, "Cowgirls Take Bull by Horns in Bid to Buck Tradition, Lasso Equal Pay," *Houston Chronicle*, 6 Mar. 1987.

4. Wright, *Universal Almanac*, 252, 254.

5. Ibid., 252.

6. Rader, *American Sports*, 330.

7. Ibid., 343.

8. Robert J. Condon, *Great Women Athletes of the 20th Century* (Jefferson: McFarland and Co., 1991), 115–18.

9. Carruth, *What Happened When,* 1056, 1069.

10. Wright, *Universal Almanac,* 1032.

11. Burke, "Effect of Current Sports Legislation on Women," 337–39.

12. Joan S. Hult, "The Legacy of AIAW," in *A Century of Women's Basketball,* ed. Joan S. Hult and Marianna Trekel (Washington, D.C.: American Alliance for Health, Physical Eduction, Recreation, and Dance, 1991), 281–308; Carruth, *What Happened When,* 1056–57; Burke, "Effect of Current Sports Legislation on Women," 337–39.

13. Trounson, "Cowgirls Take Bull by Horns."

14. Ibid.

15. Ibid.

16. "Purina to Add $30,000 to NRF Barrel Race Purse," *Women's Pro Rodeo News,* 1 Nov. 1990, 1.

17. Data compiled from *Pro Rodeo Sports News,* 27 Nov. 1991, 2; and ibid., "1991 Year End Edition," 4.

18. *The Sports Illustrated 1992 Sports Almanac* (Boston: Little Brown and Co., 1991), 291.

19. Wright, *Universal Almanac,* 624–25.

20. "Toughening Title IX," *Sports Illustrated,* 23 Mar. 1992, n.p.

21. *Sports Illustrated 1992 Sports Almanac,* 503.

22. Ibid.

23. *WPRA/PWRA Official Reference Guide,* vol. 8, 47.

24. Ibid.

25. Ibid., 34, 48ff.

26. Ibid., 54.

27. Ibid.

28. "WPRA Members Shine at Fort Smith," *Women's Pro Rodeo News,* 1 July 1990, 1.

29. *WPRA/PWRA Official Reference Guide,* vol. 8, 34.

30. "Senior Rodeo Finals Expect First Woman to Take Overall Title," Nov. 1991 press release provided by NOTRA; "Congratulations World's Champions," provided by NOTRA; NOTRA National Senior Rodeo, memo to the author, 18 Mar. 1992; *The Rodeo Roundup,* Nov. 1991–Jan. 1992; *Women's Pro Rodeo News,* Dec. 1991, 10; "Way to Go, Wanda," *Prorodeo Sports News,* 29 Jan. 1992, 2.

31. "Senior Rodeo Finals Expect First Woman to Take Overall Title"; "Congratulations World's Champions"; NOTRA National Senior Rodeo, memo; *Rodeo Roundup,* Nov. 1991–Jan. 1992; *Women's Pro Rodeo News,* Dec. 1991, 10; "Way to Go, Wanda," 2.

32. Springer, "James Heads Entire NFR Delegation," 1; "WPRA: Strong Group of Women in Pro Rodeo," *Sunday Express–News* (San Antonio), 3 Feb. 1991, 3–D.

33. *Women's Pro Rodeo News,* 1 Apr. 1992, 1ff.

34. Questionnaire sent to a random sample of fifty WPRA members, Feb. 1992; return rate 58 percent.

35. *Women's Professional Rodeo Association 1985 Reference Guide,* vol. 6.

36. Kenneth Springer, "Jimmie Munroe Named Coca-Cola WPRA Woman of the Year," *Women's Pro Rodeo News*, 1 Feb. 1991, 1; *WPRA/PWRA Official Reference Guide*, vol. 8, 36.

37. Ibid.

38. *WPRA/PWRA Official Reference Guide*, vol. 7, 5.

39. Ibid., vol. 7, 6; vol. 8, 6.

40. Ibid.

41. Ibid.

42. Kenneth Springer, "1991 WRPA/Coca-Cola Woman of the Year LYDIA MOORE," *Women's Pro Rodeo News*, 1 Feb. 1992, 2. Despite Munroe's statement, there are fewer than 1,300 names on the WPRA membership list.

43. Anderson, "Having a Barrel of Fun," 78–83; "No, Dad, I'm Going to Win It," *Prorodeo Sports News*, 4 Sept. 1985, 3.

44. "No, Dad, I'm Going to Win It," 3; Anderson, "Having a Barrel of Fun," 78–83.

45. *Prorodeo Sports News*, 18 Jan. 1989, 2.

46. Kindra Santos, "Rodman Untouchable in 1990," *Prorodeo Sports News*, 1990 year–end edition, 70–71.

47. Ibid.; Anderson, "Having a Barrel of Fun," 78–83; Springer, "James Heads Entire NFR Delegation"; Springer, "James Weds Rodman," *Women's Pro Rodeo News*, Dec. 1988, 20; "Charmayne James Rodman and Scamper Take 7th World Title," *Women's Pro Rodeo News*, 1 Jan. 1991, 1.

48. *Women's Pro Rodeo News*, 1 Apr. 1992, 24.

49. Ibid., 1 Dec. 1987, 14; Jordon, *Cowgirls*, 239–40; *WPRA/PWRA Official Reference Guide*, vol. 7, 7.

50. *WPRA/PWRA Official Reference Guide*, vol. 7, 64–69.

51. *Women's Pro Rodeo News*, Oct. 1988, 22.

52. Ibid., Jan.–Oct. 1990.

53. Ibid., Sept. 1990.

54. *WPRA/PWRA Official Reference Guide*, vol. 7, 65.

55. Ibid., 5. Only three women have won both titles simultaneously since the rules were changed in 1949: Wanda Bush in 1952, Jane Mayo in 1959, and Jimmie Gibbs Munroe in 1975.

56. *Women's Pro Rodeo News*, 1991–92; *WPRA/PWRA Official Reference Guide*, vols. 7 and 8.

57. See "PWRA," *WPRA/PWRA Official Reference Guide*, vol. 7, 70–71; telecast of 1989 PWRA Finals Rodeo.

58. "WPRA Wins Lawsuit," *Women's Pro Rodeo News*, Aug. 1990, 2.

59. Ibid.

60. *Women's Pro Rodeo News*, 1 Dec. 1991, 1, 12, 13.

61. Ibid., Jan. 1992, 7.

62. Marvine, "Fannie Sperry Wowed 'em at the First Calgary Stampede," 36; Stiffler and Blake, "Fannie Sperry-Steele," 56.

63. "World Champion Cowgirl Tad Lucas Dies at 87," 26; "Talented Lucas Blazed Trail for Rodeo Cowgirls in the 1920s," *Fort Worth Star Telegram*, 26 Feb. 1990, III-5.

64. Greenough interviews, correspondence.

65. Binford, Barton, Mosley interviews.

66. *Women's Professional Rodeo Association Reference Guide* (Fort Worth: Western Media Services, 1985), 34; *Women's Professional Rodeo Association 1987 Official Rule Book* (Blanchard: WPRA, 1987), n.p.

67. Kenneth Springer, "Wanda Bush Makes Comeback—Wins $28,500," *Women's Pro Rodeo News,* 1 July 1992, 1.

68. "Crown Royal Top WPRA Barrel Racers," *Women's Pro Rodeo News,* 1 July 1992, 1.

69. "WPRA: Strong Group of Women in Pro Rodeo," 3-D.

Bibliographical Essay

Primary Sources

The most valuable sources used in this research were interviews, archives, and trade papers. Four pioneer cowgirls, Tad Lucas, Margie Greenough Henson, Alice Greenough Orr, and Isora DeRacy Young, provided invaluable insights into life on the road, the development of rodeo, and what the sport had meant to them and their families. GRA founders Nancy Binford, Mary Ellen Barton, and Dixie Reger Mosley spent an entire day sharing their memories. They discussed the formation and early development of the GRA, and its importance in their lives, as well as their own careers. I am especially indebted to Mosley, who spent another afternoon sharing scrapbooks and memorabilia, and describing her life "growing up on the road" as a child professional.

Archives include National Rodeo Hall of Fame at the National Cowboy Hall of Fame, Oklahoma City, Oklahoma (NRHOF); ProRodeo Hall of Fame and Museum of the American Cowboy, Colorado Springs, Colorado (PRHOF); National Cowgirl Hall of Fame and Western Heritage Center, Hereford, Texas (CGHOF); and the Glenbow Museum and Archives, Calgary, Alberta, Canada (Glenbow). The three halls of fame maintain extensive files on both honorees and nominees. In addition, many honorees donate their personal belongings including scrapbooks, correspondence, photos, trophies, and prize saddles. The CGHOF is especially important as a repository of data concerning the history of the GRA and the lives and careers of its founders, many of whom have been inducted there. My notes and tapes will ultimately be donated to their collection. The PRHOF has the most exhaustive collection of rodeo programs, day sheets, and prize lists from all over the country, as well as the minutes and records of the PRCA and the National Finals Rodeo Committee. The Glenbow is the main repository of Canadian rodeo history, and is especially useful for its collection of photos and memorabilia from the Calgary and Winnipeg Stampedes, as well as the Guy Weadick Papers and his correspondence with many pioneer rodeo figures. The NRHOF has an invaluable collection of glass plate negatives from the

great rodeo photographer R. R. Doubleday. It also houses the only complete collection of the original rodeo trade paper, *The Wild Bunch,* which was published
from 1915 to 1917 and later reestablished.

While *The Wild Bunch* covered rodeo exclusively, the earliest trade paper to
include rodeo and Wild West news was the entertainment weekly *The Billboard,*
which began publication in 1897. It carried regular rodeo and Wild West show
columns from 1915 through World War II, and is the best single source for data
concerning the history of that early period, including results, gossip, editorials,
and advertisements.

From 1929 through 1955, *Hoofs and Horns* served as the "official publication"
of several rodeo associations including the RAA, CTA, and GRA. Since that time,
each organization has published its own periodical. The Barker Texas History
Center at the University of Texas at Austin has a nearly complete set of *Hoofs and
Horns* as well as several other western publications that often carried rodeo news.
These include *The Cattleman,* the *Western Horseman,* and the *Quarter Horse
Journal.* In addition to these periodicals, I relied heavily on newspapers from the
towns where rodeos took place. These allowed analysis of publicity, turnout, com-
munity involvement, and attitudes toward female contestants.

Secondary Sources

There are three recent books about cowgirls. The two mentioned in the introduction (Jordon and Roach) are not about rodeo cowgirls exclusively; they cover cowgirls of all sorts. Both rely heavily on oral history and folklore. Another, Milt
Riske's *Those Magnificent Cowgirls* (Cheyenne: Wyoming Publishing, 1983), is a
popular work about rodeo and Wild West show cowgirls, with lively prose and
extensive illustrations. Several general articles are worthy of mention: "Cowgirls
of the Rodeo, Interesting," *The Billboard,* 25 Jan. 1922, 108; "In Praise of Cowgirls," *Texas Monthly,* Nov. 1987, 110; and Bruce Anderson, "Having a Barrel of
Fun," *Sports Illustrated,* 15 Dec. 1986, 85.

Books and articles on individual cowgirls abound. The best books are Kathryn
B. Stansbury's *Lucille Mulhall* (privately published, 1985) and *Lucille Mulhall
Wild West Cowgirl* (Mulhall, Okla.: Homestead Heirlooms Publishing Co., 1992),
which came out too late to appear in my notes; and Vera McGinnis's autobiogra-
phy, *Rodeo Road: My Life as a Pioneer Cowgirl* (New York: Hastings House,
1972). The most useful article on Florence Hughes Randolph is a two-part piece
by Sally Gray, "Florence Hughes Randolph, Part I," *Quarter Horse Journal,* Mar.
1971, 42–50, and "Part II," *Quarter Horse Journal,* Apr. 1971, 142–50. Good articles about Tad Lucas include Jane Pattie, "Rodeo's First Lady, Tad Lucas," *Quarter Horse Journal,* June 1961; and Willard Porter, "Tad," *True West,* Sept. 1988.
Jim Scarboro's three-part series, "Tip Your Hat . . . Monte Reger . . . Tip Your
Hat," *Quarter Horse Journal,* Aug., Sept., and Oct. 1970, tells a great deal about
Dixie Reger Mosley's early career, as does Porter's "Dixie Lee Reger," *Hoofs and
Horns,* Sept. 1951. Finally, Fannie Sperry Steele and Helen Clark detailed Fan-
nie's long life and career in the oft-quoted "A Horse beneath Me Sometimes,"
True West, Feb. 1956; while Liz Stiffler and Tona Blake took a more scholarly

approach in "Fannie Sperry-Steele: Montana's Champion Bronc Rider," *Montana Magazine of Western History* 32 (Spring 1982).

Scholars have largely ignored rodeo history, with two notable exceptions. They are Kristine Fredriksson's *American Rodeo* (College Station: Texas A&M University Press, 1985), and Elizabeth Atwood Lawrence's *American Rodeo: An Anthropologist Looks at the Wild and the Tame* (Knoxville: University of Tennessee Press, 1982). Lawrence's book, as the title suggests, is an anthropological analysis, while Fredriksson's focuses primarily on the history of the PRCA, and is invaluable for that reason. The best-known, and probably the most authoritative, popular work is *My Fifty Years in Rodeo* (San Antonio: Naylor Company, 1952), by Foghorn Clancy, longtime rodeo publicist, producer, and announcer. Based on Clancy's experiences and magazine articles, it covers much ground and fills in many missing pieces. The biggest problem is the absence of accurate dates. Bill King's *Rodeo Trails* (Laramie: Jelm Mountain Press, 1982) provides an inside look at rodeos in the twenties and thirties.

Several writers have attempted to chronicle the history of specific rodeos. Two books each are devoted to the Calgary Stampede and the Cheyenne Frontier Days: Robert D. Hanesworth, *Daddy of 'em All: The Story of Cheyenne Frontier Days* (Cheyenne: Flintlock, 1967); Milt Riske, *Cheyenne Frontier Days* (Cheyenne: Frontier Printing, 1984); Fred Kennedy, *The Calgary Stampede Story* (Calgary: T. Edwards Thonger, 1952); James H. Gray, *A Brand of Its Own* (Saskatoon: Western Producer Prairie Books, 1985). Books also cover the histories of the Pendleton Roundup, Prescott Frontier Days, and the Burwell, Nebraska, rodeo, among others. To date, no one has undertaken the story of the Madison Square Garden rodeo.

Articles on the GRA/WPRA are difficult to locate outside WPRA publications, but three proved helpful: "Girl's Rodeo Association," *Hoofs and Horns*, May 1948, 24; "GRA," *Western Horseman*, July 1959, 10–13; and Rebecca Trounson, "Cowgirls Take Bull by Horns in Bid to Buck Tradition, Lasso Equal Pay," *Houston Chronicle*, 6 Mar. 1987.

The late Don Russell was the unquestioned authority on Wild West Shows, and his two books, *The Lives and Legends of Buffalo Bill* (Norman: University of Oklahoma Press, 1960), and *The Wild West* (Fort Worth: Amon Carter Museum of Western Art, 1970), are the definitive works on the subject. Glenn Shirley's *Pawnee Bill* (Lincoln: University of Nebraska Press, 1958) describes the other major Wild West show.

The Women's West (Norman: University of Oklahoma Press, 1987), edited by Susan Armitage and Elizabeth Jameson, provides some of the best current research on the western women's history. The best overview of the status of that research is probably the Spring 1991 issue of the *Montana Magazine of Western History*. Several books by and/or about western ranch women are also valuable. These include: Ada Moorehead Holland, *Brush Country Woman* (College Station: Texas A&M University Press, 1988); Hallie Crawford Stillwell, *I'll Gather My Geese* (College Station: Texas A&M University Press, 1991); and Donna M. Lucey, *Photographing Montana, 1894–1928: The Life and Work of Evelyn Cameron* (New York: Alfred A. Knopf, 1990).

Index

MARY LOU LECOMPTE is an Associate Professor in the Department of Kinesiology and Health Education at the University of Texas at Austin, where she has taught since 1960. A charter member of the North American Society for Sport History, she was also the 1992-93 president of the History Academy of the National Association for Sport and Physical Education. Dr. LeCompte began researching rodeo history in 1979 and since 1986 has focused her efforts on women in rodeo. She has presented the results of this research to state, regional, national, and international meetings of numerous scholarly groups, and also published extensively on rodeo history. She teaches American sport history and women's sport history.

Books in the Series Sport and Society

A Sporting Time: New York City and the Rise of Modern Athletics, 1820-70
Melvin L. Adelman

Sandlot Seasons: Sport in Black Pittsburgh
Rob Ruck

West Ham United: The Making of a Football Club
Charles Korr

Beyond the Ring: The Role of Boxing in American Society
Jeffrey T. Sammons

John L. Sullivan and His America
Michael T. Isenberg

Television and National Sport: The United States and Britain
Joan M. Chandler

The Creation of American Team Sports: Baseball and Cricket, 1838-72
George B. Kirsch

City Games: The Evolution of American Urban Society and the Rise of Sports
Steven A. Riess

The Brawn Drain: Foreign Student-Athletes in American Universities
John Bale

The Business of Professional Sports
Edited by Paul D. Staudohar and James A. Mangan

Fritz Pollard: Pioneer in Racial Advancement
John M. Carroll

Go Big Red! The Story of a Nebraska Football Player
George Mills

Sport and Exercise Science: Essays in the History of Sports Medicine
Edited by Jack W. Berryman and Roberta J. Park

Minor League Baseball and Local Economic Development
Arthur T. Johnson

Harry Hooper: An American Baseball Life
Paul J. Zingg

Cowgirls of the Rodeo: Pioneer Professional Athletes
Mary Lou LeCompte

REPRINT EDITIONS

The Nazi Olympics
Richard D. Mandell

Sports in the Western World
Second Edition
William J. Baker